Treasures of
New Mexico

by William Faubion

a part of the Morgan & Chase Treasure Series
www.treasuresof.com

© Copyright 2006 by Morgan & Chase Publishing, Inc.
All rights reserved.
No portion of this book may be reproduced or utilized in any form,
or by any electronic, mechanical or other means without the prior written permission of the publisher.

Published by:
Morgan & Chase Publishing, Inc.
531 Parsons Drive, Medford, Oregon 97501
(888) 557-9328
www.treasuresof.com

Printed by:
Taylor Specialty Books - Dallas TX

First edition 2006
ISBN: 1-933989-06-8

THE
TREASURE
SERIES

*I gratefully acknowledge the contributions
of the many people involved in the writing and production of this book.
Their tireless dedication to this endeavour has been inspirational.*
—Damon Neal, *Publisher*

Managing Editor:
David Smigelski

Senior Story Editor:
Mary Beth Lee

Senior Writer:
Gregory Scott

Proof Editors:
Avery Brown and Robyn Sutherland

Graphic Design:
C.S. Rowan, Jesse Gifford, Tamara Cornett, Jacob Kristof, Michael Frye

Photo Coordinators:
Wendy Gay and Donna Lindley

Website:
Casey Faubion, Molly Bermea, Ben Ford

Morgan & Chase Home Team
Cindy Tilley Faubion, Anita Fronek, Emily Wilkie, Cari Qualls, Anne Boydston, Virginia Arias, Danielle Barkley,
Sue Buda, Tom Corkery, Marlene Glasgow, Shauna O'Callahan, Clarice Rodriguez, Terrie West, Cindy Young

Contributing Writers:
Sharon M. Stachler, Mark Allen Deruiter, Jerry Adams, Dorothy Rosado, David Singer, Dusty Alexander, Heather Allen, Jennifer Buckner, Amber Dusk, Kiley Faubion, Rochelle Ford, Larry George, Paul Hadella, Mary Knepp, Nancy McClain, Maggie McClellen, Chris McCrellis-Mitchell, Candy Schrodek, CJ White

Special Recognition to:
Carolyn Courian, Jolee Moody, Judy Stallcop, Mike Stallcop, Kimberley Wallan

Special Thanks to:
The New Mexico Tourism Department

To the people of New Mexico,
especially Governor Bill Richardson
and New Mexico Tourism Department Secretary Michael Cerletti.
Our sincere thanks for helping us see New Mexico through reverent eyes.
Also, thanks to Sharon M. Stachler,
travel writer and photographer.
Her heartfelt efforts are on every page.

Table of Contents

- Accommodations 4
- Arts & Crafts 44
- Attractions 50
- Fashion 130
- Galleries 142
- Gardens, Plants & Flowers 194
- Health & Beauty 200
- Home 212
- Recreation 220
- Restaurants & Cafés 238
- Shopping 270
- Textile Arts 294
- Trading Posts 308
- Wineries 320
- Index by Treasure 338
- Index by City 340

How to use this book

The *Treasures of New Mexico* is divided into 14 categories, such as accommodations, attractions, galleries, restaurants, trading posts, shopping and wineries.

In the index, all of these Treasures are listed alphabetically by name and by city.

We have provided contact information for every Treasure in the book, because these are places and businesses we have personally visited, and which we encourage you to visit on your travels through New Mexico.

We sincerely hope you find this book to be both beautiful and useful.

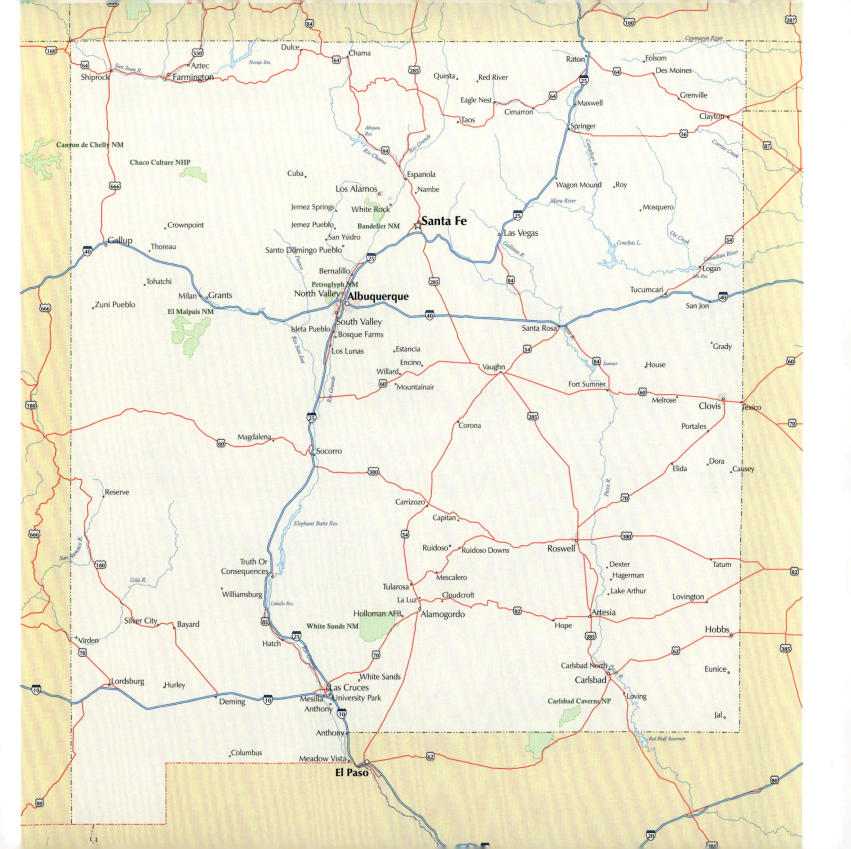

2

State of New Mexico
Office of the Governor

Bill Richardson
Governor

A Welcome Message from Governor Bill Richardson

As Governor of New Mexico, I am pleased to welcome to you to Treasures of New Mexico, *an inviting glimpse into all that makes our great state truly the "Land of Enchantment."*

New Mexico is home to vast natural beauty that has served for centuries as the setting to stories of proud cultures and intriguing characters. Here, living history in ancient pueblos and historic communities meets future innovation in our national laboratories and the world's first purpose-built commercial spaceport. The landscape, ranging from expansive desert to towering mountaintops, is breath-taking at every turn. Our rich and diverse cultural heritage, together with a world-class arts community, means great museums, galleries and entertainment possibilities abound. Whatever your interests, there is something for everyone to discover here.

New Mexico is the perfect respite for those who appreciate nature, who have a love for history, or for anyone who is just looking for great food and good-hearted people. The Treasures in this book exemplify the spirit of generosity, hospitality and beauty on which we pride ourselves. I invite you to seek them out for yourself.

With warmest regards,

Bill Richardson
Governor of New Mexico

4 • Accommodations

Hot air balloons over a New Mexico lake

Accommodations

Elaine's, A Bed and Breakfast

Step away from it all and find a peaceful retreat in the Land of Enchantment at Elaine's, A Bed and Breakfast. You'll enjoy all the pleasures of the New Mexico countryside, with an easy drive to either Albuquerque or Santa Fe. Nestled in the evergreen forests of the Sandia Peaks, this charming inn offers breathtaking views, beautiful rooms and a restful, centrally located launching pad for your adventures into area attractions. Owner and proprietress Elaine O'Neil opened the inn in 1988 and has since received high praise from innkeeping professionals and guests. Elaine's home is a wonderfully romantic, three-story, wood and stone house that has been expertly designed and tastefully furnished with European antiques. Guests choose from five specialized rooms, including the Sangre de Cristo and Sunrise rooms, which boast whirlpool tubs and kiva fireplaces. In the morning each guest enjoys a hearty and delicious breakfast, served in either the dining room or the outside patio, depending on the season. Elaine's designs numerous specialty packages for guests, which can include golf, skiing and bird watching. Make time for yourself and experience the wonders of New Mexico with a stay at Elaine's, A Bed and Breakfast, where storybook vacations come to life.

72 Snowline Road,
PO Box 444,
Cedar Crest NM
(505) 281-2467
or (800) 821-3092
www.elainesbnb.com

Accommodations • 7

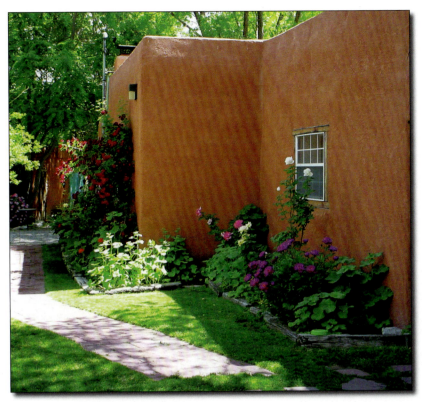

Hacienda Vargas

When you desire a romantic New Mexico getaway, take a look in the Rio Grande Valley between Santa Fe and Albuquerque and discover Hacienda Vargas. Steeped in tradition, this bed-and-breakfast inn offers a varied choice of lodging possibilities. Each suite reflects a different aspect of the spirit of the Southwest, from the suite with authentic adobe walls that is dedicated to the Acoma people to the Kiva suite with a large kiva fireplace and private Jacuzzi tub under a skylight. Breakfast in the fresh and festive dining room will satisfy your morning taste buds with delightful creations, like pumpkin pancakes with roasted piñon nuts, Southwestern potatoes and mandarin muffins. The wedding chapel and grounds lend a glorious setting for weddings. You may choose the indoor courtyard or spacious north yard for larger parties. The lush and well appointed gardens complete the nuptial scene. The interior of this 200-year-old adobe chapel reflects the historic nature of the entire premises while exuding an elegant yet cozy atmosphere. Plan your family gathering or celebrate a special occasion at the inn. The owners strive to provide a total experience of relaxation and comfort, while the history and grace of the original buildings induce a rich experience that will shine in your memory. The charming Hacienda Vargas is truly a one-of-a-kind inn.

1431 Highway 313, Algodones NM
(505) 867-9115 or (800) 261-0006
www.haciendavargas.com

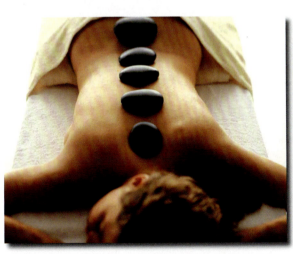   

Angels' Ascent Retreat & Spa

Named as one of Albuquerque and Santa Fe's top five spas by *Travel & Leisure* magazine, Angels' Ascent Retreat & Spa offers a rejuvenating spa experience, highlighted by heavenly mountain views and divine sunsets. This popular getaway destination opened in 1995 as a bed and breakfast. In 2000, the inn was renovated to include the current retreat and spa and the recently added tea room. Angels' Ascent is centrally located on the Turquoise Trail near the breathtaking Sandia Peak Ski Area and the Paa-Ko Ridge Golf Course. The idyllic retreat, close to both Albuquerque and Santa Fe, offers numerous amenities and features English Country décor with an angel theme. Here you can while away the hours as you indulge in a full spectrum of spa services at the Paradise Day Spa and Wellness Center, including massages, facials and body polishes. Guests enjoy relaxing in the steam room, sauna or whirlpool. Angels' Ascent offers specialized retreats, designed to improve your overall wellness via healthful foods, detoxification and stress management. Along with complimentary breakfasts and varied programs, Angels' Ascent offers a wide range of packages that cover everything from special dinners to relationship enhancement instruction. Visit the Land of Enchantment while you rediscover the balance and peace within yourself at Angel's Ascent Retreat & Spa.

20 Gilbert Place, Sandia Park NM (PO Box 4, Cedar Crest NM 87008)
(505) 286-1588
www.angelsascent.com

Pine Cone Inn

On your next vacation or family getaway, bypass the crowded hotels and campgrounds and find peaceful relaxation at Pine Cone Inn, a private vacation rental just off the Turquoise Trail in the stunning Sandia Mountains. This charming mountain home is centrally located between Santa Fe and Albuquerque, just minutes away from numerous fine dining options and the thriving artistic community of Madrid. The expansive home sleeps four to six people and offers a garden-level master bedroom, complete with a queen-sized bed and a comfortable sitting or office area. A second bedroom features bunk beds that are ideal for children. Further amenities include high-speed Internet access and an easy-to-use gas fireplace, as well as a fully equipped kitchenette, where you can whip up your favorite dishes. Stay clean, comfortable and well fed thanks to the inn's washer and dryer, gas barbecue and cable television with a VCR and DVD player. A short five-minute walk up the lane takes you to the Cibola National Forest, where you can enjoy such mountain activities as hiking, biking, skiing and rock climbing.

For those who prefer to do their sightseeing from the road, the Sandia Scenic Byway offers stellar views and great picture-taking opportunities. Enjoy a relaxing retreat that is quiet without being remote at Pine Cone Inn, a vacation rental that is well above par.

Adjacent to Cibola National Forest, Sandia Park NM
(505) 250-3629
www.VRBO.com/31227

Sarabande Bed & Breakfast

The Sarabande Bed & Breakfast fulfills a two-fold purpose: to provide a gracious and welcoming inn to visitors, and to share the beauty of New Mexico's land and culture. Named for the rose growing in its gardens, the inn is a study in Los Ranchos charm. Sculptured adobe walls punctuated by antique stained glass windows support the hand-hewn viga and latilla ceilings. The courtyard features an enticing fountain. Spacious and comfortable guest rooms can easily accommodate four guests and most contain fireplaces, jetted bathtubs and flagstone patios. Skylights are generously placed to let in the light, while leaded or stained glass windows add to the warm glow. Many rooms boast romantic French doors. Two full breakfasts are included in the package for each room, and the nominal $15 rate for each added occupant covers an additional breakfast. Licensed massage therapists are on hand. Special rates for business and extended-stay guests provide affordable comfort for the longer-term guest. The Sarabande Bed & Breakfast is the perfect place to hold meetings, reunions and special events, providing a backdrop so full of grace and style that any occasion is elevated to an elegant status. The back garden offers an in-ground hot tub and 50-foot lap pool among aromatic flowers, and you can refresh yourself with a siesta by the lily pond. No matter which path you take, you can't go wrong at Sarabande Bed & Breakfast.

5637 Rio Grande Boulevard NW, Albuquerque NM
(505) 345-4923
www.sarabandebb.com

Hotel Albuquerque at Old Town
A Heritage Hotel & Resort

Hotel Albuquerque at Old Town is surrounded by the diverse history and culture that exemplifies New Mexico. A leisurely walk will allow you to explore 400 years of history at a variety of nearby museums, along with more than 200 galleries, shops and restaurants in and around the quaint Old Town Plaza. Hotel Albuquerque is a Heritage Hotel and Resort property which has been renovated to provide a landmark hotel experience that blends the diverse cultural influences of local Native Americans, Mexico and the Old West. Along with 41,000 square feet of exhibit and meeting space, the hotel boasts two restaurants and a sophisticated multi-venue bar, as well as a swimming pool and Spanish gardens. Hotel Albuquerque at Old Town was listed in the April 2001 issue of *Travel & Leisure* magazine as one of the top 25 stylish hotels for under $200. Tucked into a private corner is a 19th-century style non-denominational chapel. Featuring a dramatic vaulted ceiling with hand-plastered and carved finishes, a spiral staircase leading to a choir loft and seating for 156 guests, the elegant simplicity provides the perfect setting for spectacular weddings or moments of quiet reflection. Submerge yourself in the traditions of the Southwest and book a stay at Hotel Albuquerque at Old Town.

**800 Rio Grande Boulevard NW,
Albuquerque NM
(505) 843-6300
or (800) 237-2133
www.HotelABQ.com**

Enchanted Trails RV Park & Trading Post

From its perch on a high mesa overlooking Albuquerque, Enchanted Trails RV Park brings the modern trailblazer a delightful mix of New Mexican charm and modern comforts. This property has been a favorite stop for travelers since the 1940s. It's been a backdrop for Western movies and its adobe building was originally the Hill Top Trading Post on Route 66. Owner Vickie Ashcraft keeps her guests informed on local events along Route 66. She also advises reservations as much as a year in advance for those who wish to view the spectacular hot air balloon festival, held each fall, from this stunning location. Enchanted Trails RV Park is well situated for jumping off into explorations of petroglyphs, Spanish ruins and Indian pueblos. It's also the perfect place to let time slide by as you lounge by the swimming pool. Guests here enjoy large pull-thru RV sites, 30 and 50 amp hook-ups, wireless Internet and a Camping World next door. A shop for RV supplies and Southwestern gifts assures everything you seek is close at hand. The 15-acre resort holds 135 comfortable campsites, available by the night, week or month. Grab your hat, pull on your boots and come visit the Old West at Enchanted Trails RV Park & Trading Post.

14305 Central Avenue NW, Albuquerque NM
(505) 837-6317 or (800) 326-6317
www.enchantedtrails.com

The Inn at Paradise

For an active vacation in a luxurious setting, visit The Inn at Paradise. You will be just steps from the first tee of the Paradise Hills Golf Course, close to trails for running and bicycling, and close to trainers who are ready to support your fitness goals. The inn sits on the West Mesa overlooking the Rio Grande Valley and the majestic Sandia Mountains. The newly remodeled rooms showcase artwork on consignment from local artists. Suites offer fireplaces and kitchens. A tranquil garden with a pond and waterfall is a favorite spot for weddings. Antoni and Natalia Niemczak are your hosts in Paradise. Antoni is a competitive runner who has won top honors in major world marathons. The premises are home to the Center for High Altitude Sports Training, where runners, triathletes and bicyclists benefit from a synthetic track, tennis courts and miles of trails. The combination of high altitude, moderate temperatures, sunny days and soaring views satisfy athletes seeking high intensity training and anyone seeking an idyllic retreat. Train with Antoni, relax in a large hot tub and eat homemade, nutritious meals designed to support your sports training or active lifestyle. A pro shop serves golfers. The Full Moon Saloon can start your day with its fiesta breakfast. Modest rates and superior amenities make the Inn at Paradise one of Albuquerque's best values. Let The Inn at Paradise and the Center for High Altitude Sports Training be your hosts in the Land of Enchantment.

10035 Country Club Lane, Albuquerque NM
(505) 898-6161 or (800) 938-6161 *www.innatparadise.com*

Böttger Mansion of Old Town

The Böttger Mansion of Old Town is shaded by massive 100-year-old Chinese elm trees, creating true Victorian elegance in the midst of Southwest splendor. Within view of Old Town Plaza and the spires of San Felipe de Neri Church, the Böttger Mansion is just steps away from shops, excellent restaurants, galleries, museums and parks. Nearby attractions include the Botanic Garden, Rio Grande Zoo, Indian Pueblo Cultural Center, Route 66 and much more, all within sight of the magnificent Sandia Mountains. Imagine living in the past, in this home on the National Historic Register, as you experience elegant décor, gracious hospitality and gourmet breakfasts, yet enjoy modern comforts such as micro fiber robes, cable television, private baths, air conditioning and wireless Internet access. Relax in the lovely courtyard, alive spring through fall with mourning doves, goldfinches, sparrows and hummingbirds. At the center of the state, Albuquerque is a delightful home base for day trips to Santa Fe, Acoma Pueblo, the Salinas National Monument, the Turquoise Trail, Bosque del Apache National Wildlife Refuge and the lava tubes at El Malpais near Grants. Hot air balloon rides, golf courses, horseback riding, hiking, skiing, concerts and festivals—so much to do and so little time. Bring your camera for a week and you'll leave your heart forever. Come as guests. Leave as friends.

110 San Felipe NW, Albuquerque NM
(505) 243-3639 or (800) 758-3639
www.bottger.com

Nativo Lodge
A Heritage Hotel & Resort

A blend of the traditional and the contemporary, Nativo Lodge offers a one-of-a-kind experience. The renovation of the Nativo Lodge adds a modern touch to the Pueblo styling and colors. Storytelling totems line the drive to the front entrance and the soaring lobby features a towering sculpture by Horacio Cordova, along with reading areas and plush seating that encourage folks to linger and socialize. The 147 guest rooms and suites offer the highest quality linens and pillows to ensure a blissful night's sleep. Each room displays historic Native American photography, along with traditional basketry and dreamcatchers. The custom carpets sport a colorful Navajo blanket design. After a restful night, enjoy a delicious hot breakfast buffet in the Spirit Wind's Restaurant with their traditional recipes, all made from scratch. A Heritage Hotel and Resort property, Nativo Lodge can accommodate groups of up to 255 people in their flexible event space, and offers a full banquet kitchen on site. One of the unique amenities is the large swimming pool that is partially indoors and partially outdoors. Enjoy the many attractions in the area, including the International Balloon Fiesta held every fall, or browse through the historic Old Town district. For a memorable stay in a truly unique hotel, visit Nativo Lodge.

6000 Pan American Freeway NE,
Albuquerque NM
(505) 798-4300
or (888) NATIVO1 (628-4861)
www.Nativolodge.com

Ojo Caliente Mineral Springs & Spa

Soothing body, mind and spirit naturally for centuries, Ojo Caliente Mineral Springs & Spa is one of the oldest health resorts in North America. Located between Santa Fe and Taos, this historic treasure was once considered sacred by local tribes, who built their Pueblos overlooking the springs. The Spaniards named it Ojo Caliente for the hot eye of a subterranean volcanic aquifer. Seven different mineral pools combine four different mineral waters. The Lithia, Iron and Arsenic springs each contain minerals believed to be beneficial for the easing of various conditions, while the Soda Spring promises deep relaxation. You may bathe *au naturel* in one of three private pools with kiva fireplaces. Lodging choices range from the historic 1916 adobe hotel to cozy cottages and private houses. Ojo Caliente is honoring its environment by switching to geothermal heating and cooling. A full-service, newly renovated spa offers massages and numerous skin care treatments. Activities abound, from easing back to read a book on the hotel porch to hiking, biking or yoga classes. You'll find conference facilities and the recently restored adobe Round Barn, an ideal location for a group retreat, workshop or wedding. The Artesian Restaurant offers an eclectic menu with global variety, local specialties and light spa and vegetarian fare, along with fine wine and beers. Listed in *Smithonian* magazine's Destination America as one of seven special places to visit, Ojo Caliente is a world-class spa that promises to be a highlight of your visit to the Land of Enchantment.

50 Los Baños Drive, Ojo Caliente NM
(505) 583-2233 or (800) 222-9162
www.ojocalientespa.com

Hacienda Nicholas

The Hacienda Nicholas in Santa Fe is a breath of fresh air in the world of stuffy hotels and starched bed and breakfasts. An old adobe home in the heart of the city, it features a central great room with 20-foot ceilings, along with a fireplace big enough to cook in. Carolyn Lee, who owns Hacienda Nicholas and two other area inns, has a tradition of naming her establishments for her children. Hacienda Nicholas was named for her son, The Madeleine Inn for Nicholas' twin sister and Alexander's Inn for their older brother. Seven distinct and beautifully decorated rooms include private baths, televisions and comfortable feather beds. Guests are provided with fluffy robes to lounge in. The scrumptious breakfast includes tempting dishes such as homemade blueberry pancakes, quiche and Southwestern frittatas. Throughout the day, guests can kick back around one of the large common tables and snack on freshly baked brownies, pies or cakes while sipping cocoa, coffee or cider. Wine and cheese are served nightly. Hacienda Nicholas is located on East Marcy Street just blocks from the historic plaza and the Canyon Road Galleries. Innkeeper Anna Tenaglia and her friendly, knowledgeable staff will do whatever they can to make your trip to Santa Fe and Hacienda Nicholas happy and memorable.

320 E Marcy Street, Santa Fe NM
(888) 284-3170
www.haciendanicholas.com

Photo by S.M. Stachler

Sportsman's Lodge

Owned and operated by Kelly Jo and Mark Drummond, Sportsman's Lodge is located on the quiet east end of Red River. It is well known to those who return yearly for its clean rooms, great rates and wonderful hospitality. The Sportsman's Lodge has a large group room with cooking facilities and specializes in reunions, groups and large gatherings. The Sportsman's Lodge has a playground for the kids, a new hot tub for adults and a stop on the Red River Miner trolley line. The Sportsman's Lodge is open all year long. Whether it is skiing, hunting or just relaxing in the cool mountains for summer vacation, Mark and Kelly Jo invite you to relax and let them help you plan your next outing at the Sportsman's Lodge.

1110 E Main Street, Red River NM
(505) 754-2273 or (800) 367-7329
www.redrivernm.com/sportsmans

The Bavarian Lodge and Restaurant

The Bavarian Lodge and Restaurant, located mid-mountain at the Taos Ski Valley, offers visitors the traditional, warm hospitality of Bavaria and you won't need your passport to get there. The owners of this incredible lodge, Thomas Schulze and his family, came from Bavaria to create a destination for travelers based upon the alpine guesthouses, or Ski Alms, of their native land. The Lodge, standing alone on the mountain, is located near several scenic hiking trails in addition to the world-class skiing that Taos Ski Valley is famous for. In the summer and autumn, you can take nature excursions that will allow you to explore the beauty of the adjoining wilderness. The lodge has a large outdoor terrace that is warmed by the sun throughout the day and has an open bar, barbecue and grill. Here guests can relax on the cushioned deck chairs or enjoy the sheepskin-covered bar stools while sipping on genuine Bavarian beers from the 600-year-old Spaten-Franziskaner Brewery. The restaurant features a nice selection of perfectly prepared, traditional Bavarian meals, including their *sauerbraten*, homemade *spatzle*, *wiener schnitzel* and other genuine entrées. Each room has been tastefully decorated with handpicked, authentic European artifacts and *objects d'art*. Room sizes and amenities vary, although each has its own bathroom, and many of the suites feature Jacuzzi tubs. The storybook Bavarian Lodge and Restaurant is the perfect place to while away a summer vacation or to enjoy a romantic ski-in and ski-out winter vacation.

P.O Box 653, Taos Ski Valley NM (505) 776-8020 or (888) 205-8020
www.thebavarian.com

Absolute Nirvana Spa, and the Madeleine Inn

Carolyn Lee knows how to create a world of luxury and splendor. In 1987, Carolyn purchased the Madeleine Inn, a stunning Queen Anne Victorian built in 1886 by Chinese railroad workers as the residence of a prominent railroad tycoon. Carolyn named this lovely establishment after her young daughter. In 2005 she added the Absolute Nirvana Spa, dedicated to the ancient healing art of using plants, herbs and spices for inner and outer beauty. The Madeleine features seven beautifully appointed guest rooms with all the amenities needed to make your stay comfortable and relaxing. In the mornings, guests receive a hearty and delicious breakfast featuring homemade baked goods and flavorful entrées. After your day of touring or relaxing, come back to sample an array of baked goodies, as well as enjoy a wine and cheese hour. The spa was recently selected by *Condé Naste Traveler* as One of the Hottest New Spas in the World. Choose from a menu of traditional Asian spa rituals and luxurious rose petal baths, as well as therapeutic, hot stone and Thai massages. These treatments, rich in history and tradition, are translated through the healing hands of a staff of master-level therapists, most of whom have 10 to 15 years of experience. The spa also features a tea room where you can sip fantastic, full-bodied chai or have a pot of one of their 50 varieties of loose teas while savoring delectable tea sandwiches and scones. The Indonesian-inspired Absolute Nirvana Spa and historic Madeleine Inn are located in a tranquil garden setting just four blocks from the plaza. Carolyn Lee invites you to book a restful, rejuvenating stay at the Madeleine Inn and Absolute Nirvana Spa.

**106 Faithway Street,
Santa Fe NM
(888) 877-7622**
www.absolutenirvana.com
www.madeleineinn.com

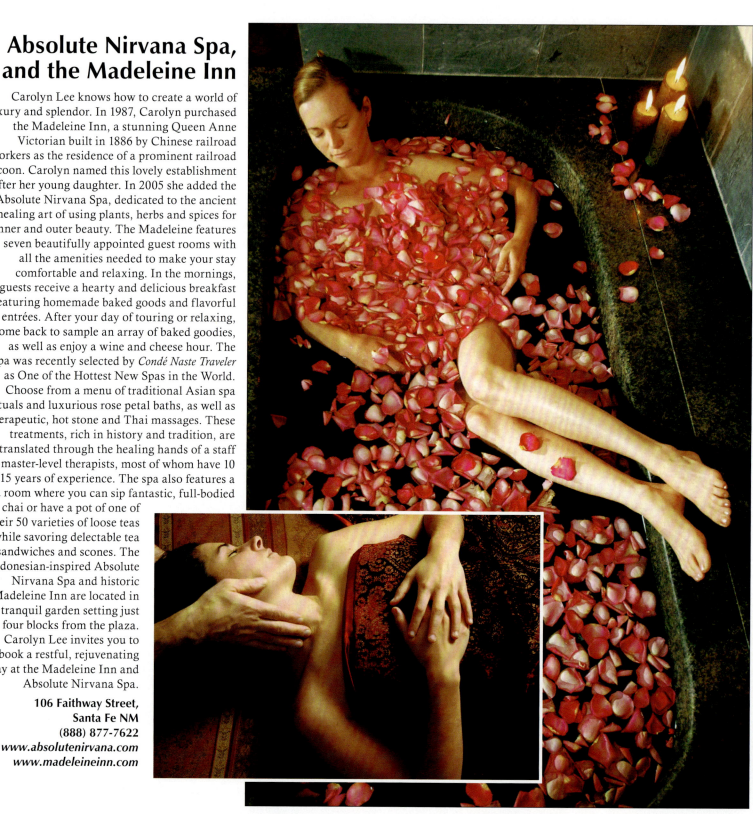

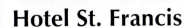

Photos by S.M. Stachler

Hotel St. Francis

The splendor of yesteryear meets the affordable luxury of today at the Hotel St. Francis. The hotel's history of hospitality dates back to 1924, when the old De Vargas Hotel, dating from 1880, burned to the ground and was rebuilt on this site. The De Vargas Hotel was first-class all the way, a handsome building in the early California Mission Revival style with a hint of European elegance. The De Vargas began a slow decline World War II. In 1986, proprietors Patricia and Goodwin Taylor remodeled the hotel and renamed it Hotel St. Francis. This beautiful hotel, just one block from Santa Fe's historic district, features 82 spacious rooms and suites with marble bathrooms and competitive room rates. It proudly provides such premier hotel services as a concierge desk, fine dining with chef Walter Manikowski and a cocktail bar. The garden patio offers a restful spot from which to enjoy the sights, sounds and clear air of Santa Fe. The hotel courts business travelers with customized business plans and rooms designed especially for them. These rooms include enhanced room lighting, work tables and wireless Internet access. A 24-hour business center provides copying, e-mail and Internet service. Whether your purpose is business or a vacation, a stay at the Hotel St. Francis will provide a luxurious retreat at the end of a busy day.

210 Don Gaspar Avenue, Santa Fe NM
(505) 983-5700
www.hotelstfrancis.com

Austing Haus Bed & Breakfast

Paul Austing wears many hats. He is the owner, chef, builder and chief bottle washer of the fabulous Austing Haus Bed & Breakfast in popular Taos Ski Valley. Austing began the project with $100 in his pocket and an eye for carving out his own American dream. The Austing Haus is the tallest timber frame structure in North America, and Paul utilized eight 18-foot trees from his own property in the construction. The bed and breakfast features 24 rooms, 16 of which have wood-burning fireplaces and one which is handicapped accessible. Austing Haus is proud to be both a smoke-free environment and a pet-friendly destination. The centralized location makes Austing Haus the ideal launching point for many different types of daytime adventures. It's only a mile and a half from Taos Ski Valley and an easy 18-mile drive to the lovely town of Taos. During the winter season, the friendly and professional staff will assist you in securing lift tickets, ski lessons and ski package deals. Summertime offers visitors a respite from the heat along with a plethora of hiking, camping, climbing and horseback opportunities. The Austing Haus staff is glad to help you find outfitters, guides and instructors for any sport you wish to enjoy. Austing Haus Bed & Breakfast is the perfect place for family vacations, romantic getaways or your next corporate retreat or conference. Each guest is greeted in the morning with a delicious breakfast and a friendly smile. With its fabulous views and friendly staff, Austing Haus Bed & Breakfast is a special place to stay year round. Make plans to visit on your next trip to northern New Mexico.

**1282 State Route 150,
Taos Ski Valley NM
(505) 776-2649 or (800) 748-2932
www.austinghaus.com**

Alma del Monte "Spirit of the Mountain" Bed & Breakfast

Since 1996, the Alma del Monte "Spirit of the Mountain" Bed & Breakfast has been offering area visitors an oasis composed of spectacular rooms, fabulous food and wonderful people. Innkeepers and owners Jan and Phyllis Waye are corporate refugees who retired from 33 years as corporate managers. Together they use their experience gleaned from years of travel and working with people from all across the globe to offer a truly exceptional bed-and-breakfast experience to every guest. The soaring ceilings and stunning architecture make an excellent backdrop for antiques and *objects d'art* that they have collected on their many travels. Alma del Monte has five exquisite rooms to choose from, each with a private bath. In-room accommodations include high thread count, 100-percent cotton linens on king-sized beds, kiva fireplaces with a sitting area, and heated floors. The private bathrooms include a whirlpool tub with separate shower and skylights. In the morning guests are treated to a luxurious three-course breakfast that includes succulent dishes like stuffed croissant Florentine, gingered honeydew and savory turkey sausage links. Alma del Monte is located near numerous attractions, including the United States' only World Heritage site, a 1,000-year-old Taos pueblo. This popular inn has received many awards, including Four Diamonds from AAA, and is a member of the New Mexico Bed and Breakfast Association. Become whole again with a stay at Alma del Monte "Spirit of the Mountain" Bed & Breakfast.

372 Hondo Seco Road, Taos NM
(505) 776-2721 or (800) 273-7203
www.almaspirit.com

Mabel Dodge Luhan House

As a salon hostess, art patroness and writer, the indomitable Mabel Dodge Luhan endeavored to forge her own utopia, and in doing so attracted some of the greatest minds of the 20th century to her Taos oasis. Mabel moved to Taos in 1918, and it was there that she and her Taos Pueblo Indian husband, Tony, hoped to teach Anglos a new way of conceiving culture by gathering the world's finest artists and thinkers together to devise a new world plan. Today the Mabel Dodge Luhan House remains dedicated to personal growth and is a welcoming sanctuary for anyone seeking spiritual, artistic or intellectual inspiration. Sleep in the room where Georgia O'Keeffe stayed while visiting Mabel, or contemplate the works of Ansel Adams in his namesake room. Guests of the Mabel Dodge Luhan House enjoy an array of soothing amenities, including kiva fireplaces, peaceful patios and enchanting, panoramic views of the sacred Taos mountains. Visitors may also choose to stay at the charming Gate House Cottage, which features multiple fireplaces, as well as a sitting room and private terrace. The main house is available as a conference center, making it an ideal place for corporate or educational retreats. A personable staff will help you organize your event to run smoothly and professionally. Meals at the house have long earned rave reviews and are served buffet style in the community dining room. Find your inspiration at the Mabel Dodge Luhan House.

240 Morada Lane, Taos NM
(505) 751-9686 or (800) 846-2235
www.mabeldodgeluhan.com

The Lodge at Santa Fe
A Heritage Hotel & Resort

Reminiscent of the building traditions of the Anasazi, The Lodge at Santa Fe is steeped in the rich colors and textures of New Mexico. A 28-foot circular kiva tower graces the entrance, and the stacked stone theme is repeated in the two-story fireplace that is the focal point of the lobby. The furnishings throughout The Lodge are handcrafted by local artisans, and traditional Navajo blanket designs are used in the custom made carpets. Guests planning longer stays have the option of booking one of the six nearby condos, complete with full kitchens and kiva fireplaces. Perched on a hill overlooking historic Santa Fe Plaza, The Lodge at Santa Fe, a Heritage Hotel and Resort property, offers incredible views of the breathtaking Sangre de Cristo Mountains. Enjoy a delicious meal at The Lodge's restaurant, Las Mananitas, and bask in the glories of a sunset while lingering over drinks on the outdoor balcony. During the summer months you can experience the passion and excitement of flamenco as world-renowned Maria Benitez Teatro Flamenco performs in the Benitez Cabaret located within The Lodge. Whether you are participating in a corporate function in one of The Lodge's tastefully appointed event rooms, or have plans to savor the history and art of Santa Fe, be sure to book a room at The Lodge at Santa Fe.

750 N St. Francis Drive, Santa Fe NM
(505) 992-5800 or (888) 563-4373
www.lodgeatsantafe.com

Best Western Kachina Lodge

The Kiva Coffee Shop in the Best Western Kachina Lodge & Meeting Center is a beautifully executed artistic and symbolic architectural achievement. It is only one of the many things that highlight the excellence that sets the Kachina Lodge apart from other hotels. Built by Edwin Lineberry, the coffee shop is patterned after an underground Native American Kiva, a traditional ceremonial meeting room. In the center is a totem pole carved by Lineberry's wife, artist Duane Van-Vechten, which supports the roof. Vigas extend from the top like the spokes of a wheel across the ceiling of the room. The lodge, owned by Dean and Sally Koop, also contains the two-room Hopi Dining Room that serves American and New Mexico cuisine and features a fireplace. Beautiful art is everywhere, including an art gallery on the premises. The outdoor pool is heated and there is also an indoor hot tub. Kachina Lodge is conveniently located near points of interest like the Taos Art Museum, Kit Carson's house and the St. Francis de Assisi Church, but there is plenty to do without ever leaving the building. Lodge activities include massage services, a billiards table, yoga and video games. Entertainment events are provided in the lounge. The staff at the Kachina will welcome you with an evening wine, cheese and cracker reception and serves complimentary hot breakfast to you in the morning when you stay at the Best Western Kachina Lodge & Meeting Center.

413 Paseo del Pueblo Norte, Taos NM
(800) KACHINA (522-4462) or (505) 758-2275
www.kachinalodge.com

Casa de la Chimeneas Inn & Spa

Seven-foot high adobe walls surround the protected paradise of Casa de las Chimeneas Inn & Spa. Inside the adobe walls, you can look forward to a formal garden with a fountain and several smaller informal garden spaces. The inn features eight rooms, each with its own name and character, and is presided over by master innkeeper Susan Vernon. All of the rooms at Casa de las Chimeneas, which means "house of chimneys" in Spanish, have a host of amenities, including cable television, stocked mini-refrigerators, hair dryers and cozy robes. Notable details make this inn special. Each room has a fireplace, vigas (beamed ceilings), a private entrance, a private bath with hand-painted Talavera tile and down pillows. Room costs include a three-course breakfast, buffet supper, use of a sauna, fitness facility and hot tub located under the starry skies of Taos. On-site spa facilities offer massage and spa treatments, including a three-hour, head-to-toe treatment called The Works. The concierge and chef provide such services as an outdoor picnic pack, ski arrangements, a list of area attractions and restaurant reviews. Meals are simple but delectable and hearty with fresh organic vegetables from a local farm. Package specials include llama trekking, hot air balloon rides and river rafting. Taos has a large art community and the inn offers the opportunity for travel sketching with a local artist. In the fall, Taos hosts many festivals and weekend events. Any time of the year, stay at Casa de las Chimeneas for rejuvenation and bliss at its best.

**5303 NDCBU-405 Cordoba Road, Taos NM
(505) 758-4777 or (877) 758-4777**
www.visit-taos.com

Touchstone Inn and Riverbend Spa

Embrace your desire to escape from everyday stress at the Touchstone Inn and Riverbend Spa, a peaceful adobe oasis in Pueblo country. This premier destination has been aptly named The Place to Stay in Taos by both *USA Today* and *Fodor's* guide. All rooms are comfortably furnished with fireplaces, luxurious textiles and intimate patios that offer spectacular mountain views. Realign your mind in the seclusion of the tall trees or take a journey through the labyrinth of lush gardens and fountains. Since 1994, owner Bren Price has been hosting her guests with the finest amenities a bed and breakfast can provide. With the addition of Riverbend Spa, relaxation at Touchstone Inn is further enhanced. Massage therapists Patty and Carol employ methods to help you after a long day of shopping, skiing or hiking. You can enjoy a traditional massage in their indoor spa room or opt to have your massage near the river or outside fountain. The spa uses quality Phytomer products and Thalesso therapy and features such decadent treatments as chocolate fondue wraps, Vision Quest facials, heated stone therapy and water therapy under a Vichey shower. After enjoying a perfect night of rest and relaxation, awaken to a delectable gourmet vegetarian breakfast. Touchstone is filled with original works by Bren Price and other artists, and with special treasures collected from all over the world. Ms. Price, whose work was featured in the book *Inside the Wind*, is mainly expressionistic watercolors with Southwestern and Oriental imagery. Supreme accommodations and artful elegance await when you visit the Touchstone Inn and Riverbend Spa.

0110 Mabel Dodge Lane, Taos NM
(505) 758-0192 or (800) 758-0192
www.touchstoneinn.com

Accommodations

Hotel Plaza Real
A Heritage Hotel & Resort

Just blocks from the Capitol and steps away from the historic Plaza of Old Santa Fe, Hotel Plaza Real displays a marvelous blend of cultural influences. The authentic territorial architecture includes private balconies that overlook a charming courtyard and incredible views of the majestic Sangre de Cristo Mountains. Jesse's, the on-site bar, is where you can go to enjoy a signature margarita and relax after a day of absorbing your beautiful surroundings. Hotel Plaza Real is a Heritage Hotel and Resort property offering 12 guest rooms and 44 deluxe suites. All rooms feature handcrafted furniture and original art works, including painting, pottery and weaving by some of the foremost artists of the Southwest. The Hotel Plaza Real is perfectly situated to allow guests easy access to the world-class art, shopping and dining that is readily available along the Plaza. Immerse yourself in the soul of Santa Fe with a stay at the Hotel Plaza Real.

125 Washington Avenue, Santa Fe NM
(505) 988-4900 or (877) 901-ROOM (7666)
www.hhandr.com/plazareal

Formed of volcanic ash 30 million years ago and sculpted by wind and water into rows of monolithic blocks, City of Rocks State Park takes its name from these incredible rock formations

Best Western Sands

Loyd and Grace Wilkins built their hotel in 1960 with only three rooms. Their daughter Peggy Baird and her husband Richard took over the business and continued to build onto the property, and today their son and daughter–Robert Baird and Donna Hilliard–continue the family tradition of maintaining the Best Western Sands hotel in Raton. The facility includes an outdoor heated pool, a hot tub, a playground and an on-premises family restaurant. The large courtyard rooms offer the comforts of home, including in-room coffee, down pillows, hair dryers, irons and ironing boards. You can indulge yourself in the hotel's luxury wing with its overstuffed recliners, refrigerators and other great amenities. This 50-room luxury hotel is AAA approved. For reservations or further information, consult the web page.

300 Clayton Road, Raton NM
(505) 445-2737 or (800) 518-2581
www.bestwestern.com

Otherworldly Landscape Near Raton
Photo by Phillip Capper

Best Western Adobe Inn

For comfortable lodging in Santa Rosa, turn to Best Western Adobe Inn. It's conveniently located just off Interstate 40 on the old Highway 66. The inn's interior courtyard design offers a quiet, secure and enjoyable stay, and its location on a raised mesa assures spectacular views. This AAA-rated hotel's spacious, air-conditioned rooms are nicely equipped with cable television, hair dryers, irons and ironing boards, coffee makers and refrigerators. Your house-broken pets are welcome, and the hotel hosts a complimentary Continental breakfast each morning. Enjoy a dip in the heated swimming pool, dine at the on-site restaurant or take advantage of the inn's high-speed Internet access. The multi-lingual staff can direct you, using English or Spanish, to nearby attractions, such as the Route 66 Car Museum, a nine-hole golf course, Santa Rosa Lake and the famous Blue Hole, a destination for scuba divers. If Santa Rosa is not your ultimate destination, chances are you still have many miles to go, which is all the more reason for taking a pleasant break at a great hotel. Get out of the fast lane and enjoy the hospitality of Santa Rosa and Best Western Adobe Inn.

**1501 Old Route 66,
Santa Rosa NM
(505) 472-3446**
www.bestwestern.com

Photo by S.M. Stachler

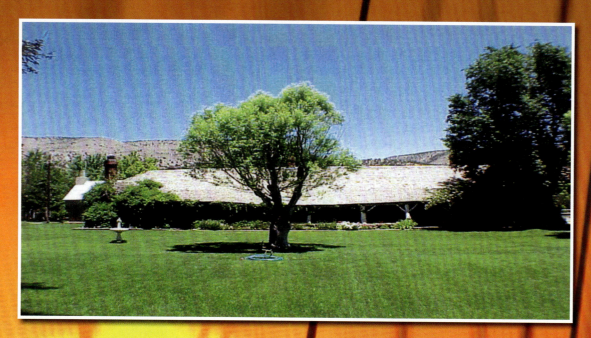

The Ellis Store Country Inn

A treasure is something of unique value, held close and to be enjoyed. This is a perfect description of The Ellis Store Country Inn in Lincoln. The Inn has been named as one of the 45 Best Inns in the West by *Sunset Magazine* and the front portal was called "A world class front porch" by the *National Geographic Traveler*. Centered in the oldest standing residence in Lincoln County, first built in 1850, surrounded by beautiful gardens and overflowing with tales of Billy the Kid, the Inn is an ideal setting for weddings, family reunions or just a quiet get-away. The guest rooms are furnished with antiques, handmade quilts, fine linens and the tranquility of a time gone by. The cuisine, for breakfast or the candlelit gourmet dinner, is prepared by owner Jinny Vigil. Jinny was named Chef of the Year for this state and has been publicized as providing one of the best dining experiences in the US. Just like finding buried treasure, discovering The Ellis Store Country Inn is the ultimate award for your vacation treasure hunt.

Mile Marker 98, Highway 380, Lincoln NM
(800) 653-6460
www.ellisstore.com

Burnt Well Guest Ranch

Experience the work and rewards of ranch life with a vacation at Burnt Well Guest Ranch in Roswell. Owners Kim and Patricia Chesser run this working ranch, a family endeavor established in 1950. Families can bunk in the Rodeo Room, which sleeps four, or take up quarters in the Indian Room with space for six. Guests can choose to be as involved as they like in the ranch life, with opportunities for roping and branding cattle, feeding animals, horseback riding, or just relaxing in the great outdoors. An open fire pit is an inviting place to gather in the evening and share stories of the day's events. Saddle sore cowboys and cowgirls will appreciate a therapeutic soak in the hot tub or relaxing in the hacienda's great room. Patricia's three hearty cowboy meals will put you back in the saddle with renewed energy. If you want to lasso something to remind you of your working ranch adventure, Burnt Well Mercantile offers gift items and souvenirs. The warm and sunny days, the sunsets and the camaraderie are certain to refresh your outlook. For a vacation on the range, make your reservation at Burnt Well Guest Ranch, and let Kim and Patricia treat you like family.

399 Chesser Road, Roswell NM
(505) 347-2668 or (866) 729-0974
www.burntwellguestranch.com

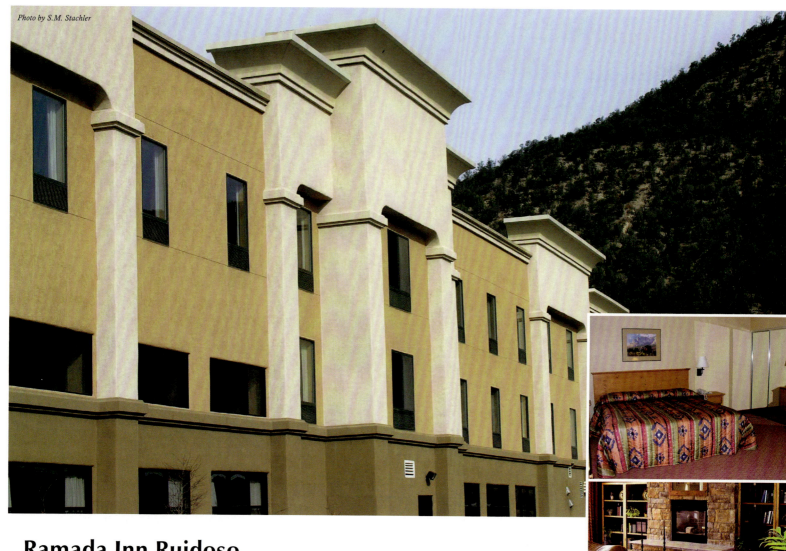

Photo by S.M. Stachler

Ramada Inn Ruidoso

The Ramada Inn in Ruidoso couldn't be in better hands. Owner Suren Sharma has been a resident of Ruidoso for 27 years and spent 24 of them in the hotel business. This two-year-old Ramada Inn offers all the amenities you would expect from a hotel of its reputation, including the most current technological amenities. Rooms have Internet access and two-line phones with data port and voicemail service. Whirlpool suites are available for those who appreciate this luxury. You can snack in your room, which comes equipped with coffee maker, microwave and refrigerator. Relax in front of the 27-inch television, connected to the Dish Network and HBO, or check out the Ramada's fitness center. Start off your day with the inn's deluxe Continental breakfast. The inn's conference rooms and business center make this the ideal location for corporate meetings. The Ramada Inn is conveniently close to Ski Apache, Billy The Kid Casino, Apache Casino and Ruidoso Downs Race Track. You can also take in the Museum Of Horses, Spencer Theater and Bonita State Park. For comfortable hotel accommodations to suit all your needs in the Ruidoso area, make your reservation at the Ramada Inn.

2191 Highway 70 W, Ruidoso Downs NM
(505) 378-1199 or (800) 2RAMADA (434-5800)
www.ramadainn.com

Accommodations • 33

La Quinta Inn & Suites Roswell

Whether you are traveling to Roswell for business or pleasure, the new La Quinta Inn & Suites is sure to exceed your expectations. From the luxurious towels and sheets to the fresh hot waffles each morning, there are many extra touches that will make your stay so comfortable you might not want to leave. These little touches are just some of what sets La Quinta apart from other hotels. General manager John R. Bolte and his helpful staff will do everything they can to make you feel like this is your home away from home. People traveling for work will appreciate the business amenities, such as workspaces in each room, high-speed wireless Internet and spacious conference rooms. La Quinta is also a great place for families, with an indoor swimming pool that's sure to keep kids happy for hours. The hotel is located a half mile from downtown Roswell. With several popular museums nearby, as well as the New Mexico Military Installation, it is the perfect home base for all of your adventures in and around Roswell. You will find everything you could want from a hotel at Roswell's La Quinta Inn & Suites.

200 E 19th Street, Roswell NM
(505) 622-8000 or (800) 531-5900
www.lq.com

Accommodations

Sierra Grande Lodge and Spa

Sierra Grande Lodge and Spa is an oasis in the desert for refueling your spirit. The lodge is a restored 1929 resort renowned for its mineral spring water. The lodge is built on an area that was known as Geronimo Springs Baths in the 1880s. Many cowboys and soldiers came to these springs to soak their aching bodies and cover their wounds with the white mud that was said to have many healing powers. The town where the Sierra Grande Lodge and Spa is located has one of the largest mineral water aquifers underneath downtown and is naturally heated by magma. The mineral water in Truth or Consequences contains 38 minerals, almost four times the amount found in other mineral water aquifers. Sixteen deluxe rooms include one suite with balcony access, four balcony rooms and 11 standard rooms. Each guest receives a complimentary 30-minute soak for each day of their stay. The restaurant offers a combination of Mediterranean and Asian cuisine. The chef creates private dinner services in the kitchen or on the balcony. Unwind at the spa with a soothing massage, custom facial or body treatment. You may choose from an indoor or outdoor pool for your mineral soak. Suits are optional in the indoor pool. Discover the healing power of the desert and mineral water at Sierra Grande Lodge and Spa.

501 McAdoo Street, Truth or Consequences NM
(505) 894-6976
www.sierragrandelodge.com

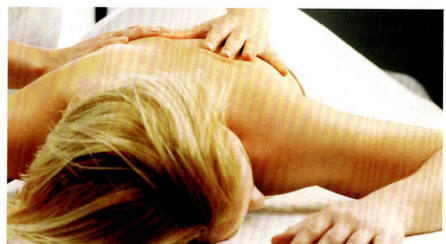

Historic Pelham House Sanctuary and Retreat

If civilization has gotten to you, come replenish yourself at the Historic Pelham House Sanctuary and Retreat. With its stunning views of the picturesque Hatch Valley, rich with tilled fields and horse corrals, you're sure to feel the stress of daily life slip away. The Pelham House can accommodate an intimate weekend getaway or a gathering of up to 60 people. Proprietors Robert and Ci Ci Gross pride themselves on the services and ambience of this retreat. You will find relaxing spa treatments, as well as private time for quiet reflection. The welcome and sense of peace begin the moment you step foot in the old adobe hacienda. A fireplace and family memorabilia grace the Grand Sala. A tiny chapel offers still one more avenue to contemplation. Other relaxing spots include the library with its rich red walls and cozy furnishings, as well as an enclosed atrium with lime and lemon trees around a central fountain. The Grosses will create a special event or occasion around any client's personal wishes. Ci Ci, a massage therapist and herbalist, can treat you to a full spa experience. Rich with history, love and faith, the restored Historic Pelham House Sanctuary and Retreat is available for your rest and renewal.

34150 S Highway 185, Hatch NM
(505) 267-5288

Best Western Mesilla Valley Inn

Las Cruces offers visitors a plethora of recreational opportunities along with art galleries, fabulous shopping venues and the historic district of Old Town of Mesilla. The Best Western Mesilla Valley Inn is a convenient launching point for all of the wonderful things there are to see and do. It's within minutes of New Mexico State University and just a short drive from NASA and the White Sands Missile Range and National Monument. Mesilla Valley Inn features 160 rooms, 51 of which are deluxe rooms in the Executive Wing. Each deluxe room comes with king beds and upgraded furnishings and lighting, along with work areas and other business amenities. Visitors quickly fall in love with the heated pool and adjacent Jacuzzi, which are centrally located to all rooms and make for an ideal family gathering spot. The pool area offers barbecues, lounge chairs and umbrella tables. When you're ready for something to eat, head to Eddie's Bar and Grill, which has a terrific menu featuring their popular shrimp bar, along with nightly entertainment and a dance room. For those who wish to dine al fresco, there is also Eddie's Terrace Bar where you can relax with a tropical cocktail while listening to talented local musicians. From arrival to departure, the inn's friendly and personable staff offers visitors a taste of true Southwestern hospitality and comfortable accommodations highlighted by thoroughly modern amenities. Enjoy hotel living at its finest at the Best Western Mesilla Valley Inn.

901 Avendia de Mesilla, Las Cruces NM
(505) 524-8603
www.mesillavalleyinn.com

Hotel Encanto de Las Cruces
A Heritage Hotel and Resort

The Hotel Encanto de Las Cruces is the perfect destination for any traveler enticed by the culture and history of New Mexico. The architecture is reminiscent of the grand Spanish Colonial style prevalent in the late 1800s and early 1900s. Its dramatic and culturally driven design features deep, vibrant colors, rich fabrics and textures, signature art pieces from Old Mexico and regional photography. Located near the majestic Organ Mountains and overlooking historic Old Mesilla, the hotel gives guests ample opportunity to explore the city's sites. This authentic Heritage Hotel features 203 guestrooms and is outfitted with an artful mix of Mexican, Western and Spanish design elements. Hand-painted wood elements and one-of-a-kind photography by local artist Miguel Gandert add intimacy and warmth to the space. The Hotel Encanto has seven executive and Jacuzzi suites, laundry and valet services, on-site car rental, free shuttle service and parking, as well as personalized room service. With more than 10,000 square feet of meeting and exhibit space, including the 5,000-square-foot San Andres Ballroom, the Hotel Encanto is perfect for weddings, business conventions and special events, as well as small intimate affairs. Guests can enjoy a variety of unique Southwestern dishes at the hotel's casual fine dining restaurant. This restaurant combines a Spanish Colonial design theme with a contemporary twist. The new bar uses a rich indigo and oxblood red color palette with gold and silver accents along with mother of pearl tile tabletops. This cosmopolitan interpretation of the high-style clubs found in Mexico and Spain will offer guests the area's best selection of liquors, cordials, imported beers, an extensive wine list and an excellent selection of premium tequilas. For a lodging experience unparalleled in New Mexico, stay at the Hotel Encanto de Las Cruces, a Heritage Hotel and Resort.

705 S Telshor Boulevard, Las Cruces NM
(505) 522-4300 or (877) 901-ROOM (7666)
http://hhandr.com/las_main.php

Bear Creek Cabins

Nestled in the tall pines at 7,000 feet, en route to the Gila River, Lake Roberts and the Cliff Dwellings, lie the scenic and popular Bear Creek Cabins. Proprietors Dawn and Billy Donnel have created a welcoming environment at the edge of Pinos Altos on Bear Creek, surrounded by the 3.5 million-acre Gila National Forest and Wilderness area. Pinos Altos is a rustic mining town that sprang up in the 1860s with the discovery of gold in Bear Creek. Today, visitors can enjoy the quality comforts of the Bear Creek Cabins while discovering all the area has to offer, including the old Hearst Church and a visit to the historic Pinos Altos cemetery, fort and museum. Visitors to Bear Creek Cabins will enjoy friendly personnel, spotless rooms that are comfortable and welcoming, warm fireplaces and barbecue grills, along with Adirondack chairs and sylvan views. The two-story, split level cabins include a full kitchen that comes equipped with a microwave, coffeemaker and additional amenities. The cabins are located near the renowned Buckhorn Steakhouse, as well as the Melodrama Theater and numerous other local attractions. Discover a land of enchantment with a stay at Bear Creek Cabins, seven miles north of Silver City on Highway 15.

P.O. Box 53082, Pinos Altos NM
(505) 388-4501 or (888) 388-4515
www.bearcreekcabins.com

La Quinta Inn & Suites of Deming

Photos by S.M. Stachler

Visitors to the southwest corner of New Mexico, where you will find Luna County and the popular community of Deming, are treated to a wealth of historical and recreational opportunities that range from hiking the mountains of the Black Range to touring the Shakespeare Ghost Town. While discovering all that this inspiring area has to offer, enjoy the casual comforts of La Quinta Inn & Suites, which is centrally located on East Pine in Deming. At La Quinta Inn & Suites, guests are made to feel at home through exceptional personalized service and a slew of modern amenities, including free high-speed Internet. With a philosophy geared toward making each guest feel right at home, La Quinta Inn & Suites outfits each room with televisions that include premium channels, movies on demand and video games along with dataport telephones, voicemail and free local calling. Additional amenities include in-room dryers, coffee makers and irons with ironing boards, as well as well-lit workspaces that include swivel-tilt chairs. The inn offers meeting facilities, a swimming pool and a fully equipped fitness center, along with airport shuttle and pet accommodations. La Quinta Inn & Suites of Deming is part of the La Quinta Organization, which is one of the nation's largest owners of limited-service hotels. Based in Dallas, Texas, the company boasts more than 65,000 rooms and offers a 110-percent satisfaction guarantee to ensure that you have the most pleasant and rewarding stay possible. Enjoy all the comforts of home at La Quinta Inn & Suites.

4300 E Pine Street, Deming NM
(505) 546-0600
www.lq.com

Casa Blanca Inn

David and Shirley Alford would like to welcome you to Casa Blanca Inn, the latest in their award-winning family of bed-and-breakfast inns in the Southwest. This paradisal inn offers a lush oasis in the high desert. Known for his green thumb, David created the gardens, which are filled with a variety of opulent and vividly hued flowering bushes, stately shade trees and soothing ponds. The gardens feature expansive courtyards, shaded seating areas and a charming gazebo. Inside, guests will find an inviting array of period antiques, hand-carved Spanish colonial furniture and other luxurious amenities to enjoy. Guests of Casa Blanca Inn are treated each morning to a scrumptious Southwestern breakfast served buffet-style in the elegant dining room. Each room in the hacienda building has an individual patio with either a courtyard or a garden view. Several rooms offer fireplaces, whirlpool tubs and wheelchair access. A few of the amenities include down pillows and comforters, in-room refrigerators, coffee grinders, microwave ovens, private phones, cable television, DSL and wireless Internet. The inn has a wonderful guest library offering a workstation and lending library. A stately living room provides just the right setting for gaming tables. Situated only a few blocks from Farmington's historic downtown, the inn is an easy walk to numerous galleries, restaurants, antique shops and trading posts.

The Alfords have provided a small gift shop which offers wonderful local wares like Navajo rugs and other necessities for your travels. Enjoy gracious hospitality and surround yourself with the quiet enchantment of the Four Corners by staying at Casa Blanca Inn.

505 E La Plata Street, Farmington NM
(800) 550-6503
www.4cornersbandb.com

El Rancho Hotel & Motel

Opened in 1937, El Rancho Hotel in Gallup was built by the brother of movie magnate D.W. Griffith and was a temporary home for many Hollywood stars during the 1940s and 1950s when Western movies reached their peak of popularity. Armand Ortega, a respected Indian Trader, owns and operates the hotel today, a restored building on the National Historic Register that epitomizes the rustic style of the Old West with huge beams, a brick floor and handmade staircases that spiral around a fireplace cove to the second-floor balcony. The rooms, named after stars who stayed here in the early days, are individually decorated in a combination of Old West and Southwest styles. Many have views of the outdoor swimming pool. Oretega stocks the hotel's art gallery with fine selection of paintings by Indian artists, jewelry, rugs, pottery, kachinas and sandpaintings. Dining at El Rancho is always satisfying, with burgers and Southwest specialties named after stars served in a setting reminiscent of Western adventure. El Rancho makes the perfect home base for adventures into the surrounding countryside with ancient ruins and natural wonders all close at hand. Gallup, in the heart of Indian Country, is the site of the world-famous Inter-Tribal Indian Ceremonial held each August. It's close to the Navajo Reservation and the Zuni Pueblo, as well as the magnificent Monument Valley, the Petrified Forest and the Painted Desert. Surround yourself with the legendary West at El Rancho Hotel & Motel, just off Interstate 40 at Exit 22.

1000 E Highway 66, Gallup NM
(505) 863-9311 or (800) 543-6351
www.elranchohotel.com

Photos by S.M. Stachler

Courtyard By Marriott

Guests of the Courtyard by Marriott in downtown Farmington are treated to tranquil views of the Animas River, fantastic dining and personalized service. The hotel offers 125 riverview guest rooms, along with three king rooms with spas and four fireplace suites all designed to pamper the weary traveler. Each room comes complete with coffeemaker and tea service, television with complimentary premium channels, ergonomic workstation and other amenities. During your stay at the Courtyard by Marriott, the friendly and helpful staff will courteously assist you with anything you might need. The hotel provides room service, free high-speed wireless Internet, guest laundry, valet and business services, as well as free airport shuttles for your convenience. Courtyard by Marriott's heated indoor pool or whirlpool can help you unwind, and you can work out all of your stresses in the fitness center. If you prefer the great outdoors, be sure to take advantage of Courtyard by Marriott's direct access to the Riverwalk, which offers more than seven miles of nature trails and scenic beauty. The in-house restaurant, the River's Edge Café, provides Farmington's finest breakfast buffet, including a made-to-order omelet bar. During lunch and dinner, you can please your palate with one of the café's wonderful entrées served indoors or al fresco. For the business traveler, the hotel offers 5,000 square feet of flexible meeting space in the convention area and catering can be provided. Relax, unwind and feel welcome at the Courtyard by Marriott.

560 Scott Avenue, Farmington NM
(505) 325-5111
www.marriott.com

Accommodations • 43

New Mexico is the only state in the Union with an official state question: "Red or Green?" This, of course, refers to the sauce made from the native chiles found in New Mexico. Unlike salsa, which is normally chunky, thin and served with chips, chile sauce is finer, thicker and more commonly served with meals.

The Rio Grande has carved out a giant gorge along its meandering path through New Mexico

Arts & Crafts

PaperGami

PaperGami carries the largest selection of handmade Japanese paper in the country, along with handmade papers from such places as India, Italy and Thailand. The festive sheets are ideal for wrapping presents, creating covers for personal journals and other creative projects. PaperGami offers hand-bound albums, books, ribbon and other items that make perfect gifts. The store features Japanese yuzen paper, the most elegant, intricately crafted paper in the world. Yuzen papermakers rely on thousands of years of tradition to create their unique papers. Black yuzen paper is the most sought after of all the yuzen papers, and it sells out quickly. "This is sort of a dying art," says owner Anne Englehardt. "Some of the people making this paper are 80 years old." Anne has traveled all over the world to study and search for papers, and she has worked as a consultant for companies that import paper from Asia. Papergami has locations in the trendy Nob Hill district of Albuquerque and in Santa Fe, next to the historic Lensic Theater. For rare and beautiful papers sure to spark your creativity, visit PaperGami.

**114 Tulane Drive SE, Albuquerque NM
(505) 255-2228 or (800) 569-2280
213 W San Francisco Street, Santa Fe NM
(505) 982-3080 or (800) 569-2280
www.papergami.com**

Stone Mountain Bead Gallery

Beads have played a long and illustrious role in human civilization that stretches back 20,000 years. We've used them for barter, for ornamentation and to denote prestige, class and power. Stone Mountain Bead Gallery in Albuquerque searches the world for beads prized by collectors and designers alike. You'll also find finished jewelry and beaded handcrafts. Robert Steinberg opened this specialized shop in 1993, and it has become a destination for anyone seeking hard-to-find gemstone, glass and ethnic beads. If beads are not already your passion, a visit to this shop is sure to spark your interest. Not only is the merchandise very special, the entire shopping experience is a distinct pleasure, with terrific music, fabulous service and a welcoming atmosphere. *Crosswinds Weekly* named the shop in its Best of New Mexico issue, and the readers of *Weekly Alibi* have been continuously voting it the Best Bead Shop since 1994. Stone Mountain Bead Gallery pleases customers looking for original handcrafts and silver jewelry, as well as collectors and craftsmen. Visit this special store, where beads continue to be a vibrant part of human affairs.

3100 Central Avenue SE, Albuquerque NM
(505) 260-1121

48 • Arts & Crafts

Santa Fe's Indian Market is an internationally famous event, drawing a crowd from all around the globe to the city's historic plaza each August. Each year the Market includes 1,200 artists from about 100 tribes who show their work in more than 600 booths. The event attracts an estimated 100,000 visitors. Buyers, collectors and gallery owners come to Indian Market to take advantage of the opportunity to buy directly from the artists. For many visitors, this is a rare opportunity to meet the artists and learn about contemporary Indian arts and cultures.

Photo by Mark Nohl, courtesy of the New Mexico Tourism Department

Beauty and the Beads

Beauty and the Beads is a contemporary crafts Mecca, turning the ancient art of jewelry making into a modern art form. The shop itself is gorgeous. Antique beaded fabrics from around the world and Indonesian Spirit figures are woven into the stimulating décor, while a vast selection beads, pearls, crystals, glass and semi-precious stones co-mingle. Expressions of delight can be seen on the faces of customers as they meander from section to section enjoying the variety of colors and textures. People can buy books, tools and anything needed to assemble their beaded projects. "I love how people can come in and enter a world of beauty and feel expanded in ways that honor their own creative process," says Madeleine Durham, owner and creator of Beauty and the Beads. Madeleine recalls starting out with a tray of beads at the local flea market, and by the end of the summer the tray had become many tables prompting her to move into a store front. For more than 16 years she has created a network honoring women's love of making things with their own hands, though she is quick to help men, as well. Beauty and the Beads is a center for creative expression. "Women have long loved to adorn themselves and we're not waiting around to be gifted, we are customizing!" said a member of her staff. Madeleine is accessible to her clients. A designer herself, she offers expert repairs, an extensive class schedule, slide shows and a place to transform your creative desires. Come to Beauty and the Beads and experience the rewarding thrill of creating your own masterpiece.

939 W Alameda Street, Santa Fe NM
(505) 982-5234 *www.santafebeads.com*

50 • Attractions

Adobe ruins at Pecos National Monument, Pecos, New Mexico

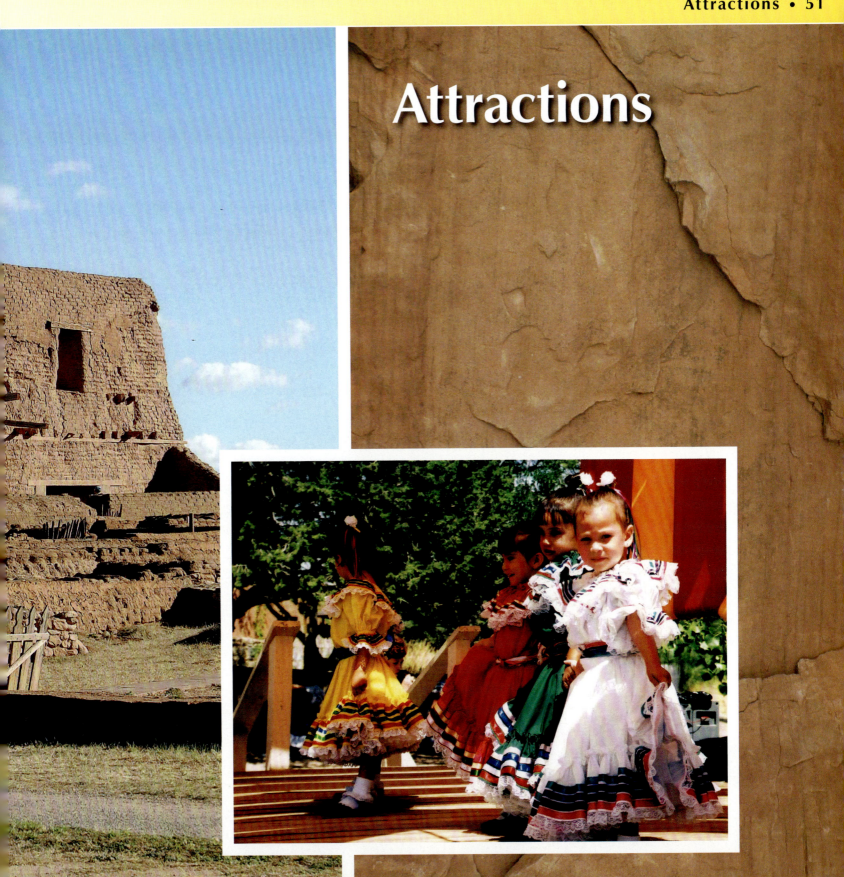

Attractions

Attractions of Sierra County

Photo by Judd Irish Bradley

Truth or Consequences Museums

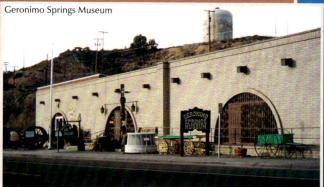
Geronimo Springs Museum

Veterans' Memorial Park

Truth or Consequences is located in an area abundantly rich in history. Fortunately, much of this history is preserved in the area's museums. The Truth or Consequences Museums reveal to us a glimpse of not only why we are who we are today, but of those who have gone before us. Preserved are snapshots of time faithfully documenting ancient Native American civilizations of the area, the history of the famous El Camino Real trail built by the Spaniards in the 1500s and mining boom towns of the 1800s. The Veterans' Memorial Park, which is home to the Wall That Heals, is a half-scale representation of the wall found in Washington D.C. It toured the United States and Ireland, honoring veterans of all conflicts from the Revolutionary War to the present day conflict in Iraq. The Geronimo Springs Museum features several rooms representing southwestern history including mastodon and mammoth skulls discovered in the area, mineral exhibits and Apache and Hispanic histories. There's also a world class collection of prehistoric pottery and a Geronimo Trail Interpretive and Visitor Center. Callahan's Auto Museum has an outstanding display of vintage and classic cars dating from 1925 through 1963, as well as a large collection of unusual memorabilia from the early days of the automobile. Be sure to stop in at all of the area's fine museums when you're in Truth or Consequences and become engaged with stories of heritage that are still being told today through their continuing efforts.

**211 Main Street,
Truth or Consequences NM
(505) 894-1968**
geronimospringsmuseum.com
truthorconsequencesnm.net

Percha Bank Museum

Rural Museums of Sierra County

There are four wonderful Rural Museums in Sierra County. The first is called the Pioneer Store Museum, owned by Don and Dona Edmund. Located in an 1880 log building, the museum store features the merchandise and bookkeeping records dating back to 1880, as well as memorabilia of early pioneer residents. The second and third museums are both located in Hillsboro. The Black Range Museum, located near the junction of NM 27, contains many artifacts of the town's history, a once-thriving gold mining town of the 1880s. Found in the old Ocean Grove Hotel building, it was once owned by the famous Sadie Orchard. The cook stove and ice box used in the old hotel are a part of the exhibit, articles owned by Sadie Orchard, as well as old photographs of the town. The Clock Museum is located adjacent to the Black Range Museum, and features antique clocks and reproductions of clocks, with hand-made clock faces. The fourth museum is called Percha Bank Museum. It is located in Kingston and displays the history of Kingston from its silver mining days in the 1880s. Housed in the original bank building, complete with the original teller windows and vault, it was organized to collect, preserve and display artifacts and photographs from the town's early mining history. There is also a gallery space where local artists show their work. The Rural Museums of Sierra County will take you on an adventure into the past.

**211 Main Street,
Truth or Consequences NM
(800) 831-9487**
sierracountynewmexico.info

Attractions of Sierra County

Turtleback Mountain overlooking Truth or Consequences

Geronimo Trail Scenic Byway

The Geronimo Trail Scenic Byway meanders through the most spectacular scenery in the southwest, from high deserts to mountain forests, spanning many distinct ecological life zones. The Geronimo Trail offers a wide variety of outdoor experiences, from the Rio Grande Valley, with the cities of Truth or Consequences and Elephant Butte, to the rugged peaks of the Black Range Mountains, with its quaint old mining towns. The lakes of Sierra County at Elephant Butte Lake and Caballo Lake State Parks offer fishing, boating and water sports of all types. Camping facilities are also available. The Gila National Forest, managing the Black Range Mountains, offers hiking, backpacking, picnicking and camping, along with breathtaking vistas. Photography and bird watching are popular pastimes in this area. The main focus of the Byway is to provide the traveler with the unique experience of traveling through a country once inhabited by ancient peoples and later the homeland of the fierce Apache tribes. As the area was settled, rip-roaring towns sprang up overnight. Eventually, conflicts between cultures resulted in the Apaches being exiled to Florida in the 1880s as prisoners of war, never to return to their homeland. The picturesque old mining towns, with few inhabitants left, are reminders of the times that once were. Today they are filled with unique shops, art galleries and studios, cafes featuring local cuisine, museums and fascinating stories of bygone days. Drive the Geronimo Trail Scenic Byway, and prepare for beautiful sights and a rich history.

**211 Main Street,
Truth or Consequences NM
(800) 831-9487**
geronimotrail.com

Attractions of Sierra County • 57

Truth or Consequences Hot Springs and Spa Association

Truth or Consequences is a small resort town with a year round population of just over 8,000. The Spa Association is a group of managers and owners of the town's ten functioning hot mineral springs bathhouses and spas. These men and women have banded together to promote Truth or Consequences as a spa destination. Languishing amidst its hot mineral springs, alongside the flowing Rio Grande, this town has remained unspoiled and has not seen local development run rampant or real estate prices rise beyond the reach of long time locals. Here the breathtaking sandstone bluffs, nearby parks and sunny, deep blue skies remain the biggest neighborhood attraction. Truth or Consequences is a preferred vacation site for the state's natives. Traditionally they have come to bathe in the soothing hot springs and participate in the many recreational opportunities in the area and at the two large lakes nearby. In the past decade the town began to gain more national attention and praise. National publications such as Where to Retire recently named the city as one of the top retirement destinations in the United States and the number of retirees relocating here continues to grow. As they reclaim their hot mineral baths heritage, now is the time to visit, relax in some of the finest rediscovered hot springs in the country and experience the charms of this quiet little town that is still an icon of the genteel old west.

211 Main Street, Truth or Consequences NM
(800) 831-9487
spa-town.com

Photo by Peter Wong

Photo by Dorothy Sturges

Attractions of Sierra County

Sierra County Arts Council

Truth or Consequences and Sierra County are premier arts destinations and home to the Sierra County Arts Council. There's a large community of artists living in the area that possess a wide variety of skills, visions and talents. As you drive through downtown Truth or Consequences, you'll discover many colorful shops and galleries displaying the work of local artists. As you stroll through town it soon becomes evident that the arts community is alive with vision and expression. Take a peek into shop windows and you'll see a wonderful variety of art, color and style on display. Beyond Truth or Consequences, in the outlying hamlets and ghost towns, you'll find even more variety. Both contemporary and historical artwork adorn Sierra County. Many public and private buildings and monuments are decorated with murals. Las Palomas Plaza fountain, which is the site of one of the earliest hot springs, displays colorful ceramic sculptures. The Sierra County Arts Council participates in sponsoring concert and theatre events, farmers' markets and other arts festivals and competitions. You're invited to visit and discover an area rich with talented artists representing a wide variety of media.

**211 Main Street,
Truth or Consequences NM
(505) 894-1968 or
(800) 831-9487**
sierracountynewmexico.info

Sierra County Birding

Sierra County lays claim to being in one of the finest birding regions in the nation in terms of habitat diversity and potential for rarities. The riparian habitat found along the famous Rio Grande and along the area's lakes is a paradise for birders. Here you'll see egrets, herons, pelicans, grebes and some pretty unusual avian sightings. Two areas in particular are stand-outs for prime bird watching. First, for land birds, is the Percha Dam State Park and secondly, excellent mountain birding habitat can be found in the Gila National Forest. Percha Dam State Park plays host to a two day springtime bird related program called Migration Sensation. Each day starts with guided bird walks where you can observe many different species of migratory birds. One of the more striking birds that are commonly seen at the dam is the brightly colored Vermillion Flycatcher. A total of 121 species of birds were recently counted around the Percha Dam and Caballo Lake State Parks, including Bald Eagles, White Pelicans, and Sandhill Cranes. Visitors may even get a close-up glimpse of a pair of roosting Great Horned Owls. Those interested in dormant trees and avian behavior will encounter a rich floral and fauna diversity where the upper Chihuahuan Desert meets the Rio Grande bosque. Both of the state parks offer ample camping opportunities. Make sure to visit this beautiful and scenic area and discover all the great birding opportunities it has to offer.

211 Main Street, Truth or Consequences NM
(505) 894-1968 or (800) 831-9487
sierracountynewmexico.info

Photos by Judd Irish Bradley

60 • Attractions of Sierra County

Elephant Butte Lake

Percha Dam

Elephant Butte Lake

Sierra County Lakes and Rivers

Incredibly vast scenic vistas of lakes, high desert valleys and rugged mountain ranges intermingled with natural mineral hot springs are what you'll find when you visit Sierra County Lakes and Rivers. A mild climate and plenty of sunshine make for abundant opportunities for year round recreation wherever you go in the region. The area features three well-equipped and maintained state parks containing eight developed campgrounds, and the county boasts 33 RV parks for summer and winter visitors. There's Elephant Butte Lake State Park which is the largest lake in the state, Caballo Lake State Park and Percha Dam State Park. The famous Rio Grande runs through the area as well. The lakes and river create a diverse paradise for water-based recreational opportunities, as well as birding. All the parks feature interesting hiking trails such as the two-mile Luchini Trail at Elephant Butte Lake, the one and a half mile Cactus Trail at Caballo Lake and the recently developed Paseo del Rio trail. It's a one-mile loop that features interpretive signs that teach visitors about the natural and cultural history of the area. The portion of the Rio Grande between Elephant Butte Dam and Caballo Lake runs high in the spring and summer months and dwindles down to a trickle during the fall and winter. Adventurous rafters can take a 15 minute float from Truth or Consequences to Caballo Lake in the summertime. There's plenty to see and do in this recreational wonderland. Visit and discover Sierra County Lakes and Rivers and see why it's often called the Oasis in the Southwest.

**211 Main Street,
Truth or Consequences NM**
(505) 894-1968 or (800) 831-9487
sierracountynewmexico.info

RioBravoFineArt, Inc.

Artists are dreamers. RioBravoFineArt, Inc. founder H. Joe Waldrum purchased a vacant ice house in Truth or Consequences and dreamt of turning it into a stylish home and art gallery. In 2000, his dream grew when the store next door became available. He and his friend, architect and art collector Andy Anderson, drew up lofty plans for living quarters that included a courtyard with organic garden and outside mineral bath. Eventually a large gallery space, the Living Room, was created upstairs. Between two areas on the main floor are the Lower Gallery and Print Room. A temporary studio is housed on the bottom floor. Before they could complete the renovation, a local painter asked if he could show his new work, The Stations, and thus a showcase gallery was born. Two more shows occurred during construction, one featuring four local artists, the other a Waldrum event. Unfortunately, Waldrum passed away in December of 2003. His dream, affectionately known as *mi fantasia gigante*, did not die with him. Eduardo Alicea, his former assistant, and Waldrum's children continue to show new work in the main gallery areas. The ice house, currently used as a makeshift movie theater, will be a sculpture garden, with a piece showing the former owner riding a mule. Come see the fruit of one man's labor and vision, and the art of many others, at RioBravoFineArt, Inc.

**110 E Broadway Avenue,
Truth or Consequences NM**
(505) 894-0572
riobravofineart.com

Attractions of Sierra County • 63

Grasshopper Silk

The origins of silk painting can be traced back to India in the second century A.D., and yet this popular and labor-intensive art form is still highly sought after for its uniqueness and delicate beauty. At Grasshopper Silk, artist Sandy Hopper continues to study, learn and improve her skills while creating stunning, one-of-a-kind pieces that are both beautiful and practical. Sandy discovered silk painting in 1999 after moving to Elephant Butte Lake State Park with her husband and renewing a friendship with fellow artist Sharon Holmes. The duo set their sights on silk painting and later attended a workshop in Santa Fe, where Sandy was introduced to Jacquard steam set dyes and became instantly devoted to the art. Many steps are required in the creation of a piece and any one of those steps can easily go awry and ruin a project. Sandy has to go through an involved process of cleaning, stretching and examining a piece before she can begin the dye application process. After a project is painted, it has to be cured for a minimum of 72 hours, carefully steamed for three to five hours, and then left to rest for two days. After that, the silk is washed to remove excess dye, rolled in terry cloth to absorb excess moisture and ironed while damp. Sandy uses this laborious process to create magnificent ruanas, art scarves and shoji screen panels, which are available for purchase by appointment only at Grasshopper Silk.

**509 Bass Road, Old Hot Springs Landing,
Elephant Butte NM**
(505) 744-4958
grasshoppersilk.com

Blue Hole
Photo by Dan Monaghan
Courtesy of the New Mexico Tourism Department

Santa Rosa, City of Natural Lakes

Halfway between Albuquerque and Amarillo on I-40, picturesque Santa Rosa is a favorite spot for travelers. Some stay for a few days. A few stay forever. It has been an oasis for motorists since 1927, when Route 66, the most famous route in America, was built through town. Santa Rosa takes its nickname, the City of Natural Lakes, from the small spring-fed lakes that form in the area's limestone rock. These lakes are connected by a network of underground, water-filled tunnels. The lakes are a rarity in the dry climate of the *llano estacado*, or staked plains. Interestingly, early settlers could make little use of the lakes, because the crystal-clear water is very hard and ill-suited for drinking or laundry. The water is fabulous for diving, however. Even before U.S. 66 arrived, Santa Rosa was important as a railroad center. Here, the Rock Island Line constructed a difficult bridge over the Pecos River. When director John Ford filmed the *Grapes of Wrath*, he used Santa Rosa for a memorable scene in which Tom Joad (Henry Fonda) watches a freight train steam over the Pecos River into the sunset. In a much earlier era, Santa Rosa was part of Billy the Kid's territory, along with the neighboring town of Puerto De Luna. Santa Rosa was settled in 1865 under the name Aqua Negra Chiquita, or little black water. Don Celso Baca, the founder of the town, changed its name in 1890 to honor his mother, Rosa. Santa Rosa's pleasant climate, historic points of interest and magnificent natural beauty are guaranteed to make your stay one to remember.

141 S 5th Street, Santa Rosa NM
(505) 472-3404
www.santarosanm.org

City of Natural Lakes • 67

Santa Rosa Blue Hole

Santa Rosa Blue Hole is one of those rare natural finds that has attracted visitors for years. This 81-foot deep, bell-shaped pool of water remains clear because 3,000 gallons per minute of new water flows in from a cave entrance at the bottom, recycling the hole every six hours. This means divers and swimmers alike can experience a deep dive in a nearly crystal-clear environment. Also, no matter what the weather is like, the water temperature of this desert oasis remains a constant 61 to 64 degrees. These two qualities have earned the spot the nickname "Nature's Jewel." An attractive watering hole in the days before cars, it is believed that native Indians as well as Spanish explorer Francisco Vasquez de Coronado and Billy the Kid may have used the spot to cool off and refresh. Today it is primarily used by scuba divers who enjoy practicing in the near-perfect conditions. Because the Blue Hole is 4,600 feet above sea level, it is a perfect place for Open Water and Altitude Diver training. Although it is open daily and nightly for public diving, be sure to obtain a diving permit from the City of Santa Rosa, as local officials monitor the site carefully and there is a $300 fine for non-compliance. Cool off, explore or just dip your feet for a spell at one of the coolest place on earth, the Santa Rosa Blue Hole.

www.santarosanm.org

Santa Rosa Golf Course & Country Club

When you visit Santa Rosa, get in a few holes at the Santa Rosa Golf Course and Country Club. You'll appreciate the low humidity and pleasantly warm days. Local and visiting golfers enjoy this challenging nine-hole, par-36 course and fun driving range, which is owned and operated by the City of Santa Rosa. In 1999, the city made $130,000 worth of improvements to the course, including new landscaping, new equipment to improve fairways and greens, a new sprinkler system and a remodeled clubhouse. Santa Rosa's elevation is 4,600 feet, and at this altitude balls travel noticeably farther than at sea level. Come prove this for yourself. The course is open year round, seven days a week. Greens fees are only $10 for 18 holes. Carts, instructors and a pro shop are all available. Santa Rosa sponsors annual charity tournaments. Come visit the Santa Rosa Golf Course and Country Club, a half mile off historic Route 66. You may find your only problem is keeping your eyes on the ball instead of on the stunning scenery that surrounds the greens.

Chuck & Dale Lane, Santa Rosa NM
(505) 472-GOLF (4653)

Santa Rosa Park Lake

Santa Rosa's water fun options include spring-fed Park Lake, the Southwest's largest free swimming pool, which features a free waterslide. The Park Lake recreation area offers family swimming, a water park and fishing. Swimming is available from Memorial Day to Labor Day. The lake has certified lifeguards, water play equipment, pedal boats and canoes. Lake Ponds is stocked with trout and is for kids and seniors only. It's free, as well. In addition to the lakes, the recreation area offers tennis, basketball and softball facilities, a kiddieland and a picnic area. You can take a hiking trail down to beautiful El Rito Creek, another spot where you can fish. Park Lake is a great place to hold company picnics. It is the home of many of Santa Rosa's special summer events, including the 4th of July celebration and the Route 66 Festival on Labor Day weekend. The old road ran into town right past Park Lake, which was a motorist campground and source of water during the Great Depression. For a day of play, bring the whole gang to Santa Rosa Park Lake.

Will Rogers Drive and Lake Drive, Santa Rosa NM
(505) 472-3 763

Billy the Kid Museum

There aren't too many names more familiar from the tales of the Old West than Billy the Kid. Several movies and countless books have immortalized and attempted to shed light on the fascinating story of this outlaw who made a name for himself even though he died at the young age of 21. If you want to get a real feel for Henry McCarty, the name his parents gave him at birth, then you'll want to visit the Billy the Kid Museum in Fort Sumner. Founder Ed Sweet wanted to own a museum when he grew up. After several jobs where he would occasionally take antiques in trade for his services and wares, he and his wife, Jewel, opened a one-building museum in 1953. With the popularity of the legendary criminal and his own collection of related items, Ed Sweet's museum was changed to the Billy the Kid Museum. Today, the museum boasts nearly 60,000 relics of the 1800s and early 1900s, from carriages to cars, stoves to signage. However, the biggest draws are the Kid artifacts. There's a rock he carved his name into, one of his rifles, chaps, spurs and even curtains from the room where he was shot. Discover an important icon of the Wild West with a trip through time at the Billy the Kid Museum.

1601 E Sumner Avenue, Fort Sumner NM
(800) 556-7049
www.billythekidmuseumfortsumner.com

Photos by S.M. Stachler

ROUTE 66 AUTO MUSEUM

Normally, if you hear someone referred to as "Bozo," you think they are being called a clown or an imbecile. That doesn't hold true around Santa Rosa. "Bozo" is the nickname of revered local, James Cordova, owner of Route 66 Auto Museum and Bozo's Garage & Wrecker Service & Body Shop. The nickname is a reference to the famous clown of classic children's programming fame, but not because James is such a joker. Back when the show aired, his family had the only television set on his side of town. Kids naturally flocked there to watch the popular clown. Thus, the nickname. While the good-natured Santa Rosa native usually sports a smile, he's serious about cars. A love of building models as a kid blossomed into tinkering with the real thing as soon as he was old enough to drive. When he's not towing stranded motorists or repairing local rides, he's restoring and re-polishing the 30-plus vehicles that inhabit his Route 66 Auto Museum. From a classic Caddie to tricked-out trucks, street rods to the sleek fins of a '57 Chevy, there's enough chrome here to dazzle any car buff. There's also Route 66 memorabilia, models, and vintage signs to peruse and purchase in the gift shop. While other museums may be a drag, you'll definitely get your kicks at the Route 66 Auto Museum. If you're lucky, Bozo will be in to entertain you with his stories and knowledge.

2766 Old Route 66, Santa Rosa NM
(505) 472-1966

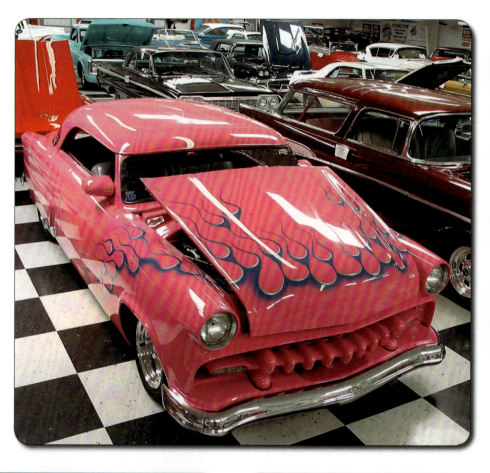

Photo by S.M. Stachler

Photo by S.M. Stachler

Photo by S.M. Stachler

City of Natural Lakes • 71

Photos by S.M. Stachler

Joseph's Bar & Grill

Joseph's Bar & Grill does more than just serve good food. It is also keeping the Santa Rosa tradition very much alive. One way is through the Fat Man logo. The chubby faced icon had been inviting travelers along Route 66 to stop by Club Café since 1935. He was a symbol of wealth, fortitude and satisfaction through several wars and American crises. Club Café fell on hard times, however, as did many businesses along the famous route when the superhighways took over. In 1991, the club closed its doors, leaving the Fat Man as a lonely sentinel on America's most famous route. A few years later, the building was bought by local restaurateurs Joseph and Carmen Campos, who made the Fat Man part of their restaurant's logo. The Campos family is the other part of the tradition here. Joseph and Carmen opened La Fiesta Drive-In in 1956, eventually expanding it into a full service, cafeteria-style restaurant. When hard times hit the area, they handed it to their children, who made it into what Joseph's Bar & Grill is today. Joseph's includes a gift shop, bar and nightclub with live entertainment and karaoke. The menu features breakfast, lunch and dinner with a heavy Southwest influence. Running the show is son Joseph, his wife, Christina, and their children, Analisa, Andrea and Jose, III. Route 66 Club Café may no longer be around, but the Fat Man and the Campos' dream of serving their community are still going strong. Get a taste of Santa Rosa tradition at Joseph's Bar & Grill.

865 Will Rodgers Drive, Santa Rosa NM
(505) 472-3361
www.route66.com/Josephs

Destination Southwest

If the idea of planning all the details of your upcoming trip to the Southwest seems daunting, Destination Southwest can help. With so many options available, you might wonder how to squeeze in all the fun things you can do in and around New Mexico. You can visit the ruins of ancient civilizations, shop in small boutiques for beautiful gifts made by local artists, or experience adventurous outdoor activities. That's where Destination Southwest comes in. The staff will custom-tailor the perfect getaway to suit your needs. Destination Southwest will give your organization or group a custom-made itinerary. They can make reservations for hotels, restaurants and a wide variety of attractions. Lydia Griego-Hansen and Sally Lane have operated Destination Southwest for more than 15 years and are ready to meet all of your tour service needs. Although Destination Southwest specializes in tours of New Mexico and the Southwest, services are available for travel throughout the West, including places like Hawaii and Yellowstone. The next time you want to plan an amazing vacation sure to please everyone in your group, call Destination Southwest.

**20 First Plaza Galeria, Suite 212,
Albuquerque NM
(505) 766-9068**
www.destinationsouthwest.com

Sandia Peak Tramway

The 10,378-foot Sandia Peak behind Albuquerque exists due to intense seismic activity in the area millions of years ago that caused the earth's crust to rise well above the surrounding flats. Today you can explore the beauty of this geologic wonder from the Sandia Peak Tramway, the world's longest aerial tramway. The tram was put in motion by Ben Abruzzo and Robert J. Nordhaus and made its first run in May 1966. Sandia Peak Tram Company, with Louis Abruzzo as president, continues to operate and maintain the tram, called a double reversible jigback aerial tramway, meaning that while one car is ascending, the other is descending. The tram takes about 15 minutes to ascend 4,000 feet to the peak and runs at an operating speed of 12 miles per hour. Each of the two cars is equipped to transport 50 passengers, and the cars' expansive windows treat riders to spectacular views as they lift above the desert to canyons and forests on the 2.7-mile sky ride. Skiers and hikers can start a day of adventure from the tramway. Sandia Peak Tramway offers two distinctive dining venues, owned and operated by Russ Zeigler and Doug Smith. Located in the lower tram terminal is Sandiago's Mexican Grill, featuring traditional New Mexican cuisine and oversized, handcrafted margaritas. High Finance Restaurant and Tavern perches atop the peak and specializes in steaks and seafood. Experience everything from a warm welcome and exceptional dining to incredible views and outdoor recreation at Sandia Peak Tramway.

10 Tramway Loop NE, Albuquerque NM
(505) 856-7325
www.sandiapeak.com

The University of New Mexico

The University of New Mexico

The University of New Mexico, the state's flagship university, is located in the heart of Albuquerque on historic Route 66. The University has branch campuses in Taos, Gallup, Valencia County and Los Alamos, providing a broad range of academic opportunities, scientific research, medical education and services. They are also the home of the UNM Lobos. Visitors delight in their unique Spanish Pueblo Revival style architecture and can explore an exciting array of museums, libraries, bookstores, and entertainment and athletic venues. For a closer look at what the University of New Mexico has to offer, visit them on the web or stop by the Welcome Center today.

Albuquerque NM
(505) 277-1989
www.unm.edu

The University of New Mexico Bookstore

The University of New Mexico Bookstore has become such a vital element of life at UNM that it is hard to imagine a time when it did not exist. Surprisingly, students once had to depend on an off campus retailer for their course materials. The bookstore as we now know it wasn't actually established until 1952. When students decided the university should be responsible for selling their own merchandise, the Associated Students' Bookstore was born. Originally housed in the old Student Union building, the store comprised 1,600 square feet and served the university's 4,000 enrolled students. Since its beginnings, the bookstore has gone through many incarnations and locations. It has been housed in the Women's Cafeteria, later known as Bandalier East (a WWII surplus barrack), and multiple Student Union Buildings. After a name change in 1970 to its present moniker, the bookstore moved to its very own building in 1974 to accommodate the ever-expanding student population. Much to everyone's delight, gone were the days of overcrowding and textbook rush tents. The Bookstore moved to its current location in 1996 in much fanfare and excitement. The 45,500-square-foot facility now contains textbooks, supplies, general books and gift apparel departments, as well as a convenience store and a Starbucks. Whether you need a textbook, a tall latte, or some Lobowear, people can depend on the UNM Bookstore to continue its long-held tradition of serving UNM students, staff, faculty and the Albuquerque community as a whole.

**2301 Central Avenue SE,
Albuquerque NM
(505) 277-5451
http://bookstore.unm.edu**

Photos by S.M. Stachler

Tractor Brewing Company

The Tractor Brewing Company™ honors the good things in life, like beer, tractors, family and good friends. Tractors are as prominent as beer at the brewery, affectionately called the Beer Farm. Outside you'll find antique tractors restored by the president of the company. Inside look for hundreds of tractor models mounted on walls and positioned on a carousel and a Ferris wheel. The tasting room continues the farm theme with a roof reminiscent of a barn. The beer is everything you could hope to find, with farm fresh flavor sure to enliven your day or evening. Try Tractor's Hay Maker Honey Wheat™ or Sod Buster Pale Ale™. Taste the naturally rich flavor of earth in the Double Plow Oatmeal Stout or the crisp flavor of the Farmer's Tan Red Ale™. The beers are natural accompaniments to Ribs Hickory Pit Barbecue, located next door to the brewery. Continue your celebration of the good life with collectible hats and shirts emblazoned with the Tractor Brewing Company logo and Getplowed.com, Tractor's catchy web address. The website is a great place to check for upcoming events sponsored by Tractor, such as the large bike rally, which touts bikes, bands, barbecue, brew and babes. For a homegrown microbrewery experience just 25 tasty miles south of Albuquerque, visit Tractor Brewing Company.

120 Nelson Lane, Los Lunas NM
(505) 866-0477
www.getplowed.com

Sierra Blanca Brewing Co.

New Mexico's largest brewery, Sierra Blanca Brewing Co., recently moved to the Albuquerque Metro Area. Richard and Suzanne Weber started the brewery 10 years ago in Carrizozo and it went on to become one of the top 100 breweries in America. Their microbrews include the top seller among New Mexico-made beers, Alien Amber Ale, as well as a Pilsner, Pale Ale, Nut Brown, Stout, IPA, Lager and Wheat. Sierra Blanca Brewing Co. also brews two sodas, root beer and ginger ale, under the label Way 2 Cool. The brewery's number one objective remains the consistency and quality of the product. Their state-of-the-art equipment plays a role in masterfully producing flavored crystal clear beers. Enjoy a gift shop and tasting room, with free tours Monday through Friday 10 am to 4 pm. Cheers!

1016 Industrial Avenue E, Moriarty NM
(505) 257-BEER (2337)
www.sierrablancabrewery.com

Sandhill Cranes at Bosque del Apache Wildlife Refuge

Albuquerque Biological Park

Whether they are baby elephants, sea turtles or butterflies, almost everyone loves to look at living creatures. Albuquerque provides some of the best opportunities in the West for viewing natural life. The Albuquerque Biological Park, or BioPark, consists of four separate facilities: the Albuquerque Aquarium, the Rio Grande Botanic Garden, the Rio Grande Zoo and Tingley Beach. The aquarium exhibits freshwater species from the Rio Grande and saltwater creatures from the Gulf of Mexico. Habitats include estuaries, coral reefs and the deep ocean. The highlight of the aquarium is a 285,000-gallon ocean tank where sandtiger, blacktip and nurse sharks swim alongside brilliantly colored reef fish, eels, sea turtles and open ocean species. Every day, divers enter the tank for feeding and other chores. The Rio Grande Botanic Garden, on 20 developed acres, offers a 10,000-square foot glass conservatory with plants from desert and Mediterranean climates. From May through September, the Butterfly Pavilion gives visitors a close-up look at hundreds of colorful butterflies. Tingley Beach on the Rio Grande sports picnic areas and a series of trout-stocked fishing lakes, including one just for children. The BioPark operates a narrow-gauge railroad that connects all its facilities, plus a sightseeing line that runs within the botanic garden. Parking is ample and free, and all sites have restaurants and gift stores. Young and old will delight in a trip to the Albuquerque Biological Park.

1601 Central Avenue NW, Albuquerque NM (aquarium and botanic garden)
1800 Tingley Drive SW, Albuquerque NM (Tingley Beach)
(505) 764-6200
www.cabq.gov/biopark

The Rio Grande Zoo

Founded in 1927, the Rio Grande Zoo is the oldest and most popular attraction at the Albuquerque Biological Park, or BioPark. The zoo hosts more than 200 species of exotic and native animals. The zoo's 64 acres are laced with two and a half miles of paths. Trees, grass, waterworks and rocks provide naturalistic habitats. The many state-of-the-art exhibits feature polar bears, lions, giraffes and Mexican wolves, among others. Adventure Africa showcases antelope, red river hogs, chimpanzees and other exotics. The Tropical America exhibit features an array of plants and animals from the American tropics. The zoo's breeding program has experienced success with cheetahs and gorillas. Boopie the baby hippo is the most recent newborn addition. Birds appear in fascinating variety, from storks and eagles to roadrunners running free. A bird show at the Nature Theater near the Cottonwood Café features parrots, raptors and other amazing avians. You can even take a camel ride, except in the winter. A narrow-gauge railroad connects the zoo with the other BioPark facilities, the Albuquerque Aquarium, the Rio Grande Botanic Garden and Tingley Beach. In addition, the Thunderbird Express Zoo Train loops through the zoo. Like the other BioPark units, the zoo hosts many special events, including the Zoo Music Summer Concert Series from June through August. Come to the Rio Grande Zoo, because you never outgrow your need for cute.

903 10th Street SW, Albuquerque NM
(505) 764-6200
www.cabq.gov/biopark/zoo

Desert sunset with boulders and Yucca in the Sandia Mountain foothills near Albuquerque

American International Rattlesnake Museum

The Rattlesnake Museum is a gift to the public from former high school biology teacher Bob Myers. The museum provides a way for adults and children to safely get close to reptiles and learn about the many ways they have influenced our lives. At this museum, people suffering from snake phobias have transformed their fear into the desire to own a snake for a pet. At the Rattlesnake Museum, common myths are debunked by hard facts. For instance, only one person in a thousand who have been bitten by rattlers actually die from the wound, placing this cause of death lower on the list than deaths caused by dog attacks, bee stings or lightning strikes. Snakes also do not chase people. Large creatures like people scare them, and they prefer to stay out of the way if at all possible. Rattlesnakes come in a multitude of varieties, colors and patterns. The museum houses a good selection of these, as well as some scorpions, a tarantula and a gila monster lizard. Fun displays such as the snake-themed beverages case, board games and toys featuring snakes, artworks and future plans for a snake song display illustrate how snakes and the image they convey touch many aspects of our lives. The Rattlesnake Museum, with the largest collection of rattlesnakes in the world, promotes the conservation of snakes and discourages the killing of snakes for sport. Tickets to view the snakes double as signed certificates of bravery. Test your courage and learn about some of the most fascinating and beautiful reptiles that grace our world.

202 San Felipe NW, Albuquerque NM
(505) 242-6569
www.rattlesnakes.com

Mottled Rock Rattlesnake

Anderson-Abruzzo
Albuquerque International Balloon Museum

The Anderson-Abruzzo International Balloon Museum is the most recent addition to the wide-ranging cultural offerings of Albuquerque, the balloon capital of the world. The Balloon Museum, a municipal facility overseen by the city's Cultural Services Department, opened in October 2005. It is located on the northern end of Albuquerque adjacent to the city's Balloon Fiesta Park, where each October hundreds of pilots participate in the world-renowned Albuquerque International Balloon Fiesta. The Balloon Museum is an educational institution with engaging exhibits and informative programs on the history, science and art of ballooning achievements. The award-winning building looks like a giant hot air balloon preparing to launch. Inside, the gallery spaces are large and airy with a ceiling over 70-feet tall. It's large enough to accommodate long-distance balloon gondolas the size of a small room, along with partial envelopes reaching to the ceiling. Exhibits display a wide variety of artifacts that trace the importance and impact of ballooning worldwide. Look for items related to the first flights in 1783, as well as scientific flights, calling cards, broadsides and postcards. You will also find collectible pins, patches, posters and fine jewelry. China from great airships and the gondola of the first balloon to cross the Pacific Ocean also make for memorable displays. The museum has a reference library, resource center and classrooms. Trained docents are always on duty to answer questions about the history of ballooning and tours can be arranged for groups. The museum's meeting and party rooms, with some of the best views in town, are available for rent. For a memorable experience, visit the Anderson-Abruzzo Albuquerque International Balloon Museum.

**9201 Balloon Museum Drive NE,
Albuquerque NM
(505) 768-6020**
www.cabq.gov/balloon

Indian Pueblo Cultural Center

The purpose of the Indian Pueblo Cultural Center in Albuquerque is to showcase the history and accomplishments of the Pueblo people. In the process, the facility manages to reflect the authentic, beautiful and creative soul at the core of the Pueblos. The cultural center, opened in 1976, is circular, like the Earth, and adorned with amazing murals painted by recognized and respected Pueblo artists. Many activities held throughout the year take place in the tranquil interior plaza, but the main focus is the 10,000-square-foot museum. In this permanent exhibit, the authentic history and artifacts of traditional cultures keep company with contemporary art works. The new exhibition galleries display changing fine art and historical exhibits of Southwest Native Americans, with strong representation of Pueblo art and history. Visitors can enjoy the Pueblo Harvest Café Restaurant and the 12,500-square-foot retail gallery and gift shop, offering a fantastic selection of authentic handmade Native American goods. Another exciting opportunity is a visit to the Children's Pueblo House Museum, an interactive adventure. A yearly calendar of special events include dance performances, artist demonstrations and special performances. The Indian Pueblo Cultural Center is owned and operated by the 19 Pueblos. Visit the website for tour and price information, but visit in person to experience the gateway to the 19 Pueblos of New Mexico.

2401 12th Street NW, Albuquerque NM
(505) 843-7270 or (866) 855-7902
www.indianpueblo.org

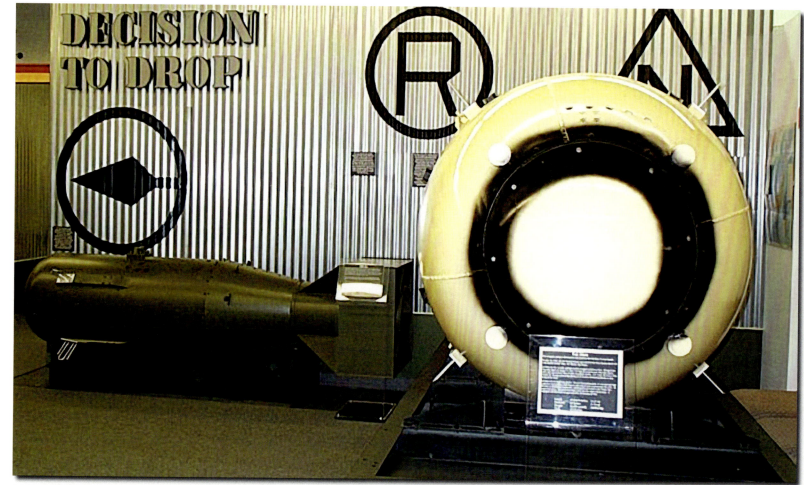

National Atomic Museum

Have you ever been to a museum that's so interesting you don't even care that you're learning? The National Atomic Museum is America's only congressionally chartered museum of nuclear science and history. First established in 1969, the National Atomic Museum is a gripping trip through the story of the Atomic Age, from the earliest days of nuclear research right through the peaceful uses of nuclear technology being explored today. Through permanent and changing presentations, exhibits and quality education programs, the museum conveys the diversity of the pioneers and events that shaped the history of the nuclear age and explores how nuclear science continues to influence the world. Here you'll find replicas of Fat Man and Little Boy, sobering reminders of the first and only nuclear weapons ever used during wartime. Exhibits and photo galleries that explain things like radiation, the Manhattan Project, and the Cold War fascinate school groups and tours. Children will get a chance to look at the possibilities inherent in nuclear medicine and participate in interactive displays where inquisitive young minds can try their hands at a variety of science activities. The National Atomic Museum is one of the region's most vital outreach educational resources and provides summer science camps, teacher workshops and Learning Adventures, plus special events and classes. The museum gift shop is a one-of-a-kind retail experience, complete with history memorabilia, educational toys, unique books and science games. The museum is planning a move to a new location in 2008, and will re-open under the new name of National Museum of Nuclear Science & History. Make sure to put the National Atomic Museum on your itinerary. It's an awesome trip into the world of our nuclear past and future.

1905 Mountain Road NW, Albuquerque NM
(505) 245-2137 *www.atomicmuseum.com*

Attractions • 85

The Turquoise Museum

The Turquoise Museum exists to educate and enlighten the public about the realities and myths of turquoise. Owners Katy and Joe Lowry and their son, Joe Dan, have amazing knowledge and passion about turquoise. Since 1993, this museum has celebrated the lifelong pursuit of J.C. "Zack" and Lillian Zachary. More than 60 mines in the American Southwest and around the world have contributed the rough, cabochon and inset turquoise extensively displayed in the collection room. The lapidary shop offers a daily demonstration and displays of the shaping and polishing process for turquoise. The Museum's education rooms provide an appraisal service and tips on what to look for when purchasing turquoise jewelry. The family has mined and cut turquoise for five generations, forming the basis for an unequaled expertise in the field. Joe Dan Lowry is a recognized and respected lecturer in museums, gift shops and organizations throughout the country. With his father, Joe Dan co-authored the book *Turquoise Unearthed*. Joe Dan's lectures are entertaining and interactive. He is a resource for the Indian Arts & Crafts Association, Santa Fe Indian Market, *Smithsonian Magazine*, *New Mexico Magazine*, *Lapidary Journal* and many other groups. Visit this rich repository, housing the largest collection of turquoise in the world, and take in the history, geology, mythology and folklore of this fascinating and singularly beautiful gem.

2107 Central Avenue NW, Albuquerque NM (505) 247-8650

Samples of turquoise from mines around the world
Photos by Davonna Lowry

Unser Racing Museum

The Unser Racing Museum, with its collection of race cars, engines and memorabilia, honors four generations of competitive Unsers, their record-setting victories and continuing love of racing. Al Unser, Sr., known worldwide as Big Al, and his wife, Susan, are the driving forces behind the museum, which opened in September 2005 in the beautiful village of Los Ranchos de Albuquerque. The museum was made possible with funds from the Unsers, private donors and the state of New Mexico. Set up like spokes in a wheel, the museum's various galleries offer tours of Unser family victories on Pikes Peak, the Unser history at the Indianapolis 500, including nine Indianapolis victories by three Unsers, and visiting exhibits. Visitors can watch racing videos and learn about changes in race car technology. They can take a close-up look at cars like the Johnny Lightning Special, in which Al won the 1971 Indianapolis 500. An area called Jerry's Garage tells the Unser family story and can be rented for private meetings. Al Sr. hopes the museum will honor the entire racing fraternity. He brings in some of racing's greatest stars for special occasions. The drive to win that is such a strong trait in the Unser family has produced a first-class museum worthy of your time and attention. For an inspiring look at an Albuquerque family who became national ambassadors for New Mexico, visit the Unser Racing Museum.

1776 Montaño NW, Albuquerque NM
(505) 341-1776
www.unserracingmuseum.com

Museum of Archaeology and Material Culture

Explore the 12,000-year legacy of Native American people at the Museum of Archaeology and Material Culture in Cedar Crest. Discover how archaeologists learn about ancient cultures by analyzing tools and ceramics and by studying the remains of humans, animals and plants. See how America's first inhabitants hunted the now extinct mammoth, as well as how they pursued horses and camels. If the weather is good, you can visit a Rio Grande-style pit house and learn what daily life would have been like in the Albuquerque area when the Clovis people lived here 12,000 years ago. The museum shows facets of history sometimes absent from other institutions, including sensitive cultural issues. Learn more about attempts to exterminate the buffalo and the importance of Cerrillos turquoise to the Anasazi Chacoan empire. The Museum's 12,000-year timeline ends with the tragic 1890 Battle of Wounded Knee. An outdoor theater presents films with historical and cultural interest, and an educational program gives school children opportunities to participate in mock excavations. As a result of the museum's ongoing efforts to preserve the past and a long-term research project in western New Mexico, museum director Bradley Bowman received the prestigious 2003 New Mexico Historic Preservation Award. For an educational and entertaining experience, visit the Museum of Archaeology and Material Culture, just 15 minutes from Albuquerque.

22 Calvary Road, Cedar Crest NM
(505) 281-2005
www.museumarch.org

J&R Vintage Auto Museum

Featuring nine classic automobiles that have competed in the Great American Race, J&R Vintage Auto Museum has been displaying antique cars and trucks for 10 years. Their display consists of 70 automobiles that range in year from 1902 to 1956. A visit to the museum will include a trip to the 2,000-square-foot gift shop where you can browse through hundreds of automotive books, porcelain signs and die cast toys. Owned by the Joiner family and the Roy family, J&R Vintage Auto Museum has had a lot of publicity thanks to *The Great Race* on Speed Vision in 2004 and 2005 and The History Channel. Museum Director Carl Anderson says that the museum has also been in the *Albuquerque Journal* and the *Rio Rancho Observer*. A must-see for the antique auto buff, the museum resides in a 15,000-square-foot building that also houses a spacious restoration shop. If you're interested in owning your own classic, there are some cars available for sale or trade. If you love antique cars and trucks, put the J&R Vintage Auto Museum at the top of your list when you visit central New Mexico.

3650 NM Highway 528, Rio Rancho NM
(505) 867-2881
www.jrvintageautos.com

Tinkertown Museum

Visitors to the mountain town of Sandia Park will find not only first-class skiing and recreation, but a folk art museum that has grown from one room in 1983 to a major roadside attraction. Drawing more than 20,000 visitors a year, Tinkertown Museum offers a whimsical kaleidoscope of carvings, inventions and collections that were assembled by the late Ross Ward, a man born to tinker and a prolific wood carver. The 22-room museum holds 40-plus years of Ross's efforts. It's been featured on such television shows as *Antiques Roadshow, Good Morning America* and the HGTV *Roadside* series, which becomes somewhat ironic when you discover one of Ross's philosophical signs that reads, "I did all this while you were watching TV." The popular destination is owned and operated by Ross's wife Carla, who co-founded the museum with her husband in 1983 and continues to keep his dream alive by offering visitors a glimpse of Ross's thoroughly entertaining world. Delights include hilarious animations, like those in a miniature Old West town populated with thousands of hand-carved figures. Eccentric collections include 132 wedding cake toppers and antique tools galore. For a quarter, Esmerelda the Fortune Teller tells your fortune. You'll find a 35-foot antique sailboat that braved a 10-year global voyage. The museum is more than a collection of miniatures and memorabilia; it's a testament to Ross Ward's determination to showcase folk art in a big way.

**121 Sandia Crest Road, Box 303, Sandia Park NM
(505) 281-5233**

Museum of International Folk Art

Folk art is the art of the everyday. The individuals who create it express the culture of the community rather than an idiosyncratic individual view. Founded in 1953, the Museum of International Folk Art in Santa Fe has become the home of the world's largest collection of folk art. The museum holds more than 135,000 objects from 100 nations and hosts regular traveling exhibitions. Recent shows have presented Japanese folk ceramics and beds from around the world. The museum's exhibitions, on display in the four wings of the building, include the museum's permanent collections. The popular Girard wing showcases folk art, popular art, toys and textiles from around the world. The Hispanic Heritage wing introduces the culture of northern New Mexico. Its permanent exhibition, Familia y Fe (Family and Faith), focuses on two of the strongest currents in regional life. The Bartlett Wing, named in honor of museum founder Florence Dibell Bartlett, contains two galleries with rotating exhibitions. The Neutrogena Wing features exquisite textiles and garments. The Treasure Chest in this wing invites visitors to explore what goes on behind the scenes in a museum. The museum building also sports a research library and two museum shops. The excellent Museum Hill Café, located next door, is another part of the Museum Hill complex. Visit the Museum of International Folk Art, a major contributor to Santa Fe's reputation as a museum city.

706 Camino Lejo, Santa Fe NM
(505) 476-1200 *www.moifa.org*

Attractions • 91

The Enchanted Forest Cross Country Ski Area offers trails groomed for both classic and freestyle skiing. Enchanted Forest is three miles east of Red River, in the Carson National Forest. The groomed trails offer stunning views and a back-country feel as they wind through the forest.
Photo courtesy of the New Mexico Tourism Department

92 • Attractions

Zozobra, who has gone up in flames every year since artist Will Shuster created him in 1926, became one of the symbols of Santa Fe. Santa Fe Fiesta has been celebrated since 1712, by proclamation of the then-governor of the province Jose Chacon Medina Salazar y Villaseor, the Marquis of Penuela. It is the oldest civic celebration of its kind in North America. The burning signifies the ridding of a year's worth of troubles and sorrows. Fiestas de Santa Fe takes place on the weekend following Labor Day.
Photo courtesy of the New Mexico Tourism Department

Museum of Indian Arts & Culture

At the Museum of Indian Arts & Culture, you encounter Native cultures and artifacts from the ancestral to the contemporary. Highlights include Southwestern textiles, pottery and jewelry. A contemporary art collection includes sculpture and works on paper and canvas. You can find collections of Mimbres and Anasazi ceramics. One of the most fascinating items is a 151-foot hunting net made of human hair around the year 1200. The museum's collections, developed through active partnership between Indians and non-Indians, include 80,000 archeological, ethnographic and fine arts objects, plus more than 10 million artifacts from archeological sites across New Mexico. The Laboratory of Anthropology, next door to the museum and founded in 1927, is charged with conserving archeological finds in the state. The museum itself, which opened in 1987 as one of four museums in the Museum of New Mexico system, is an excellent introduction to the complexity and diversity of the Native American cultures of the region. Here, you can listen to the stories and songs that tell of origins and the long history of the Native peoples, and witness the development of new forms of art. Located in the foothills of the Sangre de Cristo Mountains, the museum shares its extraordinary location with the other museums on Museum Hill. Come to the Museum of Indian Arts & Culture and discover that American Indian cultures are complex, diverse, steeped in tradition, and yet very much alive.

710 Camino Lejo, Santa Fe NM
(505) 476-1250
www.miaclab.org

Photo by Mark Nohl
Courtesy of the New Mexico Tourism Department

Kit Carson Home and Museum

Christopher "Kit" Carson was born in 1809 and moved to the Missouri frontier as an infant. Due to his father's death, he was apprenticed to a saddle maker at a young age, which limited his education. In 1826, he left home and headed down the Santa Fe Trail into New Mexico, where he developed and honed his hunting and guiding skills. He met the famous cartographer, John C. Freemont, and accompanied him on three mapping expeditions. The fact that Carson became so widely known was largely due to Freemont's reports. After the Mexican War, Carson operated a ranch near Taos and in 1853 he was made the US Indian Agent for the area. Carson went on to become a hero within his own lifetime thanks to the many dime-store novels and westerns printed during the 1860s and 70s. Today you can discover more about the exciting life of Kit Carson with a visit to the Kit Carson Home and Museum in Taos.

The home was built in 1827 and has been owned and operated by the Masonic Lodge since 1908. Newly remodeled, it includes new exhibits, storyboards and living history guided interpretive tours. The museum features a large gift and bookstore. Delve into the life of one of America's most popular heros at the Kit Carson Home and Museum.

113 Kit Carson Road, Taos NM
(505) 758-4945
www.kitcarsonhome.com

Carson wearing a beaver hat, circa 1854. (Courtesy of Kit Carson Museum)

Photos courtesy of the Kit Carson Museum

Kit Carson circa 1860

Millicent Rogers Museum

The Millicent Rogers Museum celebrates the art and culture of Northern New Mexico. The museum offers outstanding displays of Native American jewelry, ceramics, painting and weaving. You'll see Hopi and Zuni kachina dolls and Apache basketry. Hispanic exhibits include textiles, tin work and sculpture. A highlight is the special exhibit of the famed pottery of Maria Martinez. The historic and contemporary Santos (religious images) include Nuestra Senora devotions to Mary. The museum also hosts a wide range of contemporary Southwestern art. Above all, the Millicent Rogers Collection of Southwestern Jewelry contains more than 1,000 stunning pieces, many collected by Millicent Rogers herself. Mary Millicent Rogers was an American heiress and fashion icon. A passion for beauty led her to Taos. Here, she found peace and began a spiritual journey that connected her to the land. She believed the Southwestern Indian culture was a precious part of America's heritage that had to be recognized and preserved, and her legacy lives on at the museum that bears her name. Its physical setting is superb. The classic adobe building offers spectacular views of the many-hued Sangre de Cristo Mountains. The Millicent Rogers Museum is one of America's most important resources for the study of Southwestern art and design. You'll always remember your visit.

1504 Millicent Rogers Road, Taos NM
(505) 758-2462
www.millicentrogers.org

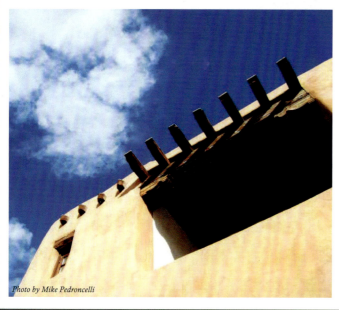

Photo by Mike Pedroncelli

Museum of Fine Arts

From the cheerful splash of the Jésus Bautista Moroles sculpture fountain in the central courtyard to the hush of St. Francis Auditorium, the Museum of Fine Arts is a feast for the soul and the senses. The Northern New Mexico Pueblo-Revival building dates from 1917, and its architecture, a synthesis of Native American and Spanish Colonial themes, has become a model for the Santa Fe style. The building forms a graceful home for a distinguished collection of 20th-century American art with an emphasis on New Mexico, the Southwest and the Taos and Santa Fe masters. The state's oldest art museum is home to more than 23,000 works of art. Its permanent collection includes items from the Cinco Pintores, works from the Taos Society of Artists, notably Robert Henri and John Sloan, and the largest collection of Gustave Baumann pieces anywhere. An important collection of Georgia O'Keeffe paintings is on display. Photographic holdings include the Jane Reese Williams Collection of women photographers. Naturally, the museum sponsors important traveling exhibitions. The Governor's Gallery is an outreach activity of the museum. Located on the fourth floor of the state capitol building near the governor's office, it presents artwork of wide interest. For an introduction to the famous art of New Mexico, visit the Museum of Fine Arts.

107 W Palace Avenue, Santa Fe NM   (505) 476-5072   www.mfasantafe.org

Photos courtesy of the New Mexico Tourism Department

Palace of the Governors

Santa Fe's Palace of the Governors is the oldest continuously occupied public building in the United States. The Spanish built it four centuries ago as the seat of government for New Mexico, and it continues to serve as the cultural heart and soul of Santa Fe. The Palace became the home of the Museum of New Mexico in 1909, and initially housed both historical and fine arts collections. The work done restoring the Palace was an inspiration for the Spanish Pueblo Revival style that became mandatory for new buildings in Santa Fe after 1912. When the Museum of Fine Arts opened in 1917, the Palace became purely a historical museum. Collection highlights include artifacts from the early Spanish colonization and the Santa Fe Trail. Art of Ancient America, 1500 BC to 1500 AD is a permanent exhibit, and the museum has a spectacular collection of Meso-American artifacts. In all, the Palace has more than 17,000 historical objects from all periods. The photo archives at the Palace contain more than 750,000 photos, negatives, illustrations and other graphic items. Under the Portal at the front of the building, Native American artists and crafters sell their wares. The 900-plus vendors represent more than 40 tribes, pueblos or villages. A Vendors' Committee enforces rules that guarantee authenticity. Learn about the colorful history of the second-oldest city in the United States at Santa Fe's Palace of the Governors.

105 W Palace Avenue, Santa Fe NM (505) 476-5100 *www.palaceofthegovernors.org*

El Rancho de las Golondrinas

Perhaps New Mexico's best kept secret is the Ranch of the Swallows, a 200-acre living history museum located just 15 miles south of Santa Fe and 45 miles north of Albuquerque. El Rancho de las Golondrinas is one of the most historic ranches in the Southwest. In the 1700s, it was the last *paraje*, or stopping point, before reaching Santa Fe on the long journey from Mexico City along the famous *El Camino Real*. Today it is an educational, historical and cultural treasure. Since 1932, many of the authentic structures have been restored to portray the essential elements of Spanish Colonial culture, including an 18th century *placita* house with a defensive tower, a 19th century home, a molasses mill, several primitive water wells, a blacksmith shop and a winery.

With costumed villagers, guided tours and Civil War reenactments, El Rancho de las Golondrinas reproduces as authentically as possible the living and working conditions of Spanish Colonial and Territorial New Mexico in the 18th and 19th centuries. After the tour, peruse the one-of-a-kind regional antiques and contemporary crafts in the museum shop. The ranch is closed to the public from November through March, but full of activity the rest of the year with events like the spring festival and animal fair, wine festivals, frontier days and a harvest festival. The ranch is also a popular place for weddings. As true as it was in the 1700s, El Rancho de las Golondrinas extends a warm welcome to visitors and locals alike.

334 Los Pinos Road, Santa Fe NM
(505) 471-2261
www.golondrinas.org

Above Right: Rafters on the Rio Grande
Left: Taos Gorge
Photos courtesy of the New Mexico Tourism Department

Big River Raft Trips

The Rio Grande Gorge is stunning whether it's seen from a ricocheting raft while dodging dangers in the white waters, coasting far above in a leisurely hot air balloon, or enjoying the ambience of the romantic moonlight. Particularly known for their May through October seasonal rafting expeditions, Big River Raft Trips offers custom tailored adventures to accommodate your interests and expertise. Every adventure includes what you need to enjoy your day. If the spray of river foam isn't on your agenda, or if your travels bring you to the area during the winter season, the Big River Crew serve as year round guides. You can join them for canyon hikes, horseback riding or mountain bike tours and benefit from their knowledge of local history, flora and fauna. They'll prepare an excellent lunch where vegetarians and carnivores alike will be equally impressed. Where else can you get the opportunity to tell your friends back home that you enjoyed ice cream along the Rio Grande Gorge during your llama trek or that you survived the Team Extreme Package, complete with a small boat and an aggressive guide? Book your Big River Raft Trip today so you can learn the true meaning of the word *Wahoo*.

**Box 16-D Pilar Route, Embudo NM
(800) 748-3746**
www.bigriverrafts.com

Aboot About Santa Fe

Santa Fe's combination of space, light, blue skies and a very different way of living is what brought Alan and Karla Jordan here from California 20 years ago. What they found was truly the land of enchantment, and since 1979 they've been sharing guided tours of the place they love with visitors from around the world. Originally called Santa Fe Walks, they changed the name to Aboot About Santa Fe to encompass the diverse range of their tours. Aboot About adventures range from historic walking tours to Aspook About ghost tours. Their tours are excursions into the heart of Santa Fe's unique essence. There are no buses, no microphones and no boring scripts. Aboot About has the best guides. These knowledgeable historians, artists and anthropologists expertly guide tours that fit your interests. Tours of Georgia O'Keefe country, historic museums, arts and artists are just a few of their offerings. If you don't see something on their pre-planned tours you really desire, let Karla and Alan know and they'll design a tour just for you. Whatever your idea, their motto is pretty much, "Yes! We can do that!" Karla and Alan were both teachers before taking over Aboot About and now they simply love sharing Santa Fe with others. They're committed to creativity, originality and value. They take great pride and pleasure in designing your program or tour, and training their wonderful guides. Their list of recent clients and glowing testimonials could fill pages, and range from Home and Garden Television to the French Embassy. Let this inspired couple show you the real Santa Fe with Aboot About Santa Fe.

**624 Galisteo, #32,
Santa Fe NM
(505) 988-2774
www.abootabout.com**

Top: Canyon Road Art; Right: Capitol; Left: Loretto Chapel
Photos by Dan Monaghan, courtesy of the New Mexico Tourism Department

The Santa Fe Opera

The Santa Fe Opera is one of the world's most beautiful open-air theaters, with spectacular sunsets and breathtaking mountain views all around. The dramatic adobe theater blends harmoniously with the high desert landscape. Ever since 1957, the Santa Fe Opera has been the summer oasis for internationally acclaimed operatic talents and opera enthusiasts. Over the years, the company has given nearly 1,600 performances of more than 130 operas, including nine world premieres and more than 40 American premieres. Casts are drawn from the world's most talented young singers, and production teams of conductors, directors and designers are international, as well. Many singers who now perform at the world's leading opera houses began their careers in Santa Fe. The company was founded by the late John Crosby, who sought an environment that allowed young singers ample time to rehearse and prepare each production. Recently performed works include traditional favorites such as *La bohème* and *Salome* plus American premieres such as *The Tempest* by Thomas Adès and Tan Dun's *Tea: A Mirror of the Soul*. Because much of the standard operatic repertoire is in Italian, German or French, the Santa Fe Opera features the innovative Opera Titles, a small screen in front of every seat that allows patrons to follow the stage action in either English or Spanish. For a stirring musical and visual experience, come to the Santa Fe Opera.

Opera Drive, U.S. Highway 84 exit 168, Santa Fe NM
(505) 986-5900 or (800) 280-4654
www.santafeopera.org

Santa Fe Opera
Photo courtesy of the New Mexico Tourism Department

Bradbury Science Museum

The crisis that became World War II at first cast no shadow on the sunny Pajarito Plateau, but soon war shook the entire world. Los Alamos, once the site of a boys' ranch school, became the home of secret efforts to develop an entirely new weapon, the atomic bomb. The Bradbury Science Museum is the chief public facility of the Los Alamos National Laboratory, where this work was done. Most visitors begin their tour of the museum in the History Gallery. Statues of Dr. Robert Oppenheimer and Gen. Leslie Groves, two of the most famous personalities of the Manhattan Project, greet you as you enter. The Defense Gallery focuses on the laboratory's main mission: ensuring the safety and reliability of the U.S. nuclear deterrent. It features a collection of missile and bomb casings, including Fat Man, a bomb casing identical to the device dropped on Nagasaki and similar to the one tested at Trinity. Visitors can learn where plutonium comes from and the risks associated with it. The Research Gallery shows the laboratory's widely varied basic and applied research on topics that include environmental monitoring, space science and mapping the human brain. The Bradbury Science Museum was founded in 1963 and named for the laboratory's director from 1945 to 1970, Norris E. Bradbury. Its exhibits draw nearly 100,000 visitors a year. Experience science and explore history at the Bradbury Science Museum in Los Alamos.

1350 Central Avenue, Los Alamos NM
(505) 667-4444 *www.lanl.gov/museum*

Dr. Oppenheimer

White Sands National Monument

The glistening white sands of New Mexico are one of the world's great natural wonders. Great wave-like dunes of gypsum sand engulf 275 square miles of desert. White Sands National Monument preserves a major portion of the dune field. Stop at the visitor's center, and then take the eight-mile scenic Dunes Drive into the heart of the dunes. Trail heads are located along the drive. The one-mile Dune Life Nature Trail is more heavily vegetated than other areas. The short Interdune Boardwalk is wheelchair-accessible and leads you to a scenic view from the top of a dune. This is the best trail for seeing wildflowers. The short, level Playa Trail leads to a small playa, a dried-up lake. If you want to see bare dunes stretching for miles into the wild, the 4.6-mile Alkali Flat Trail is for you. You do not have to hike the entire trail to enjoy spectacular scenery. The Heart of the Sands Nature Center, near the end of the drive, highlights the plants and animals that have adapted to the harsh environment. About 220 species of birds have been recorded at the park. The best places to look for birds are near the visitor's center and the Dune Life Nature Trail. Sledding down the face of dunes is a popular activity. Sledders use plastic snow saucers that are for sale at the visitor's center. Rangers hold activities such as nature walks and stargazing throughout the year. For an out-of-this-world experience, visit White Sands National Monument.

U.S. Highway 70, Holloman Air Force Base NM
(505) 679-2599 *www.nps.gov/whsa*

Photo by Dan Monaghan
Photo and information courtesy of the New Mexico Tourism Department

Montezuma Castle

In 1882 the Atchison, Topeka & Santa Fe Railroad opened the First Montezuma Hotel, built as an exclusive resort for train passengers interested in The West. The location outside Las Vegas, NM was ideal, with natural mineral hot springs, trout fishing, scenery and hiking. In 1884 the plush hotel's gas lines clogged, fire broke out, and the Montezuma burned to the ground. It re-opened that same year, rebuilt to become the state's first building wired for electricity. Within months the Montezuma burned to the ground again. In a matter of months a third resort opened, but named The Phoenix Hotel this time (rising from ashes). The new name didn't stick, as locals still called it The Montezuma. In 1904 the Montezuma closed for good as a hotel, no longer able to compete with other, newer Western resorts. In 1981, Armand Hammer bought the Montezuma Castle to house the American campus of the United World College (it had served as a seminary the previous 30 years), but it was in need of extensive repairs. UWC began using the surrounding grounds and buildings instead. In 1997 the empty castle was identified as one of America's 11 Most Endangered Historic Places by The National Trust for Historic Preservation. A year later the White House Millennium Council named it one of America's Treasures. The attention led to a massive fundraising and renovation program, and in 2002 Montezuma Castle re-opened, serving UWC as student and visitor housing.

Pendaries Village, Mountain Resort and Golf Community

Located near the picturesque village of Rociada, high in the Sangre de Cristo Mountains, you will find one of the best kept secrets in the southern Rockies. Pendaries Village is a combination mountain resort and golf community that is a great place for a vacation, but is an even better place to live. This idyllic mountain hideaway began more than a century ago when Jean Pendaries (pronounced Pan-dah-ray) emigrated from Gascony and built his home ranch here, including the old mill which still proudly stands along a meandering mountain stream. One of his daughters, Marguerite, and her husband Jose Baca, later became *patrones* of the 5,000-acre ranch, memorialized beautifully in their son-in-law Oliver LaFarge's book, *Behind the Mountains*. A part of that property is now Pendaries Village, a resort community that features an 18-hole golf course supported by a golf shop and snack bar, a rustic lodge with adjacent restaurant, the historic Moosehead Saloon, a non-denominational chapel, and a conference center that is perfect for retreats and seminars. Many visitors become so entranced by Pendaries Village they wind up moving here. Home sites, ranging from a half acre to three-plus acres, are available with stunning views and secluded woodland settings. The area is rich in recreational opportunities, with hiking in the nearby Pecos Wilderness, fishing in pristine lakes and streams, and, of course, golf at one of the region's most beautiful courses. In addition, Pendaries Village is within close proximity to Taos, Santa Fe, Albuquerque and Las Vegas. Visit Pendaries Village. Who knows, you may end up building your dream home here.

1 Lodge Road, Rociada NM
(505) 425-3561 or (800) 733-5267
www.pendaries.net

Vietnam Veterans Memorial State Park

Rising dramatically from a hillside overlooking one of New Mexico's most beautiful valleys, the Vietnam Veterans Memorial honors the men and women who served in Vietnam. On Veteran's Day 2005, the memorial became Vietnam Veterans Memorial State Park. The memorial was established in 1968 by Victor and Jeanne Westphall to honor their son, Lieutenant David Westphall, who was killed in Vietnam in 1968. When it opened in 1971, it was one of the first memorials of its kind in the United States. Until recently, it was funded and maintained by the David Westphall Veterans Foundation. Today, it is the only state park in the United States that is dedicated solely as a Vietnam veteran's memorial. Vietnam Veterans Memorial State Park provides veterans, and those who honor them, a refuge in which to reflect and heal. The memorial's textured surface captures the constantly changing sunlight, giving its walls a subtle play of color. The curving walls enclose a non-denominational chapel. The graceful structure was designed by architect Ted Luna. A visitor's center houses exhibits, videos and memorabilia. A representative from the Department of Veterans Affairs is present to offer assistance to veterans who require or request it. Veterans can use on-site computers to locate friends or loved ones. Since its inception in 1971, the memorial has received more than 2.5 million visitors.

34 County Road B4, Angel Fire NM
(505) 377-6900
www.emnrd.state.nm.us/EMNRD/parks/VietnamVets.htm
www.angelfirememorial.com

Aspens Over Trail in Angel Fire

Victory Alpaca Ranch

Garments made from luxurious Alpaca fibers are treasures that often become family heirlooms. Victory Alpaca Ranch, the largest alpaca ranch in the Southwest, provides a place for you to learn more about these lovely animals. Knowledgeable guides accompany scheduled tours. Victory Ranch is proud to have one of the finest alpaca herds in the United States and stands behind the bloodlines of its excellent breeding stock. The ranch has won many awards for both animals and fleeces. Alpacas have a life expectancy of 15 to 25 years and Victory Ranch is home to one of the oldest living alpacas, a female named Fuzzy who is now 23. The Victory Ranch Store offers alpaca products, including a wide selection of garments such as sweaters, capes and scarves. You'll find alpaca yarn, blankets and teddy bears. You can buy raw fiber, equipment for weaving and spinning and guidebooks to help you along. The shop also carries fine arts and crafts from local designers and artisans in Peru, Chile and Bolivia. The wares include jewelry, ceramics, Chacon belts and many other items. Ken and Carol Weisner are the owners of Victory Alpaca Ranch, which is managed by their daughter, Darcy. The Weisner family invites you to come and explore 1,100 acres of spectacular scenery in the mountains of northern New Mexico while enjoying the chance to hug and feed these charming and friendly creatures.

Route 434 (N of Mora on at mile marker 1), Mora NM
(505) 387-2254
www.victoryranch.com

108 • Attractions

Tooth of Time

Philmont Scout Ranch Museums

The Philmont Scout Ranch, located four miles south of Cimarron on Highway 21, is home to the Philmont Museum-Seton Memorial Library and the Villa Philmonte. Seven miles south of Philmont headquarters is the Kit Carson Museum at Rayado. The Philmont Museum-Seton Memorial Library houses the library, personal art and natural history collection of author, artist, naturalist and first Chief Scout of the Boy Scouts of America, Ernest Thompson Seton. The museum's annually changing exhibits tell the history of Seton, Philmont and the Southwest. Oklahoma oilman Waite Phillips built the Villa Philmonte on the Philmont Ranch as a summer home for his family. The Spanish Mediterranean home was completed in 1927. Restored to the period when Phillips owned the ranch, the Villa now serves as a memorial to the Phillips family and their generous support of the Boy Scouts of America. Guided tours are offered during spring, summer and fall, and reservations are booked at the Philmont Museum-Seton Library. Philmont's Kit Carson Museum is the first settlement of the Beaubien and Miranda Land Grant. The museum was built in the style of mid-19th century Mexican haciendas. The museum's rooms contain 1850s furnishings from the period when frontiersmen Kit Carson and Lucien Maxwell carved out a wilderness ranch along the Santa Fe Trail. During the summer, historically costumed Philmont staff members give tours of the hacienda and detail the life of Philmont's earliest pioneers.

17 Deer Run Road, Cimarron NM
(505) 376-2281

Spencer Theater

The visually striking, seven-storied Spencer Theater has raised the curtain on some of the finest performers and companies of our time, including Dave Brubeck, Hal Holbrook, Crystal Gayle and the Kingston Trio, as well as the Russian National Ballet and *Cats*. The creation of this stunning home for the performing arts was a long-held dream for the late Jackie Spencer Morgan and her husband, A.N. Spencer. Jackie's husband personally funded the amazing project, considered one of the greatest gifts to the state in New Mexican history. Renowned New Mexican architect Antoine Predock designed the theater to silhouette Sierra Blanca, the glacial peak that hovers in the near distance. The building, made from 440 tons of mica-flecked Spanish limestone, gleams in the desert light. The Spencer Theater features a step-like fountain, reminiscent of a clear mountain stream, and an intriguing, multi-faceted glass lobby. The 50,000-square-foot, 514-seat theater sits on 72 acres of pinon-dotted land in the Ruidoso area, and acts as an oasis in this windswept country. Jackie Spencer Morgan commissioned the world's foremost glass artist, Dale Chihuly, to create permanent glass art installations for the theater, allowing it to shine brightly and sparkle with color regardless of the season. Indulge your love of theater while seated within inspiring architecture when you visit Spencer Theater for the Performing Arts, one of the outstanding theaters in the world.

108 Spencer Road, Alto NM
(505) 336-4800 or (888) 818-7872
www.spencertheater.com

Dale Chihuly—*Sunset Tower*

Mercury in transit
Photo by Ed Hiker

Attractions • 111

National Solar Observatory

The sun, our star, has many lives. It warms our earth. It is constant yet always changing. In plain sight, it hides clues about its own life and the lives of other stars across the galaxy. The National Solar Observatory seeks to unravel those clues by giving researchers cutting-edge observational equipment. The observatory welcomes visitors, and indeed the site atop Sacramento Peak would be worth a visit if only for the spectacular view of the Tularosa Basin below. You can see Alamogordo and the shining expanse of the White Sands beyond. Dry air, an absence of pollution and plenty of sunshine make the peak a relaxing place. Guided and self-guided tours are available. You can start at the Sunspot Astronomy and Visitor's Center, which has exhibits on the sun, the observatories and the surrounding national forest. Three units are part of the observatory complex. They are the Dunn Solar Telescope, the Evans Solar Facility and Hilltop Dome. The Dunn's Vacuum Tower rises 136 feet and extends a further 220 feet below ground. You can step inside and watch scientists work with the unique rotating telescope. The Evans facility features two telescopes that observe the solar corona, flares, and other activities. The nearby, separate Apache Point Observatory watches the night-time sky instead of the sun, and its grounds are open to visitors. The National Solar Observatory also operates telescopes at Kitt Peak in Arizona. For a truly special day trip, visit the National Solar Observatory.

State Route 6563, Sunspot NM
(505) 434-7190
www.nso.edu

Photos courtesy of CG Photography

Photos courtesy of CG Photography

Grace Corn Heritage House

The Grace Corn Heritage House in bustling Roswell offers a beautiful setting in which to host an event or celebrate a special occasion. It was built in the late 1800s as a private residence. In the 1920s, Grace and Wade Corn remodeled and added a second story. The house was later bequeathed to granddaughter Jeanine Best, who beautifully modernized the home's amenities while keeping the original charm of the Southwestern-designed dwelling. The current staff will plan, organize and cater your event in the Grace Corn Heritage House for as few as two or as many as 400 people. There is entertainment, lighting and audiovisual equipment on-site to provide exactly what you need for your business meeting, award ceremony or wedding. A fully-equipped kitchen is available for use during your event, or the house's chef can provide catering. On the elegantly manicured grounds you will find a lovely outdoor dance floor and a koi fish pond complete with a waterfall. Jeanine and her staff pride themselves on exemplary service and attention to detail. Trust them to help you plan an event that will be truly memorable. If you have been looking for the perfect place to hold a theme party, such as a murder mystery or a gathering of the Red Hat Society, you have just found it. Give Jeanine a call at the Grace Corn Heritage House and make your reservations.

**412 N Kentucky Avenue, Roswell NM
(505) 624-2676**
http://graceheritagehouse.com

114 • **Attractions**

Carlsbad Caverns National Park

Carlsbad Caverns National Park is the home of the most famous caves in the United States. You can take self-guided tours of the 8.2-acre Big Room and the Natural Entrance. Guided tours of varying difficulties are available. The Big Room tour is a one-mile walk around the perimeter that passes famous features such as the Bottomless Pit, Rock of Ages and Painted Grotto. An audio guide notably enhances the tour. Elevators in the Visitor Center provide direct access to the Big Room. Many of the level and well lit trails on this route are wheelchair-accessible. The 1.25-mile Natural Entrance route follows the traditional explorer's route. The path descends more than 750 feet along steep and narrow trails through the Main Corridor. This route ends near the elevators in the Big Room. Main Corridor highlights include Bat Cave, Green Lake Overlook and the Boneyard. The caves are 56 degrees regardless of season, so dress warmly. Each evening in summer, nearly 400,000 Brazilian free-tail bats leave the caverns. Before the evening flight, a park ranger gives a free talk at the entrance. The starting time varies with sunset—check ahead for the exact time. The best flights are in August and September, when baby bats join the flight. The daily pre-dawn return of the bats is impressive. The bats re-enter the caverns from every direction with spectacular dives that may reach speeds of 25 mph or more. A visit to Carlsbad Canyons National Park is surely the trip of a lifetime.

3225 National Parks Highway, Carlsbad NM
(505) 785-2232
www.nps.gov/cave

New Mexico Museum of Space History

Celebrate the spirit of exploration with a visit to the New Mexico Museum of Space History. The museum has a special focus on New Mexico's pivotal role in the history of space technology. It contains depictions ranging from Robert Goddard's early rocket experiments near Roswell to a mock-up of the International Space Station. See astounding photographs of outer space at ViewSpace, an Internet-fed, self-updating, permanent exhibit that relies on the Hubble Space Telescope and its successor, the James Webb Space Telescope. Outdoor exhibits include the Sonic Wind I rocket sled, the Daisy Decelerator and Apollo program's Little Joe II rocket. Special exhibits feature rockets, satellites and space suits. The museum boasts New Mexico's only IMAX theater, with a wrap-around screen and surround sound. The theater also features a state-of-the-art planetarium. The International Space Hall of Fame commemorates men and women who have furthered the exploration of space. Ham, the first chimpanzee in space, is buried here. The Astronaut Memorial Garden is a tribute to the Space Shuttle Challenger and Columbia astronauts. The Museum is the repository for New Mexico's SpacePort America, the world's first space port to support private-sector launches. The Museum's educational outreach programs serve more than 10,000 students each school year. The New Mexico Museum of Space History is as large as it is fascinating, and you can easily spend the entire day touring it.

Highway 2001, Alamogordo NM
(505) 437-2840 or (877) 333-6589
www.spacefame.org

Photos by Ron Keller

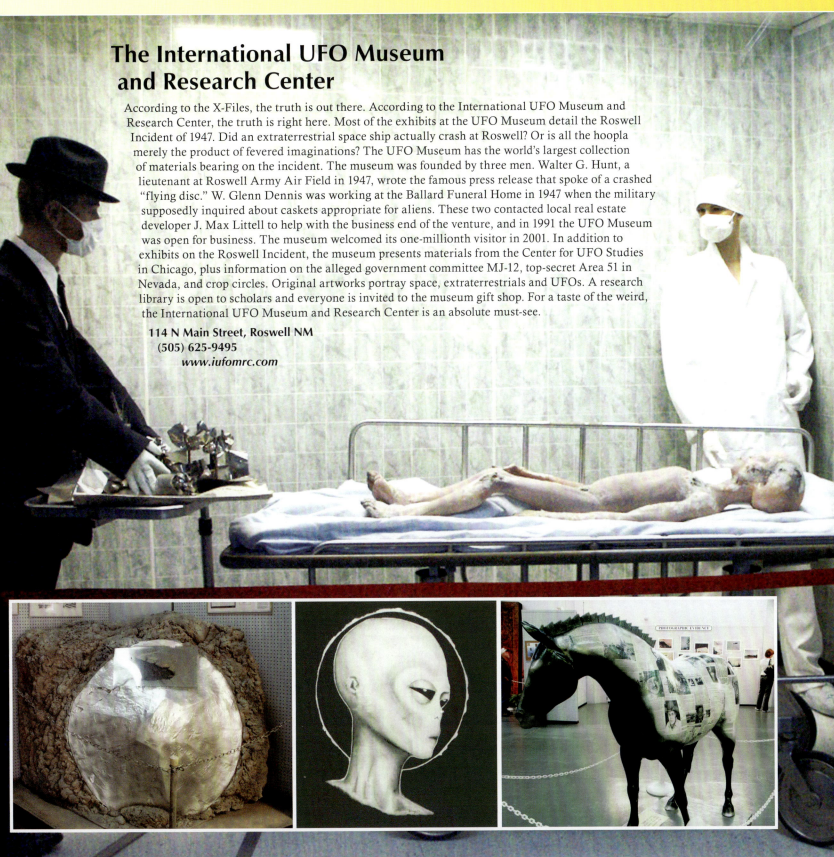

The International UFO Museum and Research Center

According to the X-Files, the truth is out there. According to the International UFO Museum and Research Center, the truth is right here. Most of the exhibits at the UFO Museum detail the Roswell Incident of 1947. Did an extraterrestrial space ship actually crash at Roswell? Or is all the hoopla merely the product of fevered imaginations? The UFO Museum has the world's largest collection of materials bearing on the incident. The museum was founded by three men. Walter G. Hunt, a lieutenant at Roswell Army Air Field in 1947, wrote the famous press release that spoke of a crashed "flying disc." W. Glenn Dennis was working at the Ballard Funeral Home in 1947 when the military supposedly inquired about caskets appropriate for aliens. These two contacted local real estate developer J. Max Littell to help with the business end of the venture, and in 1991 the UFO Museum was open for business. The museum welcomed its one-millionth visitor in 2001. In addition to exhibits on the Roswell Incident, the museum presents materials from the Center for UFO Studies in Chicago, plus information on the alleged government committee MJ-12, top-secret Area 51 in Nevada, and crop circles. Original artworks portray space, extraterrestrials and UFOs. A research library is open to scholars and everyone is invited to the museum gift shop. For a taste of the weird, the International UFO Museum and Research Center is an absolute must-see.

114 N Main Street, Roswell NM
(505) 625-9495
www.iufomrc.com

The Hubbard Museum of the American West

The Southwest is rich with history, and The Hubbard Museum of the American West is a fascinating place to learn more about it. An affiliate of the Smithsonian, The Hubbard Museum is filled with exhibits that make history come to life, including an historical look at the rodeo, artifacts of the American West and displays sure to pique the interest of all ages. Throughout the year, the museum offers an ever-changing calendar of events, including live performances and demonstrations of old-time skills. On your next visit, you just might have a chance to pan for gold or try your hand at leather crafting. The museum is home to the famous Anne C. Stradling horse collection, with bridles, saddles and carriages that span hundreds of years and come from all over the globe. When visiting the museum, be sure to walk through the awe inspiring Free Spirits at Noisy Water display near the entrance. Sculptor Dave McGary has created eight beautiful bronze horses that, although they weigh approximately two tons each, somehow look as though they are effortlessly galloping across the land. With so many things to learn and experience at The Hubbard Museum, it is a great starting point for all of your Southwest adventures.

841 Highway 70 W, Ruidoso Downs, NM
(505) 378-4142
www.hubbardmuseum.org

Photos provided by Smokey Bear Historical Park

Smokey Bear Historical Park

Six years after the Smokey Bear campaign was developed, the cub that became the personification of the caricature was found clinging with burned paws to the top of a tree in the Capitan Mountains. The fire he had miraculously survived devastated 17,000 acres of forest. Upon his death, Smokey was brought back to his birthplace and buried on a plot of land that became the Smokey Bear Historical Park, in the shadow of the mountains where he was rescued. Educational programs about wildland fire and ecology are held in the park's outdoor amphitheater, and the visitor center is full of Smokey Bear memorabilia. The Historical Park is the site of Capitan's original train depot. A playground has been built here and outdoor exhibits include interpretive plantings of New Mexico's six vegetative life zones. Indoor exhibits shed light on the history of the Cooperative Forest Fire Prevention Program and forest-related issues. No other animal has become so personally entwined with a country's culture, making Smokey Bear a fascinating study and a lasting legend. Although Smokey Bear died in 1976, after living for 26 years in the National Zoo, his name lives on. The Smokey Bear Historical Park offers a glimpse of the good works Smokey helped to propagate.

118 Smokey Bear Boulevard (Highway 380), Capitan NM
(505) 354-2748
www.smokeybearpark.com

Smokey Bear Museum

The Smokey Bear Museum rose out of efforts to promote conservation. The Museum's design was patterned after a Forest Service bulletin titled *How To Build A Log Cabin*. Using this document, Dorothy Guck, a ranger's wife, drew the plans. The Smokey Bear Museum, opened in 1960, is free to the public. A wooden replica of Smokey Bear as a cub rests in a tree in front of the museum. The first wooden Smokey was destroyed in a windstorm, but the current sculpture is a replacement crafted by Kevin Wolff, a Capitan woodworker. The one-room shrine is filled with Smokey Bear art, photographs and various memorabilia commemorating the life of the courageous bear who lived through a fire and inspired a nation. Six thick scrap books document the real bear's life through newspaper clippings, magazine articles and letters from fans. Smokey, who was awarded his own zip code when he lived in the zoo, became an icon of the times during his life. The gift shop provides souvenirs to remind travelers of their visit to the Smokey Bear Museum and the legacy of the bear it honors. The Smokey Bear Museum is closed only on Thanksgiving, Christmas and New Year's Day. That means you have 362 days of the year to get there and view this gentle piece of history.

102 Smokey Bear Boulevard, Capitan NM
(505) 354-2298
www.zianet.com/village/museum/museum.html

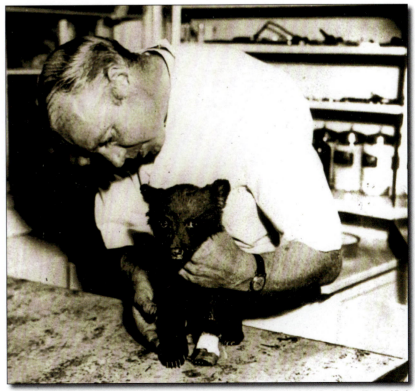

Photo provided by Smokey Bear Historical Park

Mesilla Valley Maze

If you're looking for something fun to do this autumn that is both exciting and educational, then head to the Mesilla Valley Maze in Las Cruces. This incredible maze is a joint venture between New Mexico State University's Survey Department and the Lyles Family Farms, which began entertaining and educating the community in 1999. Each January preparation for the year's maze begins with a pencil sketch that represents that year's curriculum, such as the 2005 Spirit of the West Maze entitled Water Works which depicts a giant windmill and stylized flowing water. The sketch is then turned over to Dr. Steve Frank, who is the department head for the university's Survey-Engineering Program. He, along with a small group of students, then digitalizes the drawing and calculates ground coordinates for Global Positioning Satellites. The first week in July, the corn is planted and when the crop grows to about knee-high the maze design is staked out. The maze is then cut with a small farm tractor that has been mounted with specialized GPS equipment. A few weeks later the team flies over the maze to take aerial photographs. In conjunction with the nine-acre corn maze, visitors are treated to hay rides and a trip through the huge pumpkin field, along with face painting, a trike trail and picnic tents. Whether you're planning a school field trip or a fun family outing, head to Mesilla Valley Maze at Lyles Family Farms, where education and recreation merge to make great memories.

3855 W Picacho, Las Cruces NM
(505) 526-1919
www.mesillavalleymaze.com

Town of Mesilla

Take a trip to southern New Mexico if only to visit the historic town of Mesilla, a place that strongly echoes its colorful past with a plaza that has been designated a State and National Historic Monument. Many of the almost 2,200 residents are direct descendants of the early town settlers, and they pride themselves on maintaining the original character that has made this town the best known and most visited historic community in this part of the state. Mesilla is a shopper's paradise, with a lively mix of galleries, gift and antique shops. An old theater now shows alternative and foreign films nightly. Casual or fine dining and wonderful lodging options, including a bed and breakfast inn and a boutique hotel, guarantee your comfort. Tap your foot to live music at the cantina or wander through the plaza's year round Sunday crafts market. You can relax on a plaza bench surrounded by stately territorial-style buildings, visit a museum or hike the ditch banks that criss-cross pecan orchards. Take a walking tour through the streets once visited by Billy the Kid, Pancho Villa and Pat Garrett. Plan your visit to celebrate a traditional Mexican Fiesta weekend from May through November and bring a camera, the light is perfect for photographing some of the finest adobe architecture in the Southwest.

(505) 524-3262   *www.oldmesilla.org*

Las Cruces City Museums

The City of Las Cruces sponsors its own system of museums free to the public. Among the most fascinating is the Las Cruces Museum of Natural History, located in the Mesilla Valley Mall. This museum is dedicated to explaining the environment of New Mexico and the Chihuahuan Desert. The Chihuahuan Desert Nature Center houses more than 40 live animals from the desert, and children can experience them hands-on at scheduled encounters. Other regularly scheduled events include lectures on the desert and sky safari, a guided tour of the night sky using the museum's own high-powered telescopes. The ZOOMzone is a fun place for the youngest to try science activities and games with the staff and the Junior Docents. The museum continuously sponsors special exhibits. Recent topics have included dinosaur eggs, wild weather and river life. A few of the museum's activities require a fee, such as the popular field trips into the desert and the summer day camps for children. The city sponsors two other museums. The Railroad Museum is still under development and is open only on Saturdays. The Museum of Art is open free of charge six days a week. In addition to the permanent collection, visiting exhibits change frequently. The Museum of Art has a major educational program for children and adults in painting, ceramics, photography and other media. The Las Cruces city museums are definitely worth a visit.

700 S Telshor Boulevard #1608, Las Cruces NM (Museum of Natural History)
(505) 522-3120
490 N Water Street, Las Cruces NM (Museum of Art)
(505) 541-2137
www.museums.las-cruces.org

The Organ Mountains as seen from Las Cruces
Photo courtesy of the New Mexico Tourism Department

New Mexico Farm & Ranch Heritage Museum

The New Mexico Farm and Ranch Heritage Museum comprises 47 acres packed with real stories about real people. The interactive museum, which has welcomed visitors from all over the world, brings to life the 3,000-year history of farming and ranching in New Mexico. The main building contains more than 24,000 square feet of exhibit space, along with a restaurant, gift shop and theater. Fun and learning go hand in hand as visitors can watch a cow being milked, stroll along corrals filled with livestock, and enjoy any of several gardens. Drop by the blacksmith shop to watch a demonstration. The Heritage Kitchens demonstration area cooks up free samples such as cowboy coffee, stews and bread. The Adventure Corral is an educational and play area for children 3 to 10. It includes a fiberglass cow that children can milk, a teeter-totter with saddles and peddle-powered tractors. School classes regularly tour the state-owned museum. The New Mexico Farm and Ranch Heritage Museum inspires memories in some visitors, educates others and provides a fun-filled day for everyone.

4100 Dripping Springs Road, Las Cruces NM
(505) 522-4100
www.frhm.org

The Fountain Theatre

If you would like to see movies that are a little more sophisticated than Hollywood's special-effects shoot'em-ups, the Fountain Theatre is an invaluable resource. The oldest theater in New Mexico, the Fountain today is run by the non-profit Mesilla Valley Film Society. The society presents alternative, foreign and indie films to the southern New Mexico and El Paso/Juarez areas—downtown El Paso is only 45 miles away. At the Fountain Theatre, you can see top rated documentaries such as *Grizzly Man*, *Who Killed the Electric Car?* and *Super Size Me*, along with many other lesser-known but excellent titles. Well known fiction titles shown recently include *Rabbit-Proof Fence* and *Amélie*. The Fountain Theatre is also the home of CineMatinee at the Fountain. This popular program screens films that usually have a New Mexico or western connection. The Fountain has 120 seats. The building, which was built in 1905, is adobe in style, with hand-painted murals on the inside walls. The theater takes its name from the Fountain family, which still owns it. In the early days, it presented both cinema and vaudeville, and in the 1930s you could sometimes see the entire Fountain family, including children, on stage performing with the band. If you are inspired by the scent of real butter on popcorn or a passion for movies, you must come the Fountain Theatre.

**2469 Calle de Guadalupe, Mesilla NM
(505) 524-8287**
www.fountaintheatre.org

Mesilla is a small town by today's standards, but 150 years ago it was the major stop for travelers going between San Antonio and San Diego. Near New Mexico's southern border with Mexico, Mesilla hasn't changed much over the years allowing visitors to see what an 1800s border town looked like.
Photo courtesy of the New Mexico Tourism Department

City of Rocks State Park is between Silver City and Deming in southwestern New Mexico. Over 30 million years wind and water eroded the soft volcanic stone into upright shapes reminiscent of England's Stonehenge.
Photo courtesy of the New Mexico Tourism Department. Photo by Mark Nohl.

The Silver City Museum

Southwestern New Mexico's history is made up of ancient Indian artists, mountain men and buffalo soldiers. Lawmen chased outlaws; miners dug for silver and copper. Hispanic cowboys, Jewish merchants and some extraordinarily resourceful women helped fill in the mix. You can find out more about this history at the Silver City Museum, a department of the Town of Silver City supported by the Silver City Museum Society. Continuing exhibits at the museum include Settling Southwest New Mexico, Two Centuries of Mining in Southwest New Mexico, and I'm Goin' into Town: Early Commerce in Silver City. The museum contains reconstructions of a period parlor and mine office. You can learn how Silver City was almost washed away by a series of floods 100 years ago. The discovery of silver in 1870 gave birth to Silver City. The young town boasted Victorian brick buildings, electricity and telephone service. The collapse of the silver boom in 1893 was a heavy blow, but the town reinvented itself as a resort for tuberculosis patients. In 1910, large-scale copper mining began, which continues to this day. The Silver City Museum, which records all this, is located in one of the finest Italianate mansions of the 1880s. The building eventually became city hall and for 40 years, the local fire station. It became home to the museum in 1967. Discover the fascinating past at the Silver City Museum.

312 W Broadway, Silver City NM
(505) 538-5921
www.silvercitymuseum.org

Photo courtesy of NRAO/AUI

The Very Large Array Radio Telescope

The Very Large Array (VLA) radio telescope is one of the most spectacular sights in a spectacular state. This gigantic instrument has made more scientific discoveries than any other ground-based telescope in history. The VLA consists of 27 radio antennas in a Y-shaped configuration on the Plains of San Augustin west of Socorro. Each arm of the Y can be up to 13 miles long. The data from the 82-foot antennas is combined electronically to give a resolution equivalent to an antenna up to 22 miles across. The National Radio Astronomy Observatory (NRAO) manages the VLA, plus additional radio telescopes in West Virginia. Scientists from around the world use these powerful tools to study the sun, planets and other objects in our solar system, as well as distant stars, galaxies and quasars. The VLA Visitor Center is open every day. Start at the theater, where a brief video provides an overview of radio astronomy. Then explore the exhibits. Discover how to move the VLA's antennas. Learn about the Very Long Baseline Array, managed from Socorro. This project combines images from a line of radio telescopes extending from Hawaii to the Virgin Islands. Then take a walking tour to the base of one of the 230-ton antennas. Climb up to the observation deck for a view of the array itself. The VLA offers special guided tours twice a year. During the summer weekends, students provide free tours. Come see the Very Large Array radio telescope, storied in film and fiction.

1003 Lopezville Road, Socorro NM
(505) 835-7000 *www.nrao.edu*

Indian kiva at Pecos Historic Park

Gallup Historical Society

Gallup has been called the Indian Capital of the World for its location in the heart of the lands of the Navajo, Zuni, Hopi and other tribes. Most of the Indian crafts from the nearby reservations passes through Gallup. Three out of every eight Gallup residents is an American Indian. Hispanics make up a full third of the population. Even the Anglos in Gallup are astonishingly diverse because of the town's history as a coal-mining center. The mines drew experienced miners from Pennsylvania, New York and Ohio, but also immigrants from a dozen European nations, including Britain, Germany, the Austro-Hungarian Empire, Italy, Serbia and Greece. By 1929, Gallup's 57 mines loaded a 70-car coal train every day, the largest volume of shipping to originate from any center between Kansas City and Los Angeles. (Even today, the mines load a 30-car coal train daily.) The Atlantic and Pacific Railroad hauled the coal from 1881, and a certain David Gallup was the railroad paymaster. Miners, railroad workers, farmers and sawmill owners all were paid by Mr. Gallup, who was soon the most famous man in the area. Many museums are in or near historic Gallup, including the Rex Museum of the Gallup Historical Society. Others include the Red Rock State Park Museum and the Storyteller Museum of the Southwest Indian Foundation. The Navajo Code Talkers Communication Center is in next-door Rehoboth. The A:shiwi A:wan Museum, Navajo Nation Museum and Ramah Museum are all nearby.

300 W Historic Route 66, Gallup NM (Gallup Historical Society's Rex Museum) (505) 863-1363
ggsc.wnmu.edu/mcf/museums/rex.html
ggsc.wnmu.edu/mcf/museums.html (Other Gallup area museums and festivals)

The Annual Inter-Tribal Indian Ceremonial is now more than 80 years old. The Ceremonial takes place each August, with all-Indian professional rodeos, Ceremonial Indian Dances, a downtown Gallup parade (America's only all-Indian non-mechanized parade), daily performing arts, and Indian foods.

Courtesy of the New Mexico Tourism Department.
Photograph by Gary Romero

The St. Francis Of Assisi Catholic Church in Ranchos De Taos.

Fashion

Celebro Natural Fiber Clothing

For comfort, for style, for life, Celebro Natural Fiber Clothing is the premier boutique in Albuquerque's historic Nob Hill. From easy care and relaxed styles in cotton, linen, rayon, hemp and tencel to hand-loomed and one-of-a-kind art wear from around the globe, the racks at Celebro Clothing runneth over with natural fiber fashions for women and men that express your unique personal style. For more than 15 years, Melinda and George Kenefic, and Roswell, the official greeter dog, have maintained a commitment to product quality, personalized service and community growth. Most of their suppliers are small businesses who work with their employees to develop economic independence through fair wages, access to health care and safe working conditions. Stop by Celebro Clothing and experience for yourself the rich colors and textures that make wearing natural fibers exceptional. And don't forget to check out the wall of socks, the wide array of scarves and shawls, and, of course, designer jewelry. For women and men, from small to generous sizes, shop Celebro, naturally.

109 Carlisle NE, Albuquerque NM
(505) 265-6403
www.celebroclothing.com

Photos by Kyle Zimmerman

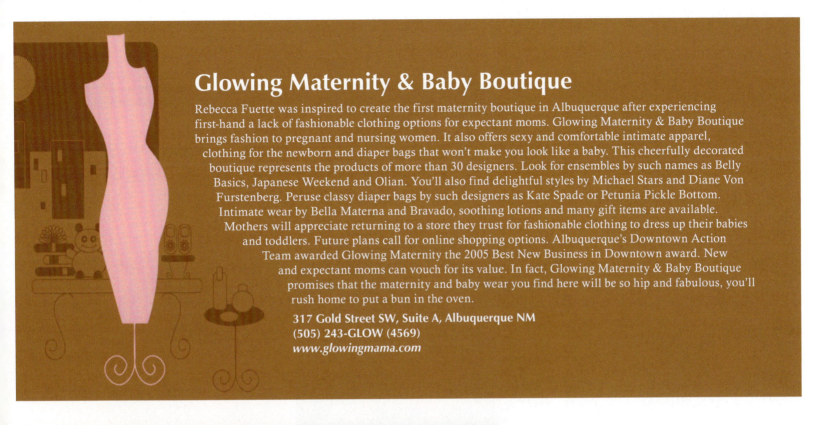

Glowing Maternity & Baby Boutique

Rebecca Fuette was inspired to create the first maternity boutique in Albuquerque after experiencing first-hand a lack of fashionable clothing options for expectant moms. Glowing Maternity & Baby Boutique brings fashion to pregnant and nursing women. It also offers sexy and comfortable intimate apparel, clothing for the newborn and diaper bags that won't make you look like a baby. This cheerfully decorated boutique represents the products of more than 30 designers. Look for ensembles by such names as Belly Basics, Japanese Weekend and Olian. You'll also find delightful styles by Michael Stars and Diane Von Furstenberg. Peruse classy diaper bags by such designers as Kate Spade or Petunia Pickle Bottom. Intimate wear by Bella Materna and Bravado, soothing lotions and many gift items are available. Mothers will appreciate returning to a store they trust for fashionable clothing to dress up their babies and toddlers. Future plans call for online shopping options. Albuquerque's Downtown Action Team awarded Glowing Maternity the 2005 Best New Business in Downtown award. New and expectant moms can vouch for its value. In fact, Glowing Maternity & Baby Boutique promises that the maternity and baby wear you find here will be so hip and fabulous, you'll rush home to put a bun in the oven.

317 Gold Street SW, Suite A, Albuquerque NM
(505) 243-GLOW (4569)
www.glowingmama.com

Ooh! Aah! Jewelry

Walk into Ooh! Aah! Jewelry and you will find a treasure trove of rings, bracelets, necklaces and earrings. Mary Vigil opened her original shop in Nob Hill in 1990, following her passion for jewelry and design. She now has a second location in downtown Albuquerque. Both of Mary's shops promise affordable style in silver, white and yellow gold, along with stunning platinum wedding jewelry. Look for diamonds, garnets, amethyst, topaz, turquoise, pearls and many other exotic gems from more than 100 jewelry lines from around the world. Albuquerqueans will tell you it's their favorite place to find a gift by a local artisan. The collection features contemporary and traditional designs for both men and women with a wide range of prices and styles. Once inside, you will find yourself saying, "Ooh, Aah," and surely find that unique piece that catches your eye.

311 Gold Avenue SW, Albuquerque NM
(505) 242-7101
110 Amherst SE, Albuquerque NM
(505) 265-7170 or (866) 266-4224
www.oohaahjewelry.com

Desert Designs

Desert Designs Boutique, Inc. is one of the most unique women's clothing boutiques in the Southwest. Owner Margaret Holmes has a wonderful way with colors and design. She follows her heart and instincts when supplying her shop with treasures from all over the world. Incredibly, Margaret began designing and sewing her own clothing when she was only 13 years old and had already developed her own clothing line by 1996. Her selections are personal, always attractive, and you can often hear her joking that she buys everything for herself and then sells it. Margaret and her knowledgeable staff of fashion consultants treat each customer like a valued friend. She creates a cheery atmosphere, serving tea, cookies and bottled water, and has even made a space for companions to relax while their partners shop. Margaret does trunk and fashion shows in New Mexico and as far away as Canada. In 2005, Desert Designs became a movie set for First Snow, starring Guy Pearce. To Margaret's delight, the cast and crew loved the shop and ended up buying many of her wonderful treasures. The socialble Margaret loves the Red Hat Society and has devoted a whole room to fulfilling their needs. She does countless fashion shows dedicated to them, punctuated with trademark flair and gusto, making such a reputation for the boutique that the Red Hat Ladies often come to visit her shop by the busload. At Desert Designs, you will walk in looking for something different, and will walk out looking gorgeously different. Come by for a truly excellent shopping experience.

206½ San Felipe Street Northwest,
 #7 Patio Market, Albuquerque NM
(505) 217-0011
www.ddboutique.com

Seventh Goddess

Downtown Albuquerque's Seventh Goddess is filled with high-end lingerie and accessories sure to make you feel feminine. The staff will treat you to truffles and tea as you browse displays filled with imported lingerie, including handmade corsets, flirty camisoles and silky undergarments. The designer lines are upscale, exotic and worth it. Everything about Seventh Goddess is rich and rewarding, from the merchandise to the deep red color of the walls and the warm wooden floors. Owners Deborah Reese and Chasie Soliz set out to create a safe environment where women can explore the possibilities and feel empowered to be sexy and confident, whether they are seeking adorable pajamas or soft Chantilly lace boy panties and bras. You'll find a range of sizes suitable for every figure. Enhance your best features with intimate apparel by Claire Pettibone and Arianne. Let styles by Le Mystère and OnGossamer change your mood and spark fantasies. In a departure from lingerie, look for alluring shoes and jewelry that any well dressed goddess would admire. Immerse yourself in sensual choices with a visit to Seventh Goddess. While you are there, take a look at the fine lineup of shops that are revitalizing Gold Avenue.

317 Gold Avenue SW, Suite B, Albuquerque NM
(505) 243-8025
www.seventhgoddess.com

Silver Sun

In 1976, recently retired schoolteachers Deanna Olson and Cheryl Ingram toured rodeo circuits looking for buyers for their small collection of natural American turquoise jewelry. In 1979, they opened the Silver Sun Gallery in Santa Fe, and in 1985, they launched Silver Sun Wholesale in Albuquerque. The pair searches the Southwest for the finest and rarest turquoise and for the Native American artisans who can turn it into such forms as concho belts, bracelets and buckles. The "fallen skystone," which in its natural form is so hard and beautiful it requires no special treatment, has been mined by Native Americans in places like Cerrillos Mine south of Santa Fe for at least 2,000 years.

The finest Silver Sun turquoise comes from small Southwestern mines, as well as from miners mining individual claims and from old, personal caches. A select group of Navajo silversmiths make most of the jewelry with several Pueblo artists contributing one-of-a-kind pieces. Silver Sun also creates an affordable line of jewelry using a variety of stones, including coral, rhodochrosite and spiney oyster. The company belongs to the Indian Arts and Crafts Association, an organization devoted to promoting and protecting Native American handmade arts and crafts. Trade shows, the Albuquerque showroom and wholesale representatives make Silver Stone jewelry available to shops and galleries throughout the nation, including places like the Heard Museum in Phoenix and the Museum of Natural History in New York City. Visit Silver Sun for Native American jewelry of lasting beauty and value.

2011 Central Avenue NW, Albuquerque NM (Silver Sun Wholesale)
(505) 246-9692 or (800) 662-3220
www.silversunalbuquerque.com
656 Canyon Road, Santa Fe NM (Silver Sun Gallery)

Fashion • 137

Santa Fe by Moonlight

Kioti

In bustling, upscale Santa Fe you'll find Kioti, a delightful and vibrant shop filled with beautiful clothing and terrific people. At Kioti, you will find unusual and original patterns and textiles blended together to create comfortable, relaxed clothing designed to fit your lifestyle. Exotic styles and vivid fabrics merge to give you affordable clothing with a chic, Asian influence. Owners Linda Prager and David Mueller began 20 years ago importing antiques and folk art from Indonesia during their extensive travels. As the antique market became less viable they switched their focus to the clothing and textile industry and opened Kioti boutique. In 2002, the couple traveled again to China to adopt their daughter, Zoë, now five years old. Eighty percent of their stock comes from Indonesia, with the remainder coming from China, Thailand and small American companies. Specializing in women's clothing and accessories, they carry a diverse and stunning selection of jackets, sweaters and dresses. Each item is distinct and many are handcrafted. The quality clothing and comfortable, friendly service at Kioti will keep you coming back often to peruse the latest merchandise. On your next visit to the Santa Fe area, make time to stop in and see David, Linda and Zoë. They are waiting to show you the latest fashions filled with Eastern flair at Kioti.

500 Montezuma Suite 114, Santa Fe NM
(505) 984-9836

Back At The Ranch

Back At The Ranch is a place where fabulous form meets quality function. Owner and designer Wendy Lane produces handmade, custom cowboy boots that are truly remarkable and thoroughly astounding. Back At The Ranch is a fun destination store located in a charming historical adobe building in Santa Fe. Along with her own designs and custom projects, Wendy stocks between 800 and 900 pairs of boots at a time. She also offers an excellent selection of the finest belts, buckles and accessories. Some of the designers who share shelf space alongside Lane's own Back At The Ranch Private Label include Rocketbuster, Liberty, Kimmel and T.O. Stanley. Wendy's creations mix everything from basic calf leather to the most exotic and wild skins in unusual colors: fuchsia alligator, the store's most popular blue denim ostrich, stingray and exotic lizards. The incredible designs and amazing craftsmanship must be seen to be believed. Vivid reds, dazzling yellows and a rainbow of other colors are on display when you enter the shop. Upon close inspection, you will find elegant, artistic scenes and patterns that come alive on these quality-crafted boots. Bears in a forest, chili peppers, or playing cards on a field of green are just a few of the amazing vignettes that you will see on the boots at Back At The Ranch. Wendy, who is known for her collaboration with high-profile clients such as Tom Ford, Brooks & Dunn and Don Imus, is able to decorate any boot or design with anything you can imagine. If you can't visit the store in person, Wendy will send a packet to trace your foot and take measurements, ensuring a perfect fit. Find the boot that fits your style as well as your foot at Back At The Ranch.

**209 E Marcy Street,
Sante Fe NM
(888) 96B-OOTS
(962-6687)
www.backattheranch.com**

Solano's Boot & Western Wear

This is the story of Solano's Boot & Western Wear, a 50-year, three-generation family business that was founded on principle, built with sweat and branded a treasure in time. Solano's began humbly in 1956 when Andy Solano opened a small boot repair shop in downtown Raton. In 1968, after many late nights and early mornings of resurrecting tired old cowboy boots, Mr. Solano had the opportunity to purchase the building that now houses Solano's daily operations. His wife, Fabie, who founded the retail side of the business, joined him in 1971, followed by their eldest son, Raphael, a decade later. The trio continued to build a dynasty that has stood the test of time and become timeless in its own right. Step inside and find yourself a world away, in a simpler time and place that is brought to life again. Browse their most unique array of merchandise and you're bound to find a treasure trove of rarities in pairs. One may even find Grandfather's hat up on display as the cemetery there remembers them each passing day. No matter what your walk of life or where you choose to hang your hat, an experience at Solano's is one you'll not soon forget.

101 S 2nd Street, Raton NM
(505) 445-2632
www.solanoswesternwear.com

Native Jackets

Native Jackets in Santa Fe creates and carries a spectacular collection of Native American blankets, jackets and vests. At the heart of this incredible company is owner John Andrews. John opened the doors to Native Jackets in 1998, offering outstanding quality, selection and service.

Their newest line is the American Classic Trade Blankets collection, featuring patterns from the golden age of trade blankets that lasted from approximately 1892 to 1929. All of the blankets at Native Jackets are of the finest quality, manufactured with the very highest standards and offered to the public at affordable prices. Designed not only for aesthetics, these Native blankets and jackets can keep you warm in temperatures as low as 20 degrees Fahrenheit. With a spectacular selection to choose from, John is able to offer the majority, if not all, of the traditional Navajo patterns and design elements. Native Jackets also carries an equally extensive collection of antique trade blankets, including some early Pendleton blankets from just before the turn of the century. These beautiful blankets and garments are not only pleasing to the eye, they are also practical objects of art that inspire the imagination and represent American history. Like the quilts of the pioneers, these stunning blankets tell stories and hold memories. Find your own link to the past and create new stories and memories at Native Jackets.

66 E San Francisco Street, Suite 14, Santa Fe NM
(888) 420-0005
www.nativejackets.com

142 • Galleries

The Organ Mountains; so named for their resemblance to the pipes coming up out of a pipe organ. The "pipes" are the remnants of volcanic vents that have been exposed by thousands of years of erosion.

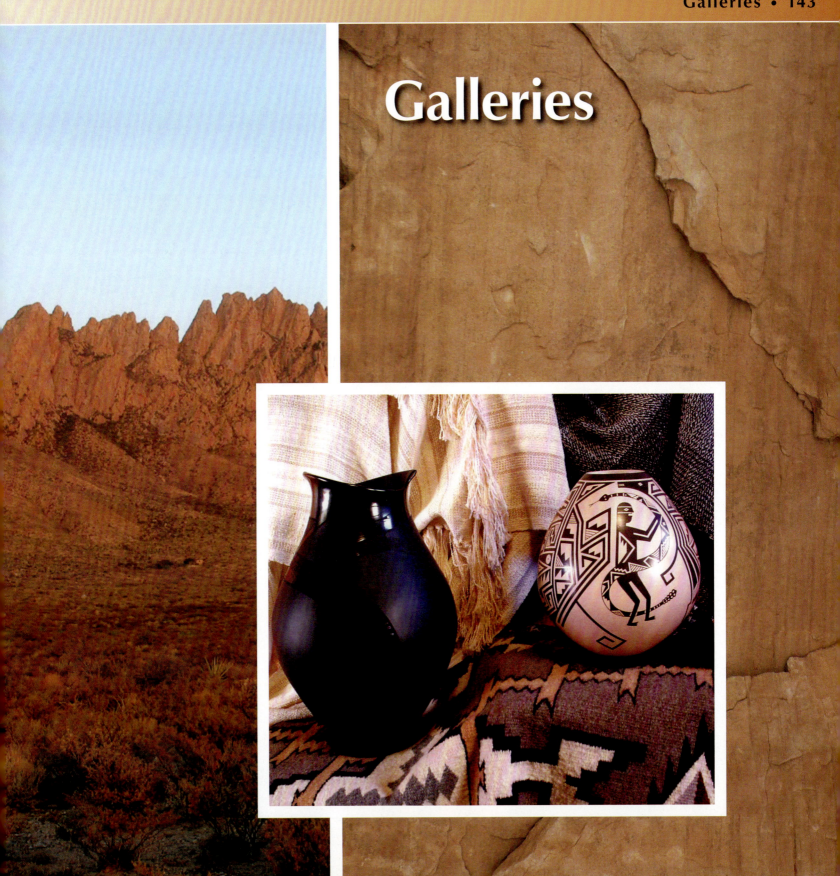

Galleries

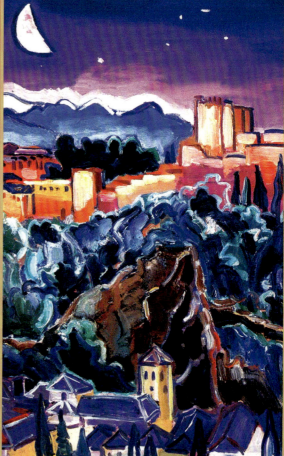

Taos Gallery Association

Taos is cradled by the soaring Sangre de Cristo Mountains of northern New Mexico. To the west, the land fans out toward mesas and sagebrush-covered plains. Taos has been a magnet for artists for more than a century. The history of art here begins with the legendary broken wagon wheel of 1898 that forced artists Ernest L. Blumenschein and Joseph Henry Sharp to linger in Taos. It runs through the formation of the Taos Society of Artists in the early 20th century. The town's storied history as an artists' community is as colorful and vibrant as the arts and crafts emanating from its adobe and hollyhock-lined streets. The Taos Gallery Association is organized to help you experience the special magic of Taos and the Taos art community. You can check out the many upcoming events in the area by visiting the Association's website. Come to the heart of art in New Mexico. Come enjoy Taos and its many galleries.

www.taosgalleryassoc.com

Inger Jirby's Taos Guest Houses

To truly immerse yourself in historic Taos, stay in a 200-year-old adobe compound in the center of town. Inger Jirby's Taos Guest Houses are luxuriously remodeled and decorated with a uniquely Southwestern flair, complete with original paintings by one of the most popular artists of the area. Painter Inger Jirby's three suites are located in the same adobe haven that contains her home, gallery and sculpture garden. The guest houses, or *casitas,* offer all of the conveniences of home, including entertainment centers, separate bedrooms and full kitchens stocked with staples. Inger has decorated each of the three casitas in its own distinctive style, with bright and interesting décor and colors and lots of her own art. The casitas sport flagstone floors, rugs and beautiful spiral staircases. Light comes from huge bright windows and skylights, and heat from kiva gas fireplaces. Each suite boasts more than 1,000 square feet of living space, giving you plenty of room to relax. Within easy walking distance of many local landmarks, such as the Taos Plaza and the Blumenschein Museum, the guest houses are convenient to everything on your sightseeing agenda, yet they grant you privacy at the end of the day. Stay at Inger Jirby's Taos Guest Houses and experience the true magic of Taos.

**207 Ledoux Street, Taos NM
(505) 758-7333**
www.jirby.com/pages

Photos by: SM

Inger Jirby Gallery

Artist Inger Jirby loves color. She expresses her emotions and her vision of the world around her using rich reds, blues, yellows and other vibrant hues. Visitors feel wonder and awe at the beauty of everyday life when they view the paintings at the Inger Jirby Gallery. Inger was born in the far north of Sweden, a land of blazing colors. Her earliest memories are bathed in the colors that fill her passion-filled fauvist paintings today. She began painting as a small child and was able to support herself as an artist by her early 20s. Inger was influenced by many artistic greats, beginning with Van Gogh and then the great colorists Matisse and Bonnard. Her style, though, is entirely her own. After living in the Greek islands, then Paris, Venice, Jamaica and New York, Inger discovered New Mexico. Taos, with its stunning landscapes and colors, offers countless subjects for Inger to paint, but she also continues to travel, painting and immersing herself in the cultures of the world. Inger's pieces hang in major museums and important private collections worldwide. Outside the walls of the Inger Jirby Gallery, a Sculpture Garden provides a space for whimsical metal creations by Fredrick Prescott, clay murals by Priscilla Hoback and works by other talented artists. Come experience the energy and color on display at the Inger Jirby Gallery.

207 Ledoux Street, Taos NM
(505) 758-7333
www.jirby.com

Brazos Fine Art

Brazos Fine Art, located in the heart of the Taos Historic District, is a destination gallery for the finest traditional and contemporary artwork in a diversity of genres and styles. The elegantly designed gallery has an Old World charm and graciousness that is unique to Taos. Established in 1992, the gallery represents nationally acclaimed local and regional artists who work in oils, watercolors, acrylics, pastels, functional and decorative fused glass, and one-of-a-kind jewelry. Brazos Fine Art also carries bronze sculptures of wildlife, along with turned wood vessels. Each month, the gallery highlights the work of one of its artists. Owner and director Jennifer Howell invites you to spend time in the gallery, or take a virtual tour on their website. The Gallery is open daily, call for hours.

119 Bent Street, Taos NM
(505) 758-0767
www.brazosgallery.com

Farnsworth Gallery Taos

Farnsworth Gallery Taos features fine art and photography from the 40-year career of Taos artist John Farnsworth. You can contemplate vintage scenes from John's early work on the Navajo and Hopi reservations and among the Pueblos of Arizona and New Mexico. Watercolor and oil paintings of Kachina dolls and other Native American subjects are on display. You can see the more recent larger-than-life portraits of horses and cattle that have become this internationally known artist's trademark. Paintings and drawings of Mexican Charros, or cowboys, are on the gallery walls, along with paintings of flowers and clouds. You can also view photographs of John's travels in Mexico, Peru and Europe. Farnsworth Gallery Taos is located in an historic adobe house amid the gardens and courtyards of Café Renato and the Taos Center for the Arts, just north of the Taos Inn and a short stroll from the Taos Plaza. Thea Swengel, the artist's wife, invites you to stroll through Farnsworth Gallery Taos and get to know the work and history of John Farnsworth, a truly special American artist.

Jd Challenger Studio/Gallery

Jd Challenger is one of the foremost contemporary artists in the world today. He was born in Oklahoma with a creative fire that began to smolder when he was very young. After moving to Taos, Challenger enjoyed success painting landscapes. Privately, he drew and painted Native Americans, but was reluctant to show his paintings in public for fear of offending a people he greatly admired. His wife, Denise, encouraged him to show his work to his Native American friends, one of whom was a holy man. When he did so, he received their blessing and was told, "The Creator chooses His own messengers." Challenger takes his role seriously, but declines credit for his remarkable gifts. "I'm just the instrument." Challenger paints the stories of a people rich in heritage and traditions; stories that demand to be told. His gallery welcomes visitors from everywhere who come to see his passionate portrayals of our country's first residents.

221 Paseo del Pueblo Norte, Taos NM
(505) 751-4677 or (800) 511-6773
www.jdchallenger.com

Wilder Nightingale Fine Art

Wilder Nightingale Fine Art has helped new and seasoned art collectors acquire original art since 1990. The gallery represents more than 35 leading and regional artists. The works are eclectic and range from traditional landscapes in oil, pastel and watercolor to contemporary and abstract styles. Leading artists such as Rory Wagner, Ray Vinella, Tom Noble, Carolyn Douglas, Phil Epp, Greg Moon, Margaret Nes and Stephen Day make this gallery a must-see when you are visiting Taos. Wilder Nightingale has a considerable collection of bronze and ceramic sculpture, some of it representational and some of it highly whimsical. The gallery has been featured in many national publications, including *Art & Antiques, Cowboys and Indians, Luxury Living, American Style* and *Distinction Magazine*. Wilder Nightingale has a relaxed and comfortable atmosphere. Proprietor Robert Wilder Nightingale looks forward to your visit, whether to collect or simply to enjoy the beauty that Taos has to offer.

119-A Kit Carson Road, Taos NM
(505) 758-3255 or (800) 845-4173
www.wnightingale.com

Art Divas Gallery

Art Divas Gallery features fine art by women and a few good men. Owner Sue Williford believes that everyone should follow their dream, and she hopes that Art Divas will allow the featured artists to do just that. At the same time, customers can enrich their lives by bringing home one or more of the beautiful works. In addition to paintings, Art Divas displays sculpture, fine crafts, jewelry and mixed media pieces. Sue spotlights the works of many talented up-and-coming and established artists. All pieces are sold on consignment. Sue explains that it is very difficult for an artist to make a living entirely by artwork. Therefore, Sue passes a larger share of the income from each sale on to the artists than most other galleries. Experience the serene landscapes of painter Kate Starling or the kinetic sculptures of Mark White. Silver bracelets gleam next to rustic beaded chokers. You can experience the beauty of drawings, glasswork and turned wood. Each piece highlights the special talents of the artist. Come to Art Divas Gallery, across from Kit Carson Park. You can help artists make art their career and at the same time bring home a genuine treasure.

208 Paseo del Pueblo Norte, Taos NM
(505) 737-0515
www.artdivasartgallery.com

Starving Artists Gallery

The image of an artist, passionately immersed in the joy of creating and expressing emotion, but also having to hold down a side job to keep food on the table, is one that nearly everyone is familiar with. At the Starving Artists Gallery, owner Stephen Daniels showcases the works of 20 emerging and established artists. Proceeds from the artwork allow artists to succeed in their craft as a career, as well as benefiting the community. A percentage of the profits are donated to two local nonprofit organizations established to feed the hungry in Taos. Experience quiet watercolor landscapes, or the energy of an abstract painted in oil. The gallery displays a variety of media, including wood carvings, sculptures and Native American jewelry. Zuni fetishes, small carvings believed to have the power to protect, heal or assist hunters, are carefully handcrafted in New Mexico. The gallery represents the talents of Jan Oliver, Jean Whetnall, Lisa Connor and many other local artists. Visit the Starving Artists Gallery in Yucca Plaza and help the artists, and the entire community, be fed.

216C Paseo del Pueblo Norte, Taos NM
(505) 758-0166

Photo by S.M. Stachler

Galleries—Taos Gallery Association • 153

Zane Wheeler Gallery

The line between art and fashion is not just blurred, but completely removed, at the Zane Wheeler Gallery in Taos. Donna Brunton, gallery owner of more than 20 years, features local artists who create in a variety of media, including jewelry, clothing and glass. Donna is an accomplished knitter. She is so skillful, in fact, that one knitting book author recognizes her as one of the best knitters in America, and describes her as "an artist that paints with yarn." Many of Donna's tunics, cardigans and children's sweaters are available at the gallery. Sheena Cameron combines various metals and clay to produce exciting artistic jewelry. Glass blowing artist Ira Lujan creates glass versions of everyday Pueblo objects, such as water jugs, canteens and baskets, instantly transforming day-to-day objects into delicate works of art. In his latest works, Ira creates glass sculptures depicting the interconnectedness of people and the earth. These original pieces have earned Ira a great deal of recognition, including an award for Best of Show and placement in several museums. Many artists, including Jim Rabby, Thom Wheeler and Barbara Ehrilch, display their talents in oils, acrylics, pottery and other materials. Come to the Zane Wheeler Gallery and discover what happens When Art and Fashion Meet.

107 N Taos Plaza, Taos NM
(505) 751-7220
www.zanewheeler.com

Glass blowing furnace
Photo by Jonas Bengtsson

Elodie Holmes Liquid Light Glass

Elodie Holmes Liquid Light Glass is a contemporary glass studio and gallery located in the Baca Street Art District at Baca Street Studios, a complex of six studio/galleries. Elodie is the owner of the complex, as well as one of the resident artists. Visitors can watch Elodie blow glass in her studio, and shop in her gallery. They can also visit the other artists at work in her complex or shop in their galleries. You can see whimsical glass art, lamp-worked glass, and bronze sculpting in the complex. Gold, silver and stone jewelry is available, and photography is on display, as well. Elodie Holmes has been blowing glass in Santa Fe for 25 years. Her highly individual pieces are hand-sculpted using the traditional techniques of glass blowing and sculpting molten glass with special tools. Through flame work, cutting, polishing and etching, Elodie creates sculptures, ornaments and decorative furnishings such as vases, bowls, platters and paperweights. Elodie's art glass can be found in museums across the country and around the world. Come see the spontaneity that marks the work at Elodie Holmes Liquid Light Glass.

926 Baca Street #3, Santa Fe NM
(505) 820-2222
www.liquidlightglass.com

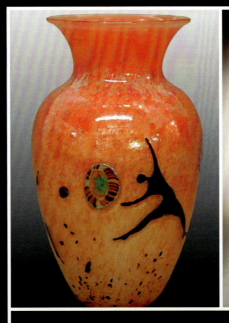

Prairie Dog Glass

Prairie Dog Glass is located inside Jackalope, a shop with home furnishings and outdoor living merchandise. Prairie Dog Glass represents more than 10 artists. At Prairie Dog Glass, you can watch artists blowing glass every day and then shop for that perfect hand-blown piece of art glass. The glass creations include glass garden art such as water basins, glass flowers and pond floats. Much of the garden glass is functional as well as decorative—for example, the bird seed feeders, hummingbird feeders and oil lamps. The artists at Prairie Dog Glass create seasonal glass art, including pumpkins, Christmas tree ornaments, valentines and eggs. You can also find fine art pieces such as vases, platters and paperweights. Prairie Dog Glass offers hands-on experience sessions to individuals who want to try glass blowing. Participants create their own works of art glass. Come to Prairie Dog Glass and admire the striking creations of glass artists.

**2820 Cerrillos Road, Santa Fe NM
(505) 471-8539 ext. 125**
www.pdogglass.com

Dragonfly Journeys

Although Pamala Dean and Karen Fielding are award-winning artists, Dragonfly Journeys does not exclusively display their works. Their gallery retreat provides a haven for others to come and create. Dean has had her own psychotherapy practice, where she drew from Jungian perspectives with a creative arts approach, in addition to enjoying success with her art and sculpture. Fielding's areas of expertise are her black-and-white photography and pottery. Both are concerned with the rapid shrinkage of wild lands and joined with community members and agencies to found Healthy Forest-Happy Potters (HFHP). This non-profit organization protects and preserves the area of Pot Creek. This area is known for the abundance of ancestral pottery discovered there. The HFHP also works to prevent wildfires. At Dragonfly Journeys, there is an inspirational creek where hummingbirds and butterflies frequent the retreat gardens. The gallery displays an array of pottery, mixed media and photography. Up to six guests can stay overnight, take workshops and reserve time to work in the studio. Master kiln-builder, technician and potter John Bradford has built a 16-foot kiln, a combination of tunnel kiln with a single catanary arch salt chamber, which produces endless wood fire effects. Raku firing is done the third Friday of the month. Pieces are available for purchase, or bring your own high fired bisque-ware and they will provide the glazes. Take the time to revive your spirit and express your memories in your own artwork in the juniper forest retreat at Dragonfly Journeys.

6690 Highway 518, Taos NM
(505) 751-3220
www.taosartretreat.com

Garcia's Colonial Gallery

The natural ambience of wood is the first thing you notice when you enter the Garcia family home and gallery. Garcia's Colonial Gallery showcases Andrew Garcia's beautiful hand-carved furniture that he mills from locally grown trees. His style is reminiscent of Spanish Colonial, carefully crafted using mortise and tenon joinery and often embellished with hand-forged iron work. Lorrie Garcia's exquisite hand-carved santos and retablos follow a tradition of using homemade gesso, natural or water-based pigments, piñon sap varnish and beeswax. The power of her work, often described as inspired, is evident in the serene faces of her caricatures. This award-winning husband-and-wife team offer notable pieces, often displayed in museums and galleries and collected by religious devotees, art collectors and interior decorators. Their work can also be seen or purchased at the prestigious Spanish Market held annually in July in the historic Sante Fe Plaza. Galleries that display their work include Red Eagle in Taos, El Potrero in Chimayo and Blue Sage Gallery in Scottsdale, Arizona. Garcia's Colonial Gallery is open by appointment only, so give them a call and plan a visit on your next trip to northern New Mexico.

1325 State Road 75, Peñasco NM
(505) 587-2968

Peterson-Cody Gallery, Ltd.

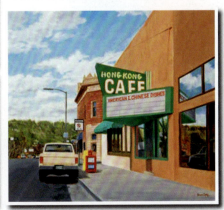

Stepping into the spacious and uncluttered elegance of the Peterson-Cody Gallery, you cannot help but feel propelled powerfully through space and time as high quality realist paintings and the intricate sculptures of George Alexander draw you across the room. Charlene and Bruce Cody have spent years in Santa Fe, gathering a select group of academically trained artists into a living entity capable of birthing works of intense energy and beauty. Representing a score of individuals at any given time, they are extreme in their quest to share with you those who have given their all and dedicated their lives to their work. Bruce Cody is the top seller in the forum. He weds the past and the present with pieces representing Contemporary Realism. Seen through his eyes, the mundane becomes a silent testament to not only humanity's impermanence but to its ability to thrive and leave a piece of itself and its dreams woven into the tapestry of everyday life. Blended into the Gallery's plethora of painted media are David Foley's serene landscapes governed by the same intense chaos found in nature, Peter Holbrook's mastery of merging oil painting and photography and Stephen Day's impressionistic ability to capture the world as it emits an intense and alluring light. View these impressive works at Peterson-Cody Gallery, Ltd.

130 W Palace Avenue, Santa Fe NM
(505) 820-0010 or (800) 752-1343   **www.petersoncodygallery.com**

Photos from www.petersoncodygallery.com

Rare Earth Studio Gallery

From their off-the-grid home studio, Rare Earth Studio Gallery, lifetime artists Sheena Cameron and Joseph Ciaglia interpret a world view that values open space and the Western landscape. A photographer for 40 years, Joseph specializes in digital techniques. He reenergizes traditional landscape photography's super-wide panorama with the help of his computer and digital camera. Joseph takes a series of five or six overlapping photographs and joins them by hand to create the illusion of a single photograph. He prints his large panoramas, sometimes 40 inches or longer, on specialty papers with archival inks to ensure the best defense against fading. Joseph's work is shown year round at Sage Fine Art in Taos. Sheena is a mixed media artist working in ceramic sculpture and jewelry making. She especially likes working in clay, her first artistic passion, which she finds immediately and personally satisfying. In demand at galleries and shows, Sheena's horse sculptures are rich symbols of energy and instinct. A melding of contemporary, primitive and folk influences, each of Sheena's horses is uniquely marked. The pieces, designed as freestanding or wall-hung sculptures, use decorative elements that employ Sheena's jewelry-making skills. Sheena's work brims with her values of wellness, free spirits and the rural lifestyle. Take a trip off the beaten path and visit two singular artists at Rare Earth Studio Gallery.

2236 Highway 68, Embudo NM (505) 579-4500 *www.rareearthnewmexico.com*

Galleries • 159

Tad Tribal Art Gallery

Tad Tribal Art Gallery in celebrated Santa Fe offers patrons an exquisite selection of quality tribal art from North and South America, Africa, Australia, Indonesia and the South Pacific. Owners Taylor (Tad) and Sandy Dale originally had a gallery on the Oregon coast before living in London for several years. They opened Tad Tribal Art Gallery in 1987 after relocating to Santa Fe for an improved quality of life in a smaller city. The couple has a superb selection of inspiring tribal art pieces. Among the pieces on display are several shields from Tad's private collection which have been featured in museum exhibitions. While visiting the gallery, you will see textiles, tribal paintings, sculptures and many other shining examples of tribal art. Tad Tribal Art carries an extensive inventory and is one of the few galleries in the U.S. to carry such a diverse selection of quality, antique tribal art. The Dales also do a series of antique tribal art shows throughout Europe and the United States, including shows in New York City, San Francisco and Los Angeles. Come enjoy the rich, relaxing and culturally rewarding art of Tad Tribal Art Gallery, where Tad and Sandy are on hand to welcome you and answer all of your tribal art questions.

**401 W San Francisco Street, Santa Fe NM
(505) 983-4149**
www.tadtribalart.com

Oviedo Carvings & Bronze

When Marco Oviedo carves traditional wooden saints and figures from Southwest Hispanic and Indian cultures, he follows a carving tradition that goes back seven generations in his family. When he replicates those sculptural forms in bronze using the lost wax technique, his creations become innovative and adventurous artistic statements. A visit to the Oviedo Carvings & Bronze Gallery in picturesque Chimayo is your opportunity to connect with the artist and his work, which ranges from traditional to abstract forms, in sizes from miniature to monumental. Oviedo's work explores Southwestern traditions and designs. When he renders traditional carved wood saints, or santos, in bronze, he produces a final patina that simulates a color similar to the natural pigments used in traditional santos. His admiration and respect for Native American prehistoric art has taken him into the creation of bronze animal fetishes and figures derived from ancient petroglyphs. These sculptures—sometimes contemporary and sometimes traditional—capture the essence of the mythical and cultural life of a people. For more than 30 years, Oviedo has honored history and the spirit of place with his inspired creations. He has garnered many awards, and his work graces museums in the Southwest, as well as the Smithsonian Air and Space Museum in Washington, D.C. Meet this talented artist and take a tour of his foundry at Oviedo Gallery in Chimayo, on a hilltop overlooking the high road to Taos.

961 State Road 76, HC64 Box 23A, Chimayó NM
(505) 351-2280
www.oviedoart.com

Galleries • 161

Santa Fe Weaving Gallery

After more than a quarter century of beating strongly at the heart of town, Santa Fe Weaving Gallery has become a veritable institution for those seeking their own statements in fashion. Each piece begins with an artist's idea, weaving its way through many incarnations, until it solidifies before you in richly textured splendor. Dozens of different artists strive to bring out the essence of local flavor, spun from the loom with the whisper of silk, or the myriad of processes used to create pieces with their own personality and substance. Unusual ideas are embraced, such as the ancient Japanese dyeing process known as Skiboki, or combining several different techniques to birth a fabric, or cut, unlike any previously seen. Creations include custom-made separates and jackets, coats, hand-woven hats, vests and scarves. Owners Barbara Lanning and Jill Heppenheimer have also expanded their catalogue of exquisite designs to include a diverse voice in artistic jewelry, with pieces individual enough to join your collection in such a way as to complete and not compete. Stop at the Santa Fe Weaving Gallery and catch a current artist's show for a glimpse of what lies on the horizon of fashion.

124 ½ Galisteo, Santa Fe NM
(866) 982-1737
www.santafeweavinggallery.com

Tailwater Gallery & Fly Shop

A perfect marriage of interests shared by husband-and-wife team Stephanie and Jack Woolley resulted in the Tailwater Gallery & Fly Shop in Taos. At Tailwater, displays include Stephanie's captivating natural paintings of fish, wildlife, landscapes and people of the region, as well as a complete line of fly fishing equipment. Stephanie's command of realism is eloquently expressed through her acrylic and watercolor paintings. The balanced use of color she unfailingly achieves in each new work is her signature. Influences from her childhood near the Brandywine River Valley in Pennsylvania and her life in Taos shine through her vividly painted canvasses. Her work is a celebration of the same triumphs and pleasures that prevail in the world of fly fishing. Fly fishing aficionados love new opportunities for fishing adventures and Tailwater caters to this desire by providing a booking service for fly fishing expeditions. At Tailwater, you can book fly fishing adventures for northern New Mexico or southern Colorado. These localized trips are booked with Van Beacham's Solitary Angler Service. International trips are also available with Mark Cowan's Pescador Solitario. If art is taking what is consequential in this world and expressing that meaning to others in a beautiful fashion, Tailwater has admirably fulfilled the definition. This is a fine chance to experience what happens when life's passions are channeled into art. Jack and Stephanie invite you to rejoice in the outcome at Tailwater Gallery & Fly Shop.

204 B Paseo del Pueblo Norte, Taos NM
(505) 758-5653 or (866) 502-1700
www.tailwatergallery.com

Artwork by Stephanie Woolley

San Francisco de Asis Church in El Rancho de Taos

Andrews Pueblo Pottery & Art Gallery

Andrews Pueblo Pottery & Art Gallery is owned by Bob Andrews, a multi-generation New Mexico native. For more than 30 years in Albuquerque's Old Town, his establishment has offered authentic works of Native American art created meticulously by hand following thousand-year-old traditions. Most are purchased directly from the artists. The shop is both educational and an historical treasure trove of wonderful art. The staff includes the very knowledgeable Arlette, Jan, Eason and Yvonne, all of whom are familiar with the type of art that represents each particular tribe. For instance, the Zuni are renowned for their stone fetish carvings, while the Hopi create cream, buff, orange or red pottery and katsina carvings. The beadwork offered here is created from authentic, historical patterns and made by traditional methods. Serigraph landscapes by Doug West, one of America's premier silkscreen artists, are each hand-pulled by Doug himself. Sheldon Harvey's Ye'ii figures, masks and paintings are expressions of his Navajo spirituality and have been created with the permission of the tribal elders. Andrews Pueblo Pottery & Art Gallery appreciates your patronage, rewarding it with reciprocal generosity. If you mention visiting their website when you stop by the store, they just might present you with a set of Doug West note cards.

**303 Romero NW,
Albuquerque NM
(505) 243-0414 or (877) 606-0543
www.andrewspueblopottery.com**

Oil on canvas, 48"X48" by Sheldon Harvey, Navajo: "What Can We Do for You?"

Jicarilla Apache baskets, circa 1940–1960

Galleries • 165

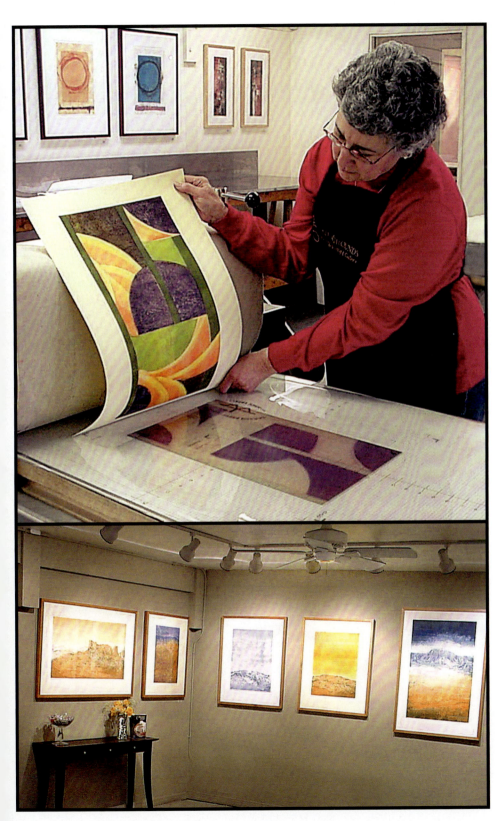

New Grounds Print Workshop & Gallery

At New Grounds Print Workshop & Gallery in the Nob Hill Art Complex, art lovers will find 3,500 square feet devoted to the art of print-making. The gallery displays traditional and contemporary works by more than 40 print-makers from New Mexico, Europe, Japan and Mexico. You will also find works from the estate of the late Reginald Gammon, an African-American artist. Founder and director Regina Held has successfully operated the organization since 1996. She has specialized in non-toxic print-making and holds regularly scheduled classes in monotype, etching, gravure and mezzotint. The workshop offers access to print-making equipment on an hourly and membership basis. The public can tour the studio or request a print-making lecture. This facility is the recipient of both the 2002 Magnifico and the 2005 Bravos award for Outstanding Arts Organization. New Grounds and her neighbor, Coleman Gallery of Contemporary Art, both participate in the monthly First Friday Artscrawl, an opportunity to sample the variety of art in Albuquerque. Whether you are an artist looking for a place to study or practice printmaking, or an art lover searching for original mezzotints, monotypes, etchings, paintings, photographs or drawings, find your way to the award-winning New Grounds Print Workshop & Gallery.

**3812 Central Avenue SE, Suite 100 B,
Albuquerque NM
(505) 268-8952**
www.newgroundsgallery.com

Art is OK Gallery & Sculpture Garden

The steel sculptures of O.K. Harris remind the viewer of the simple joys of youth. These mature, yet whimsical, forms are on display at the Art is OK Gallery & Sculpture Garden in Albuquerque's American Square Shopping Center, along with the work of 175 other artists from New Mexico and beyond. Rosemary Drexel and her artistic partner O.K. Harris own the gallery, which has been in its present location for almost 25 years. O.K. is a native New Mexican who has spent most of his life in the Albuquerque area working on his magnificent steel sculptures. He works out of a large studio in the North Valley, where he grew up and found inspiration from his grandfather, who was a master welder. Harris's creations are masterfully crafted and explode with childlike exuberance, humor and playfulness. Each of his lively sculptures is infused with an emotional appeal that easily transcends physical limitations like age, culture and social history. He paints some sculptures and leaves others completely natural, so they can develop a patina in keeping with the Southwest's particular climate and aesthetics. Art is OK Gallery & Sculpture Garden also houses a custom framing shop owned by Chris Maes, where your artwork and special treasures will receive the attention they deserve. Whether you're in search of a giant steel dragon to watch over your garden or a snappy frog on a unicycle to add whimsy to your desk, you're sure to find something pleasing and unexpected at Art is OK Gallery & Sculpture Garden.

3301 Menaul Boulevard NE, Suite 28, Albuquerque NM
(505) 883-7368
www.artisok.com

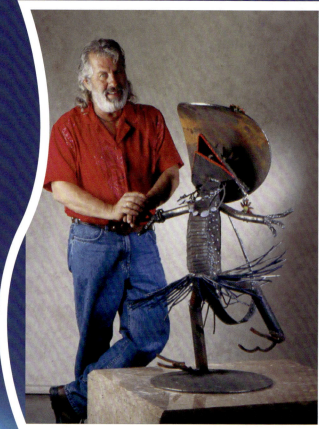

Galleries • 167

R.C. Gorman/Nizhoni Gallery

For those who have an interest in art but are new to the art world, the R.C. Gorman/Nizhoni Gallery is the ideal place to feed the fires of artistic appreciation and glean the basics that turn novices into serious collectors. Located in Albuquerque's Historic Old Town, this welcoming gallery is focused on helping its clients find the ideal artwork to personalize and add warmth to their homes and lives. The R.C. Gorman/Nizhoni Gallery staff is further dedicated to continuing the legacy of renowned artist R.C. Gorman, who was once hailed by the *New York Times* as the Picasso of American Indian art. Born in July of 1931 in Chinle, Arizona, Gorman, who was son to the famed Navajo painter and WWII Code Talker Carl Gorman, followed in his father's artistic footsteps and went on to carve new pathways for Native American artists who were fighting against unrealistic artistic definitions and native-art stereotypes.

In conjunction with the new and classic works of R.C. Gorman, the Nizhoni Gallery also features other acclaimed artists, such as Martha Pettigrew, Robert Rivera, Amado Pena and Bev Doolittle, along with Guilloume, Lawrence Vargas and Howard Terpning. Luxuriate in the vivid colors and stirring, awe-inspiring works that represent Southwest and Native American imagery at its finest with a tour of the R.C. Gorman/Nizhoni Gallery.

323 Romero NW, Suite 1, Albuquerque NM
(505) 843-7666 or (800) 399-2970
www.rcgorman-nizhoni.com

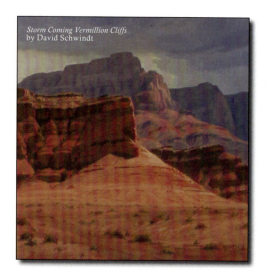
Storm Coming Vermillion Cliffs by David Schwindt

First Dance by Thais Haines

The Gazebo by James A. Messimer

Mesa and Stormclouds By David Schwindt

Framing Concepts Gallery

Tucked into the Shops at Mountain Run, in Albuquerque's popular Northeast Heights district, Framing Concepts is a spectacular gallery combined with a professional frame shop and a delightful array of original gifts. Master framer Colgate Craig opened the gallery to showcase precision workmanship and quality artwork for discerning customers. Framing Concepts Gallery offers New Mexico's largest selection of framing materials and is one of the most distinctive galleries for landscape art in the Southwest. Highly acclaimed regional artists, such as David Schwindt, Thais Haines and James Messimer exhibit here, and exhibits rotate frequently. The gallery offers a terrific selection of Native American crafts, including sculpture and stained glass art objects, as well as ceramics and stoneware. Colgate, along with wife, Stella, opened the gallery in 1988 after Colgate retired from a career in engineering. Since then he has become a certified picture framer and member of the Professional Picture Framers Association, where he serves as treasurer for the Zia chapter. Colgate takes an active interest in the arts business and serves on the board of directors for the Albuquerque Art Business Association and the Artscrawl People. Have your special treasures exquisitely and expertly framed, or find new and original artwork for your home and office with a visit to Framing Concepts Gallery.

5809-B Juan Tabo Boulevard NE, Albuquerque NM
(505) 294-3246
www.framingconceptsgallery.com

Adobe Silver at Naranjo's Arts

When it comes to jewelry and distinct *objets d'art*, no one knows her stuff better than Stella Naranjo. Four generations of expertise and more than 37 years in the business of Southwestern and Native American jewelry and distinctive objects of art are behind her. Stella owns and operates Adobe Silver at Naranjo's Arts in Albuquerque's historic Old Town. Her education and accomplishments are many and countless articles have been published about Stella as a jeweler, artist, poet and activist. Stella wants you to be completely satisfied with your purchases, and gain an understanding of quality jewelry. Here you'll find expertise in gold and silver creations, repairs and appraisals. If you're looking for a terrific souvenir to remind you of your travels, you'll find jewelry, pottery, crafts and anything else you could want at Adobe Silver. Stop by and check it out for yourself.

522 Romero NW, Albuquerque NM
(505) 248-1087
www.naranjosarts.com

Coleman Gallery Contemporary Art

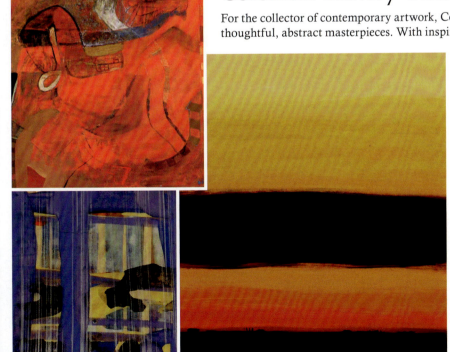
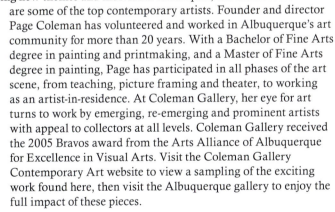

For the collector of contemporary artwork, Coleman Gallery Contemporary Art is just the place to find colorful, thoughtful, abstract masterpieces. With inspiring new themes and individual techniques, the artists featured here are some of the top contemporary artists. Founder and director Page Coleman has volunteered and worked in Albuquerque's art community for more than 20 years. With a Bachelor of Fine Arts degree in painting and printmaking, and a Master of Fine Arts degree in painting, Page has participated in all phases of the art scene, from teaching, picture framing and theater, to working as an artist-in-residence. At Coleman Gallery, her eye for art turns to work by emerging, re-emerging and prominent artists with appeal to collectors at all levels. Coleman Gallery received the 2005 Bravos award from the Arts Alliance of Albuquerque for Excellence in Visual Arts. Visit the Coleman Gallery Contemporary Art website to view a sampling of the exciting work found here, then visit the Albuquerque gallery to enjoy the full impact of these pieces.

4115 Silver Avenue SE, Albuquerque NM
(505) 232-0224
www.colemancontemporary.com

Nancy Kozikowski at DSG Fine Art

DSG Fine Art, originally Dartmouth Street Gallery, exhibits contemporary art from top Southwestern artists in a 75-year-old adobe structure. It specializes in vibrant oil paintings that capture the mystery, majesty and creativity of the enchanted New Mexico landscape. DSG Fine Art is also home to the private studios of internationally acclaimed tapestry designer Nancy Kozikowski. Nancy is one of the most prominent of the more than 60 artists represented at DSG. She learned to weave from a native Navajo and worked side by side with Northern New Mexico weavers who brought their traditions with them from Spain. Nancy's husband John Cacciatore is the president and owner of DSG. Currently, Nancy and John are extending their reach to China, and they have opened a studio and gallery in Beijing. They are lecturing at universities across China and represent a dozen or more new Chinese artists at DSG. In addition to handwoven wool tapestries, Nancy paints and draws. A native of Albuquerque, Nancy was drawn to weaving as a medium that is "natural to the community and culture I was born into." As a child, she was inspired by such artists as Picasso. Her current hero is Professor Lin Le Cheng, the top fiber artist in China. Art lovers cherish time spent at DSG Fine Art in Albuquerque, and the work of Nancy Kozikowski adds to the allure of this special place.

510 14th Street SW, Albuquerque NM
(505) 266-7751 or (800) 474-7751
www.dsg-art.com

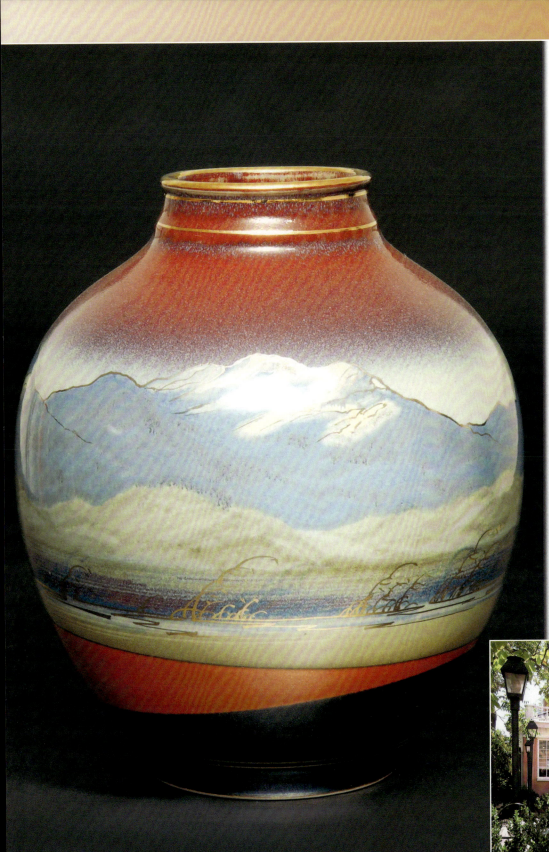

Schelu Gallery

Many customers walk into Schelu Gallery for the first time, fall in love with the pottery and fine art and go on to become collectors. The Old Town Albuquerque shop charms them in much the way it first captured the heart and imagination of its owner Jensi Kessler. She quit her job in 2001 to purchase and operate the gallery, started by Doris Scheer and Dick Lusk in 1973. The gallery is best known for its handmade, functional stoneware, although you'll also find fine art, fiber art and furnishings. Kessler's knitting habit led to the addition of a room full of hand-dyed yarn. The gallery draws many tourists, but relies on its local following and its longtime potters. Most potters have been supplying Schelu for 15 to 25 years, and Kessler has even met mothers who had bridal registries with the gallery and are now doing their daughters' registries. Kessler uses the cozy rooms of this 1880 adobe Territorial house to create inviting displays. She lives in a studio in the back of the building, so is in a position to see the ghost that New Mexico Ghost Tours (*nmghosttours.com*) calls Sarge. During the Civil War, seven cannons were buried on the Schelu grounds, but only five were later recovered. Many believe Sarge guards the remaining cannons. Whether you are in the market for fine art and pottery or just ready to let some of the Old Town magic work on you, be sure to visit Schelu Gallery.

306 San Felipe NW, Albuquerque NM
(505) 765-5869 or (800) 234-7985
www.schelu.com

Photo by Paul Kohlman

Lesley Nolan—*Eric Wore His Favorite Shirt*, fused glass wall panel, 18 x 25 inches

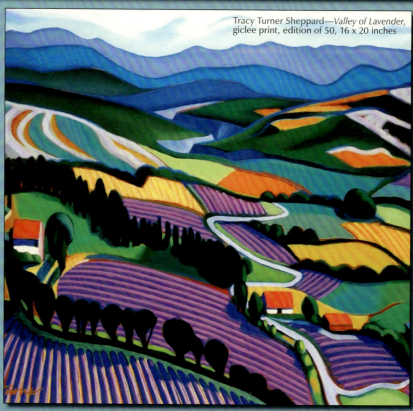
Tracy Turner Sheppard—*Valley of Lavender*, giclee print, edition of 50, 16 x 20 inches

Palette Contemporary Art & Craft

When you'd like an alternative to Southwestern and Native American Art, visit a gallery that specializes in a broad spectrum of contemporary art in many media. Palette Contemporary Art & Craft, in Albuquerque's Mossman Center, is such a place. Palette searches locally, nationally and abroad to assemble contemporary art and craft with a colorful edge and a clean look. Look for their international collection of Australian fine art glass, Aboriginal and abstract paintings, limited edition signed prints and mixed media pieces. The gallery also features handmade jewelry, marbles and ceramics by both emerging and renowned artists. If you love modern art in all of its forms, this gallery is for you. A great time to visit Palette Contemporary Art & Craft is during one of its many receptions and exhibition events, including the citywide First Friday events. Palette's website can familiarize you with their represented artists and exhibition calendar. Palette Contemporary Art & Craft is sure to provide a unique Albuquerque gallery experience, as well as offer pieces you will want to acquire to enhance your home or office environment.

7400 Montgomery Boulevard NE, Suite 22, Albuquerque NM
(505) 855-7777
www.palettecontemporary.com

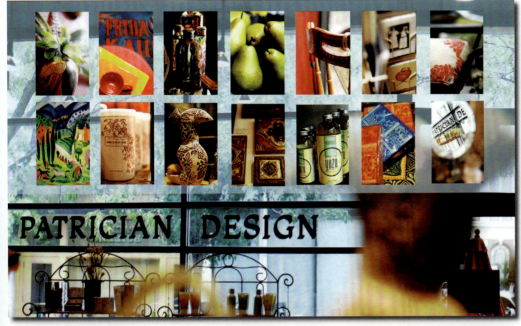

PATRICIAN DESIGN
Caliente, It's Hot!

Located in a vintage storefront in downtown Albuquerque, PATRICIAN DESIGN Caliente, It's Hot! Studio and Gallery is an art boutique that promotes artists from all over New Mexico. The gallery represents more than 60 artists, who work in a variety of media, including paint, pottery and jewelry. The gallery displays weavings, handcrafted furniture, iron and tin sculpture and distinctive decorative accessories. PATRICIAN DESIGN began in 1985 as the interior design studio of licensed interior designer Patti Harrell Hoech. Patti was a true pioneer in revitalizing downtown Albuquerque. Over the years, she has been a major force in promoting the now booming Gold Avenue Shopping District. Patti's primary professional practice continues to be interior design. Her vast portfolio ranges from state-of-the-art healthcare facilities and elegant federal court justices' offices to exclusive private residences. Her source library is matchless. Manufacturers' representatives attest that PATRICIAN DESIGN has perhaps the broadest range of samples and catalogues for fabrics, lighting and decorative accessories in all of New Mexico. PATRICIAN DESIGN became an art gallery almost by accident as Patti allowed her artist friends to display at the studio. In 1992, the Albuquerque Arts Business Association asked her to join as a member gallery, and she launched Caliente, It's Hot! Whether you need interior design services or wish to shop for unique gifts, decorative accessories or select a fabulous piece of fun, funky and functional artwork for your home or office, visit PATRICIAN DESIGN Caliente, It's Hot! Studio and Gallery.

**216 Gold Avenue SW, Albuquerque NM
(505) 242-7646**
www.collectorsguide.com/patrician

Sumner & Dene

Add touches of whimsy and fun to your everyday life with the diverse collection of fine art, furnishings and jewelry found at Sumner & Dene in Albuquerque. This delightful shop is owned and operated by Roy Sumner Johnson, a noteworthy art dealer for more than 25 years. Johnson holds a Bachelor of Fine Arts degree from the University of San Francisco, along with a degree in advertising and illustration from the San Francisco Academy of Art. He is well recognized throughout New Mexico for his work in developing the first national advertising campaign for the arts, as well as various efforts to promote New Mexico's artistic community. He has mounted traveling art exhibitions throughout the five-state area of New Mexico, Arizona, Colorado, Texas and Oklahoma. Johnson established Sumner & Dene in 1996 as an adjunct to his premier art gallery, the Variant Gallery in Taos. Sumner & Dene exhibits the work of more than 120 different artists from around the world, ranging from contemporary to true Southwestern. The work is original and unlike pieces you will find elsewhere. The shop carries an extensive array of furniture from Normand Couture along with dazzling jewelry from Dawn Estrin. Additional artists include husband-and-wife team Walker and Moore, who each work on the same canvas, and Heather Ramsey, who specializes in figurative mixed media. Find gifts and home décor that reflect your fun side at Sumner & Dene.

517 Central Avenue NW, Albuquerque NM
(505) 842-1400
www.sumnerdene.com

Wright's Indian Art

Filled with stunning turquoise and silver jewelry, Navajo and Zapotec rugs, pottery and much more, Wright's Indian Art is an homage to Native American culture. Here you can find kachinas, fetishes, Navajo folk art, masks and anything else that Indian artists create. Some of the pieces are unusual and unexpected. Modern Indian artists now work with blown glass, gold and opals in addition to more traditional materials. "We buy as if we were keeping each piece ourselves," says Wayne Bobrick, the director. Wright's buys directly from individual artists and has been dealing with some families of artists for three generations. Likewise, decades of loyal clients have relied on Wright's for uncompromising authenticity, quality and personal service. Charles Wright first opened the business in 1907. His widow Kathryn ran it until the early 1950s, when she sold it to the late Sam and Marguerite Chernoff. Sam was a Russian immigrant to Chihuahua, Mexico, and Marguerite was the daughter of the French consul in that town. They had just arrived in America with their children and knew nothing of Indian art except that they loved it. They looked, listened, learned and gradually developed their own inventory, establishing solid friendships with artists such as Maria Martinez and Pablita Velarde. Wayne is their son-in-law and together with his wife, Tania, has zealously maintained their passion and high standards. Immerse yourself in Native American culture with a visit to Wright's Indian Art.

1100 San Mateo Boulevard NE, The Courtyard (at Lomas), Albuquerque NM
(505) 266-0120 or (866) 372-1042
www.wrightsgallery.com

Weems Galleries and Framing

Albuquerque's Weems Galleries welcome you to a lifestyle of art for every interior and taste. The selection of art is immense, with two galleries representing more than 200 artisans. Whether you are looking for prestige artists or newly discovered talent, Weems is the place to shop. Voted Albuquerque's Favorite Galleries by locals, the work displayed includes every medium. From pottery, bronze, distinctive oils and glass to gifts and framing, collectors place their trust in Weems. Weems has two convenient Albuquerque locations and a frame shop where you can bring any art for a creative treatment using an innovative selection of mouldings and mattings. The frame shop also specializes in the restoration and repair of old or damaged artwork. At Weems, the staff greets visitors like honored guests. Visit Weems Galleries, where the artwork is delightful and the services are all you could desire, including gift wrapping, hanging services and decorative consultation.

2801-M Eubank Boulevard NE, Albuquerque NM (505) 293-6133
303 Romero Street NW, Albuquerque NM (505) 764-0302
www.weemsgallery.com

Guilloume's Fine Art

Guilloume focuses on the core essence of his subjects, translating his vision by emphasizing and celebrating the commonalities among all people, rather than the differences that separate us from each other. In his sculptures and paintings, he pares down the details and uses rounded forms to capture the emotions and substance of who we are. This Bolismo style, as he has named it, allows him to study and comment on the human interactions, from the mundane to the complex, that we experience as a socially driven species. Already an artist at an early age in his homeland of Colombia, Guilloume completed his studies and emigrated to New Mexico in 1958, where he expresses his talent in oils, pastels and watercolors. He sculpts in stone and bronze, and his artwork is shown in numerous galleries across the country and in collections on several continents. Recently named by *Sculpture Magazine* as one of the 10 most important sculptors of our day, Guilloume presents a personal style that has a clean elegance and appeal. "I believe art to be one of the universal languages, and I have always sought to create beauty that speaks to people from all corners of the earth, from all walks of life, from all political spectra, from all age groups," says Guilloume. Experience the mastery of his work with a visit to Guilloume's Fine Art in Sandia Park.

16 Dinos Road, Sandia Park NM
(505) 286-9710
www.guilloume.com

Old Pass Gallery

Southwestern art and culture exhibit a vibrant and exciting life of their own. A single piece of such work can add a special kind of warmth and excitement to any room. At Old Pass Gallery, located near the Raton Railroad Depot, lovers of distinctive Southwestern art can revel in the wonderful and masterfully crafted pieces that line the walls. Operated inside a restored Wells Fargo Express building completed around 1910, this sprightly gallery offers original and astonishing views of the places, people and objects that make up life in northeastern New Mexico. Owned by the Raton Arts and Humanities Council, this inspiring gallery houses the work of more than 100 regional artists in a series of exhibits on display throughout the year. At Old Pass Gallery, you will find an almost dizzying array of watercolors, acrylics and photographs alongside examples of clay and stone sculptures. The tapestries will leave you breathless. Old Pass Gallery stocks a wonderful selection of products that let you take a piece of New Mexico home with you. These items, found in the gallery gift shop, feature handmade jewelry, paintings and sculpture. They also have stained glass work and lovely Christmas ornaments that will add a delicate touch of the desert to your holiday tree. Bring a touch of the Southwest to your home with a visit to Old Pass Gallery. This project is made possible in part by New Mexico Arts, a division of the Office of Cultural Affairs, Raton Lodgers Tax and the National Endowment of Arts & the Macroon Foundation.

145 S First Street, Raton NM
(505) 445-2052 or (877) 278-2489
www.ratonarts.com

Galleries • 179

Cozy Jewel Gallery

Diane Moreno has been creating works of art at Cozy Jewel Gallery for the last 16 years. Her passion for working with her hands prompted her to leave her job in the corporate world in 1988. She found her dream property overlooking the Pecos River, and began building nichos in earnest. Nichos are little cabinets inspired by those created and placed in adobe walls by Spanish colonials. Nichos are very popular items in New Mexico, because they can be used to store personal treasures or as shrines, making them functional as well as decorative art. Most of Diane's works are made from recycled wood or rough-cut local lumber. These cabinets have latches made of juniper or pinon that actually work. Adornments are made of handcrafted tin and mixed materials. Two seasons ago, she was inspired to design metal figurines made from small tin cans she has been collecting for years. The results are funny and unusual characters that bring delighted smiles from viewers. When it comes to her birdhouses, Diane incorporates the same enthusiasm and tender loving care that she puts into her nichos. These are also fashioned from recycled materials to craft a cozy shelter for birds in all seasons. Special pieces can be made to order. Come tour the Cozy Jewel Gallery. It is well worth the beautiful drive.

233 Entrada de San Ysidro, Ilfeld NM
(505) 421-2314
www.elvalle.com/nichos

Photos by S.M. Stachler

Christopher Thomson Ironworks

"I am drawn to the fire and the transformation of humble materials into expressive form," says Christopher Thomson, proprietor of Christopher Thomson Ironworks. Christopher has been plying a malleable medium to perfection for 21 years. Hand-forged steel architectural lighting is Christopher's specialty. His award-winning talents have been featured in *Architectural Digest* and are recognized worldwide. While continuing to study the time-honored traditions of his craft, Christopher draws inspiration from his flute music, working with clay, and the Southwest's deserts and canyons. Those who insist on the highest standard of craftsmanship and the lasting elegance of museum quality home furnishings will find these hand-forged creations are perfect. Christopher and his partner and marketing director Susan Livermore invite you to visit the on-site gallery and tour the forge. Call for an appointment, directions or a catalog. They're located at the foot of Rowe Mesa in Ilfeld, about 40 minutes from Santa Fe. Experience the work of a true craftsman in Christopher Thomson Ironworks Studio.

5851 I-25 Frontage Road, Ilfeld NM
(505) 421-2645 www.ctiron.com

The Gallery Between & Head in the Clouds Productions

The Gallery Between features an eclectic collection of works from local and regional artists. The wide-ranging mix consists of jewelry, sculpture, pottery and painting. The works represent several genres and include installation art. If you can consider something to be art, it will probably show up at the Gallery Between at some point in the near future. Shows change frequently and the number of artists represented in any one show varies considerably. The Gallery Between is located in historic downtown Raton, which supports a developing art community. Dorothy, Alan and Alana Best invite you to view the fascinating works on display at the Gallery Between. The gallery shares a small mall with several other businesses, notably Head in the Clouds Productions, which provides motion picture pre- and post-production services, especially for digital equipment. Head in the Clouds won a 2006 Telly Award for *Walking Home along the Trails of Sugarite*, a documentary it produced for the New Mexico State Parks. This community-minded enterprise contributes to the Coalition for the Valle Vidal and the New Mexico Heritage Preservation Alliance. When you have a story to tell, Head in the Clouds Productions can help you tell it well.

125 S 2nd Street, Raton NM
(The Gallery Between)
(505) 445-9315
101 S 2nd Street, Raton NM
(Head in the Clouds)
(505) 445-5005
www.thegallerybetween.com

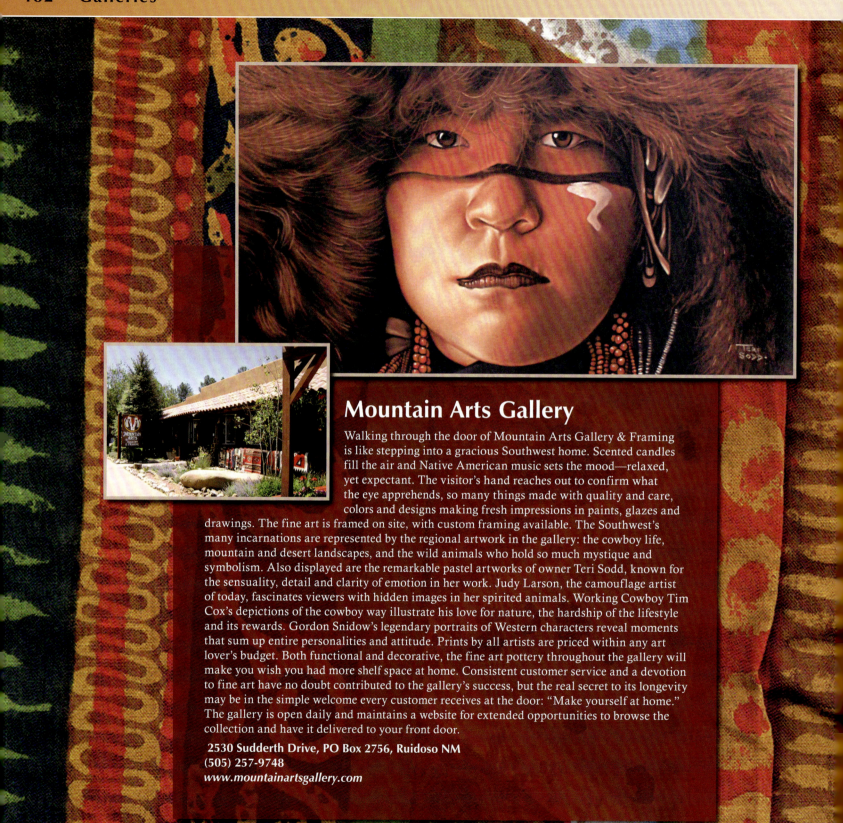

Mountain Arts Gallery

Walking through the door of Mountain Arts Gallery & Framing is like stepping into a gracious Southwest home. Scented candles fill the air and Native American music sets the mood—relaxed, yet expectant. The visitor's hand reaches out to confirm what the eye apprehends, so many things made with quality and care, colors and designs making fresh impressions in paints, glazes and drawings. The fine art is framed on site, with custom framing available. The Southwest's many incarnations are represented by the regional artwork in the gallery: the cowboy life, mountain and desert landscapes, and the wild animals who hold so much mystique and symbolism. Also displayed are the remarkable pastel artworks of owner Teri Sodd, known for the sensuality, detail and clarity of emotion in her work. Judy Larson, the camouflage artist of today, fascinates viewers with hidden images in her spirited animals. Working Cowboy Tim Cox's depictions of the cowboy way illustrate his love for nature, the hardship of the lifestyle and its rewards. Gordon Snidow's legendary portraits of Western characters reveal moments that sum up entire personalities and attitude. Prints by all artists are priced within any art lover's budget. Both functional and decorative, the fine art pottery throughout the gallery will make you wish you had more shelf space at home. Consistent customer service and a devotion to fine art have no doubt contributed to the gallery's success, but the real secret to its longevity may be in the simple welcome every customer receives at the door: "Make yourself at home." The gallery is open daily and maintains a website for extended opportunities to browse the collection and have it delivered to your front door.

2530 Sudderth Drive, PO Box 2756, Ruidoso NM
(505) 257-9748
www.mountainartsgallery.com

Grasshopper Silk

The origins of silk painting can be traced back to India in the second century A.D., and yet this popular and labor-intensive art form is still highly sought after for its uniqueness and delicate beauty. At Grasshopper Silk, artist Sandy Hopper continues to study, learn and improve her skills while creating stunning, one-of-a-kind pieces that are both beautiful and practical. Sandy discovered silk painting in 1999 after moving to Elephant Butte Lake State Park with her husband and renewing a friendship with fellow artist Sharon Holmes. The duo set their sights on silk painting and later attended a workshop in Santa Fe, where Sandy was introduced to Jacquard steam set dyes and became instantly devoted to the art. Many steps are required in the creation of a piece and any one of those steps can easily go awry and ruin a project. Sandy has to go through an involved process of cleaning, stretching and examining a piece before she can begin the dye application process. After a project is painted, it has to be cured for a minimum of 72 hours, carefully steamed for three to five hours, and then left to rest for two days. After that, the silk is washed to remove excess dye, rolled in terry cloth to absorb excess moisture and ironed while damp. Sandy uses this laborious process to create magnificent ruanas, art scarves and shoji screen panels, which are available for purchase by appointment only at Grasshopper Silk.

509 Bass Road, Old Hot Springs Landing, Elephant Butte NM
(505) 744-4958
www.grasshoppersilk.com

GALERIA 200

Deming, located 33 miles north of the Mexican border, offers visitors an exciting collection of art galleries and studios that celebrate native art and ancient crafting techniques. Among these is the new GALERIA 200, which opened in February of 2006 under the ownership of Richard and Lyn Orona. The couple had previously operated a successful silversmith business in California's San Francisco Bay Area. They were in the midst of searching for a change of scenery when they happened upon Deming, a land of flowing desert rock, inspiring beauty, and nearly endless sunshine. The Oronas' goal is to continue their silversmith and jewelry work in the new gallery, while bringing in additional local artists from the area. Eventually they intend to house 20 hanging artists along with textile, glasswork, and pottery artisans. GALERIA 200 is currently home to featured artists such as Sandra Hopper, who creates stunning silk art, and Penny Duncklee, a watercolorist who is beyond compare. Other artists include D.R. Vance, who creates marvelous gourd art, and Carolyn Rice, who uses oil as her medium to paint vivid and thought-provoking pieces. Treat yourself to a visual feast that will feed your spirit and imagination with a trip to GALERIA 200 in Old Town Deming.

**200 S Gold Avenue, Deming NM
(505) 546-9590**
www.galeria200.com

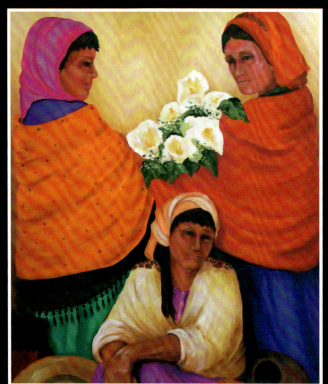

Photos by S.M. Stachler

Photo by S.M. Stachler

The Potteries

Take three gifted potters with 100 years of combined experience, give them a studio and what do you get? The Potteries, the source of some of the finest ceramics you will ever see (with some colorful clay on canvas paintings thrown in for good measure). Owners Janice and Bill Cook and Jeanne Rundell all have extensive education in fine arts. Janice, who received a degree in art education from Arizona State University, shows locally in Las Cruces at the Patio Art Gallery and at Ojo Sarco Gallery on the high road to Taos. Her specialty is brightly colored functional porcelain dinnerware, trays and large decorative plates. Jeanne, with a BFA and MA in ceramics and glass, has spent the last 25 years showing throughout the United States. She creates teapots as art, each one telling a story in white stoneware that has been painted with acrylics and sculpted to become something unique. Bill, with a BFA from Northern Arizona University and a sixth sense for finding clay, searches the mountains of New Mexico and Arizona for earthenware clays that become art. He also crafts architectural fixtures, such as wall sconces and chandeliers. The Potteries is located in the historically and culturally rich town of Mesilla in a building handmade by the potters and their friends. For ceramics that are evocative of the desert Southwest, come to The Potteries. You will be inspired by what these artisans have created.

2260 Calle de Santiago, Mesilla NM (505) 524-0538

Elemental Arts

Elemental Arts in historic Silver City offers art patrons a wealth of creative and inspiring pieces created by artist, owner and operator Valerie M. Milner. Valerie is a talented artist who is proficient in numerous media, but her passion lies in the creation of the fine gourd masks and gourd vessels she makes using her signature Southwest style. She made a move into the art world in 1987 and has since honed her skills while utilizing a wide range of finishes and textures in order to draw immeasurable beauty from the gourds' wood-like exterior. Between the interesting and natural variables of the gourds themselves and Valerie's own inventive techniques, no two pieces will ever be identical. While all of Valerie's work is original, much of it is influenced both by the indigenous designs of the Southwest and by the remarkable pottery of Mata Ortiz. Many consider Valerie's work to consist of a fine balance between elegance and honesty, attributes that are often applied to the artist herself. In conjunction with the works displayed at Elemental Arts, Valerie also has pieces on exhibit at other popular galleries across New Mexico and the Southwest, such as Nash Gallery in Mesilla and Galleria Tubac in Tubac, El Presidio in Tuscon and Diane Grimshaw Fine Art in Taos. Learn more about Valerie and her exquisite gourd art and many more fine artists at Elemental Arts.

106 W Yankie Street, Silver City NM
(505) 590-7554 *www.gourdweb.com*

Art by Valerie M. Milner

Painting by Paul Wilson

Pottery by Mata Ortiz

Photos by John Rohovec

Blue Dome Gallery

In the heart of Silver City's historic district, at the intersection of Texas and Yankie Streets, is the gateway to a fabulous and diverse art community filled with wonderful crafts and original pieces that will both inspire and delight the viewer. Nestled in among these is the highly popular and always exciting Blue Dome Gallery, where owners John Rohovec and Linda Brewer have created an oasis for the exhibition of American influenced craftwork. Here an eclectic community of local, national and international artists can meet and display their passions while also having an opportunity to meet and get to know the patrons who revere and collect their work. According to John and Linda, "Each piece reflects the handprint and creative force of the artist." Blue Dome Gallery hosts five shows annually, including shows that are tied into other community events, such as the Blues Festival in May. The welcoming and spacious gallery is home to contemporary yet timeless art pieces in a myriad of media, including ceramics, paintings, prints and glass art, along with jewelry and a spectacular array of pottery. The Blue Dome Gallery is located within easy walking distance of numerous other galleries and popular area eateries, making it the ideal place to begin or end an adventurous day of art discovery. Learn more about these amazing artists while savoring the beauty and craftsmanship of their work at Blue Dome Gallery.

307 N Texas Street, Silver City NM
(505) 534-8671
www.bluedomegallery.com

Leyba & Ingalls Arts – Supplies and Gallery

Leyba & Ingalls Arts – Supplies and Gallery offers a fabulous array of artistic creations in a multitude of media, including pottery, sculpture and silk painting, along with some truly fabulous photography and paintings. The gallery features collections and pieces from numerous local and national artists, including Teri Matelson, Zoe Wolfe and Wil Hanson, as well as Phillip Parotti and gallery owner and operator Diana Ingalls Leyba. Leyba & Ingalls Arts offers numerous exhibits and showings throughout the year. In conjunction with the gallery, Leyba & Ingalls Arts offers an extensive selection of art supplies from popular venders, including Sculpey, Golden Artist Colors and Strathmore, along with Prismacolor, Princeton Art and Brush Company, and Logan Graphic Products. Leyba & Ingalls Arts hosts a number of classes that teach budding artists of all ages the techniques and skills required to master such arts as printmaking, landscape painting and silk painting. They also offer courses in the book arts, where you can learn the process of bookmaking and scrapbooking. Leyba & Ingalls Arts also offers a custom-framing department for your completed projects. Let your imagination and creativity run wild, and find everything needed for the artistic lifestyle, at Leyba & Ingalls Arts – Supplies and Gallery.

315 N Bullard Street, Silver City NM
(505) 388-5725
www.leybaingallsARTS.com

Lois Duffy Art

Those who view the world through the eyes of the renowned contemporary artist Lois Duffy are treated to a delightful and fascinating view of the cosmos that subtly combines the old and new, real and surreal. At Lois Duffy Art, located in the popular art district of Silver City, art patrons can enjoy her latest works from the in-house studio and perhaps even discuss them with the artist herself. Lois studied art at the acclaimed Pratt Institute in Brooklyn, New York, as well as North Adams State College in Massachusetts. Her vivid and richly colored characters nearly leap off the canvas in their realism, while Lois' sense of humor and the absurd neatly mesh into exquisite and thought-provoking pieces. In conjunction with her own gallery, Lois' work is on permanent exhibition as part of the Capitol Art Collection at the Capitol Art Foundation of Santa Fe, the John and Mable Ringling Museum of Art in Sarasota, Florida, and the Williams College Museum of Art in Williamstown, Massachusetts. Additionally, Lois has opened her studio to fellow artist and woodworker Rob Winston, who creates stunning practical art in the form of beautifully crafted furniture. Rob uses a variety of hardwoods, such as cherry, oak and mesquite, along with the same tools and techniques that master furniture makers have been using for centuries to create incredible tables, rocking chairs and other custom pieces. Explore the world as Lois Duffy sees it with a visit to Lois Duffy Art.

101 N California Street, Silver City NM
(505) 534-0822 *www.loisduffy.com*

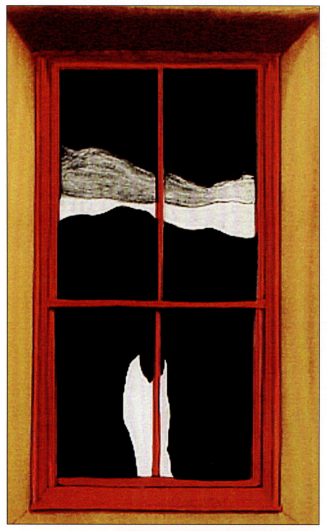

RioBravoFineArt, Inc.

Artists are dreamers. RioBravoFineArt, Inc. founder H. Joe Waldrum purchased a vacant ice house in Truth or Consequences and dreamt of turning it into a stylish home and art gallery. In 2000, his dream grew when the store next door became available. He and his friend, architect and art collector Andy Anderson, drew up lofty plans for living quarters that included a courtyard with organic garden and outside mineral bath. Eventually a large gallery space, the Living Room, was created upstairs. Between two areas on the main floor are the Lower Gallery and Print Room. A temporary studio is housed on the bottom floor. Before they could complete the renovation, a local painter asked if he could show his new work, The Stations, and thus a showcase gallery was born. Two more shows occurred during construction, one featuring four local artists, the other a Waldrum event. Unfortunately, Waldrum passed away in December of 2003. His dream, affectionately known as *mi fantasia gigante*, did not die with him. Eduardo Alicea, his former assistant, and Waldrum's children continue to show new work in the main gallery areas. The ice house, currently used as a makeshift movie theater, will be a sculpture garden, with a piece showing the former owner riding a mule. Come see the fruit of one man's labor and vision, and the art of many others, at RioBravoFineArt, Inc.

110 E Broadway Avenue, Truth or Consequences NM
(505) 894-0572
www.riobravofineart.com

Pecos Pueblo, Pecos, New Mexico

Galleries • 193

Artifacts Gallery and The Studios

The idea behind Artifacts Gallery and The Studios has been a dream of Bev Taylor's for a long time. Bev, a local artist and lifetime resident of Farmington, dreamed of creating a vibrant art center within the walls of the family's old lumber and hardware building. Farmington Lumber and Hardware Co., which closed in 1995, was started by Charles Mumma in 1905, grandfather of Bev's husband, Tom. It was a major supplier of the building needs in Farmington and the surrounding communities. After the business closed in 1995, the building was divided into 12 artist's studios where the artists work in a variety of media, including oils, watercolor, acrylic, collage and printmaking. In 1999, Artifacts Gallery opened as a formal display space, featuring the work of 40 area artists. In 2000, a large classroom area was added for lessons and workshops that are offered throughout the year. In 2003, the ever-changing family-owned business added a Chile Store, which features New Mexico-made chile food products. Owner Bev Taylor is a calligrapher, woodcarver, watercolorist and book artist. Her co-owner is her daughter, Tara Churchill, who is also an accomplished bookmaker, photographer and mother of two small boys. Together Bev and Tara have a prime corner on the art market at Artifacts Gallery and The Studios. Both operations serve as a great visitor's center and a delightful place to get acquainted with the area and its history. Visit Artifacts Gallery for an experience you won't soon forget.

302 E Main Street, Farmington NM
(505) 327-2907

194 • Gardens, Plants & Flowers

White Sands National Monument is part of 275 square miles composed of white sand dunes made of gypsum crystals. Only because the area is landlocked can the alabaster plain exist.

Gardens, Plants & Flowers

Tropic of Capricorn

Nestled in the foothills of the Sangre de Cristo Mountains is a delightful oasis filled with the scents and sounds of the tropics. Tropic of Capricorn is a home, garden and gift store that specializes in peace and relaxation. Owner and designer Michael Clark combines practical efficiency with pleasing aesthetics to create a welcoming and calming atmosphere. Clark uses the ancient Chinese art of feng shui to create an unobtrusive and harmonious space for guests to explore. The spacious main entry room has several doors leading from it, each with something new and exciting to discover behind it, while the gentle bubble of fountains adds to the intimate ambience. For the home, Tropic of Capricorn carries a wide selection of tropical plants and flowers, orchids and cacti. They also have fountains, folk art and pet accoutrements. Create your own backyard paradise with their selection of statuary, wind chimes and patio furniture. Tropic of Capricorn has a lovely variety of gift items, as well, including bath and body products, New Mexico foods, gifts and music. Clark is deeply involved with his community and hosts free classes on horticulture and landscaping, called Get Green with Michael, monthly. Clark has a degree in agriculture, has worked as a horticulturist and co-founded the Santa Fe Botanical Garden. Experience the joy and serenity found at Tropic of Capricorn.

86 Old Las Vegas Highway, Santa Fe NM
(505) 983-2700

Gardens, Plants & Flowers • 197

Hot air balloons taking off

Santa Fe Greenhouses/ High Country Gardens

Santa Fe Greenhouses serves the needs of anyone who wants to buy individual plants or create a landscaped wonderland. Long recognized for its dedication to drought-tolerant perennials, this full-service nursery and garden center has won nine Green Thumb awards for introducing new plants to the mail-order gardener. A knowledgeable staff can answer all your questions on using plants and trees that thrive in the Southwest and in many other parts of the West. Santa Fe Greenhouses publishes the nationally distributed *High Country Gardens* catalog, a resource for anyone searching for colorful low-care plants. The catalog features perennials, shrubs, grasses and cacti, along with pre-planned garden kits, books, tools, soil builders and critter repellents. Tour the gardens at Santa Fe Greenhouses any time during business hours or take a guided tour from late May through August. A visit to the gardens in late August or September offers inspirational blooms and visits from large numbers of hummingbirds. Beyond a fine selection of native plants, look for pottery, garden furniture and tools. Chief horticulturist David Salman is a recognized expert in his field, honored by Garden Club of America for his contributions to ecological conservation and preservation. David and the staff of Santa Fe Greenhouses invite you to browse their online catalog or visit their facility for a revealing look at the world of water-wise planting.

2904 Rufina Street, Santa Fe NM
(877) 811-2700 or (800) 925-9387
www.santafegreenhouses.com
www.highcountrygardens.com

Photos © High Country Gardens

Photo © High Country Gardens

Salman Raspberry Ranch and La Cueva Historic District

The Salman Raspberry Ranch and the La Cueva Historic District are nestled on the Eastern slopes of the Sangre de Cristo Mountains. Six acres of expertly cultivated river bottom land yield enough fresh berries to fill the baskets of tourists and locals alike. Visitors can pick straight from the field or buy flats at the Salman Ranch Store, which is open year round. Across the road from the store is the Salman Ranch Café, open during the you-pick season, offering such delicious homemade New Mexican treats as tacos and tamales, tasty sandwiches with locally baked bread and soft serve ice cream drenched in Salman Ranch raspberry topping and fresh raspberries from the field. Other attractions in the area are the beautifully restored Mission Church of San Rafael, the three-story adobe mill with its water wheel, and the nearby two-story Romero-Salman adobe hacienda dating to the 1800s. The hacienda is still the home of descendants of Colonel William Salman, who purchased the ranch in the 1940s. The buildings, gardens and acequia invite the painter and photographer in all of us. A day with your family at the Salman Raspberry Ranch will be well spent. Once you've picked plenty of berries, feel free to have your lunch under the beautiful willow trees that line the ancient acequia. Just across from the picnic area is one of New Mexico's most colorful gardens. The Ranch Store carries a large variety of drought resistant and sun loving seeds. The store features the famous Salman Ranch Raspberry jam, topping and vinegar, along with other gourmet food products, ranch-grown dried floral bouquets, farm-grown vegetables and fine art photography and ranch mementos. The raspberry season usually starts in early August and ends with the first killing frost in mid to late October. Be sure to call their toll-free number before visiting to check on field conditions.

**Junction of NM 518 and 442, La Cueva NM
(505) 387-2900 or (866) 281-1515**
www.salmanraspberryranch.com

200 • Health & Beauty

Though far from any paved roads, Fajada Butte in Chaco Canyon is well worth the drive.

Health & Beauty

La Bella Spa and Salon

La Bella Spa and Salon is a palace for pampering. Home designer and owner Dawn Davide turned her architectural talents to her other passion: a $3 million luxury spa and salon where you can receive world-class hair cuts, spa services and personal luxuries. Dawn is an award-winning hair stylist who has competed in international contests. She loves taking something and building it from the ground up, whether it is a home or hairstyle. At La Bella Spa and Salon, guests are recognized as individuals who can realize their true potential through therapists and technicians who are grounded as people, qualified as professionals and caring as guardians. The atmosphere at La Bella is inviting, with its Tuscan-influenced architecture and comfortable furnishings. The lower level of La Bella includes stations for hair styling and manicure rooms. Le Café Miche Bistro at La Bella Plaza is an outpost of the state's finest French restaurant. The menu reflects the country French cuisine served at Le Café Miche, plus daily specials available only at La Bella. An impressive boutique features many items, such as the Phytomer skin care and cosmetic lines from France, as well as jewelry and custom treatment baskets. The second floor, where the spa treatments are performed, opens to a scenic, natural vista and a relaxation area on the balcony. Here you'll find the men's lounge, featuring a large-screen television and computers with Internet connections, and a luxuriously appointed women's lounge.

All spa personnel are dedicated to health-conscious principles. There is a staff nutritionist available for personal consultation, as well as a professional physician. Events and classes are offered and clients are encouraged to take advantage of discounts offered monthly from the website. Come to La Bella Spa and Salon, the ultimate luxury for mind, body and spirit.

10126 Coors Boulevard NW, Albuquerque NM
(La Bella Spa and Salon) (505) 899-5557

800 Central SW, Albuquerque NM
(Labella on Park) (505) 244-0310

2201 Uptown Loop NE, Albuquerque NM
(AB2 Uptown) (505) 899-5557

www.labellaspasalon.com

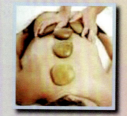

Bodywise Massage & Day Spa

Bodywise Massage & Day Spa is the perfect get-away. The well trained body care specialists utilize a smorgasbord of massage techniques to pamper you. The range of therapies includes Reiki, sports massage, deep tissue massage, relaxation massage, hot stone massage and pregnancy massage. Spa services include such delights as salt glows, herbal wraps, seaweed treatments and hydrating treatments. Their nail technician offers natural manicures and pedicures using professional products, including those that are formaldehyde free. Their esthetician offers nine different kinds of facials and a full range of body waxing for areas such as eyebrows, underarms, legs, bikinis and backs for both men and women. The facials include a skin brightening system, power regeneration treatment, Teen Clean Express and an enviromentally sensitized treatment. All of these treatments use Dermalogica products. Bodywise Massage & Day Spa accommodates the special needs of men by offering two types of facials, as well as manicures and pedicures. You are invited to spend some quality time at Bodywise Massage & Day Spa by experiencing one of their many packages. The Queen Package, for example, allows you three-and-a-half hours of pampering. This includes an herbal wrap, Power Regeneration facial, a one-hour massage and a spa pedicure. All treatments are customized for your individual needs. Susanne Greif established Bodywise Massage & Day Spa in 1996 when she fell in love with the Village of Corrales in the Rio Grande Valley after moving here from Canada. She began her business in just one room and grew it into the full-fledged day spa it is today. Susanne and her staff invite you to come to Bodywise Massage & Day Spa for a session of pampering unlike you have ever experienced.

4627 Corrales Road, Corrales NM
(505) 792-1340
www.bodywisedayspa.com

Day Spa at Serenity Gardens

If you're dreaming of an escape, then the Day Spa at Serenity Gardens is the place to go. Owned by Barbara Kline Hammond and created to provide a nurturing, natural environment just for you, this day spa is unparalleled when it comes to relaxation. Bring a friend, partner or group if you like. Generous treatment rooms in the striking adobe building with beautiful lighting, aromatherapy, cool gardens and a mystical labyrinth are waiting to invigorate you. Top quality services are offered along with the most natural base products available. On the menu are a variety of massages, facials and body wraps and other treatments to help you look and feel your best. If you're sensitive to chemicals, you'll be pleased to know that only organic products are used. This is a haven for those going through cancer treatments. You can choose from a number of spa package deals, and even sign up for a Hatha Yoga class. The Day Spa at Serenity Gardens is filled with magical wonders that you've only dreamed about. Escape today and you'll be hooked forever.

**3824 Corrales Road, Corrales NM
(505) 899-5707**
www.serenitygardensnm.com

Casa Verde Salon and Spa

At Casa Verde Spa, you journey into a sensory and tactile realm unlike any you have experienced before. The Casa Verde team fosters tranquility, beauty and rejuvenation in a creative environment that respects your dignity. For nearly two and half decades, Casa Verde has been offering clients the highest level of professional salon services. Locally owned and operated by the Maestas family, Casa Verde grew into its own in 1996 when it became a certified Aveda Concept Salon. Aveda hair and body products are based on pure flower and plant essences and provide sensory exhilaration. Today, the spa has assembled a team of technical experts and fashion advisors who share the Casa Verde vision. The salon side of the business provides complete hair care services, including styling and color. The salon also provides a full range of body waxing services. The spa provides therapeutic massage, body treatments, skin care and spa packages. Typically, packages include a steam room experience, massage and facial, plus additional treatments depending on the package. Special packages are available for men, expectant mothers and brides-to-be. Manicures, pedicures and make-up make-overs are available, as well. Consider joining the more than 1,000 clients on Casa Verde's text message list who receive special offers. Let the experts at Casa Verde Salon and Spa pamper you body and balance your soul.

5113 Comanche Road NE,
Albuquerque NM
(505) 881-0464
www.casaverdesalonspa.net

The Inn at Paradise

For an active vacation in a luxurious setting, visit the Inn at Paradise. You will be just steps from the first tee of the Paradise Hills Golf Course, close to trails for running and bicycling, and close to trainers who are ready to support your fitness goals. The inn sits on the West Mesa overlooking the Rio Grande Valley and the majestic Sandia Mountains. The newly remodeled rooms showcase artwork on consignment from local artists; suites offer fireplaces and kitchens. A tranquil garden with a pond and waterfall is a favorite spot for weddings. Antoni and Natalia Niemczak are your hosts in Paradise. Antoni is a competitive runner who has won top honors in major world marathons. The premises are home to the Center for High Altitude Sports Training, where runners, triathletes and bicyclists benefit from a synthetic track, tennis courts and miles of trails. The combination of high altitude, moderate temperatures, sunny days and soaring views satisfy athletes seeking high intensity training and anyone seeking an idyllic retreat. Train with Antoni, relax in a large hot tub and eat homemade, nutritious meals designed to support your sports training or active lifestyle. A pro shop serves golfers. The Full Moon Saloon can start your day with its fiesta breakfast. Modest rates and superior amenities make the Inn at Paradise one of Albuquerque's best values. Let the Inn at Paradise and the Center for High Altitude Sports Training be your hosts in the Land of Enchantment.

10035 Country Club Lane, Albuquerque NM
(505) 898-6161 or (800) 938-6161
www.innatparadise.com

Angels' Ascent Retreat & Spa

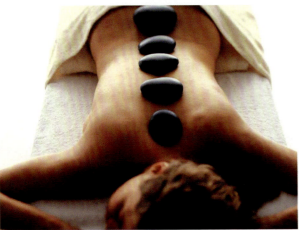

Named as one of Albuquerque and Santa Fe's top five spas by *Travel & Leisure* magazine, Angels' Ascent Retreat & Spa offers a rejuvenating spa experience, highlighted by heavenly mountain views and divine sunsets. This popular getaway destination opened in 1995 as a bed and breakfast. In 2000, the inn was renovated to include the current retreat and spa and the recently added tea room. Angels' Ascent is centrally located on the Turquoise Trail near the breathtaking Sandia Peak Ski Area and the Paa-Ko Ridge Golf Course. The idyllic retreat, close to both Albuquerque and Santa Fe, offers numerous amenities and features English Country décor with an angel theme. Here you can while away the hours as you indulge in a full spectrum of spa services at the Paradise Day Spa and Wellness Center, including massages, facials and body polishes. Guests enjoy relaxing in the steam room, sauna or whirlpool. Angels' Ascent also offers specialized retreats, designed to improve your overall wellness via healthful foods, detoxification and stress management. Along with complimentary breakfasts and varied programs, Angels' Ascent offers a wide range of packages that cover everything from special dinners to relationship enhancement instruction. Visit the Land of Enchantment while you rediscover the balance and peace within yourself at Angel's Ascent Retreat & Spa.

20 Gilbert Place, Sandia Park, NM
(505) 286-1588
www.angelsascent.com

Refugio Verde

According to a Chinese proverb, "Life begins when you plant a garden." Refugio Verde is a collection of quiet, breathtaking gardens that Coral and Jeff Clark have created over the past decade. In an obvious labor of love, dedication and devotion, Coral and Jeff have designed this green oasis from what was once a barren field. By building their home out of straw and local lumber, using rescued and other appropriate plants and gardening techniques, they have a sustainable lifestyle. Based on their philosophy that life is what you sow, they now offer a line of natural handmade soaps and a nursery of plants and meditation gardens. With Jeff's degree in horticulture and Coral's background in commercial design, they were drawn by the promise of a balanced and healthy life in one of the most beautiful and spiritual places in the Southwest along the Pecos river. In addition to their gorgeous gardens, they make exquisite jackets and hats from handspun yarn courtesy of sheep and goats owned by ranchers in the area. They sell hand-woven garments, handspun and dyed yarns and flowers on Tuesdays and Saturdays at Santa Fe's famous Farmer's Market. Their gardens and nursery, where they also sell herbs, handmade soaps and other botanicals and landscape plants, are open to the public on Sundays. Reservations are required to experience their meditation garden retreat. Experience the beauty of their green refuge with a visit to Refugio Verde.

Route 3, HCR 72, Ribera NM   (505) 421-2961   *www.refugioverde.com*

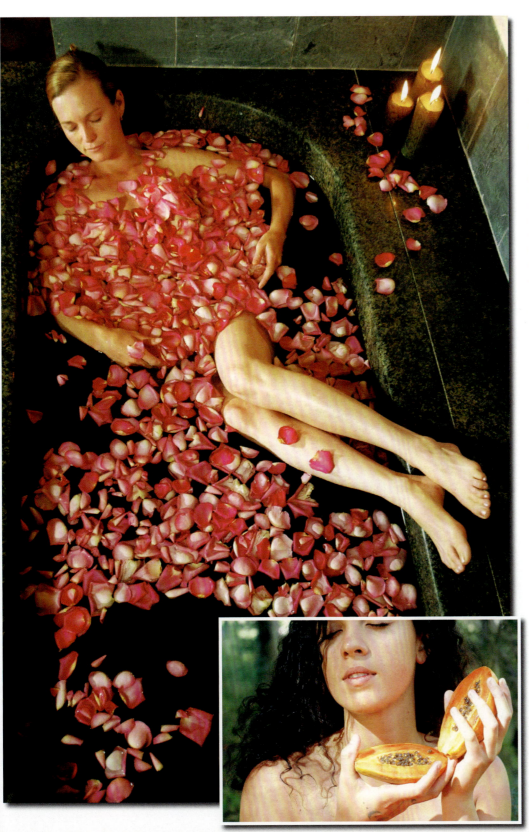

Absolute Nirvana Spa and the Madeleine Inn

Carolyn Lee knows how to create a world of luxury and splendor. In 1987, Carolyn purchased the Madeleine Inn, a stunning Queen Anne Victorian built in 1886 by Chinese railroad workers as the residence of a prominent railroad tycoon. She named this lovely establishment after her young daughter. In 2005 she added the Absolute Nirvana Spa, dedicated to the ancient healing art of using plants, herbs and spices for inner and outer beauty. The Madeleine features seven beautifully appointed guest rooms with all the amenities needed to make your stay comfortable and relaxing. In the mornings, guests receive a hearty and delicious breakfast featuring homemade baked goods and flavorful entrées. After your day of touring or relaxing, come back to sample an array of baked goodies, as well as to enjoy a wine and cheese hour. The spa was recently selected by *Condé Naste Traveler* as, "One of the hottest new spas in the world." Choose from a menu of traditional Asian spa rituals and luxurious rose petal baths, as well as therapeutic, hot stone and Thai massage. These treatments, rich in history and tradition, are translated through the healing hands of a staff of master-level therapists, most of whom have 10 to 15 years of experience. The spa also features a tea room where you can sip fantastic, full-bodied chai or have a pot of one of their 50 varieties of loose teas while savoring delectable tea sandwiches and scones. The Indonesian-inspired Absolute Nirvana Spa and historic Madeleine Inn are located in a tranquil garden setting just four blocks from the plaza. Carolyn Lee invites you to book a restful, rejuvenating stay at the Madeleine Inn and Absolute Nirvana Spa.

106 Faithway Street, Santa Fe NM
(888) 877-7622
www.absolutenirvana.com
www.madeleineinn.com

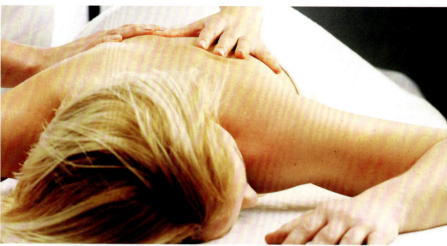

Sierra Grande Lodge and Spa

Sierra Grande Lodge and Spa is an oasis in the desert for refueling your spirit. The lodge is a restored 1929 resort renowned for its mineral spring water. The lodge is built on an area that was known as Geronimo Springs Baths in the 1880s. Many cowboys and soldiers came to these springs to soak their aching bodies and cover their wounds with the white mud that was said to have many healing powers. The town where the Sierra Grande Lodge and Spa is located has one of the largest mineral water aquifers underneath downtown and is naturally heated by magma. The mineral water in Truth or Consequences contains 38 minerals, almost four times the amount found in other mineral water aquifers. Sixteen deluxe rooms include one suite with balcony access, four balcony rooms and 11 standard rooms. Each guest receives a complimentary 30-minute soak for each day of their stay. The restaurant offers a combination of Mediterranean and Asian cuisine. The chef creates private dinner services in the kitchen or on the balcony. Unwind at the spa with a soothing massage, custom facial or body treatment. You may choose from an indoor or outdoor pool for your mineral soak. Suits are optional in the indoor pool. Discover the healing power of the desert and mineral water at Sierra Grande Lodge and Spa.

501 McAdoo Street, Truth or Consequences NM
(505) 894-6976
www.sierragrandelodge.com

Health & Beauty • 211

View from the inside of an Earthship in Taos

One of the many adobe buildings in Albuquerque; the southwestern adobe style architechecture found throughout the state of New Mexico has its roots in the buildings of Native Americans who had been using these same materials for centuries.

Home

Ernest Thompson Furniture

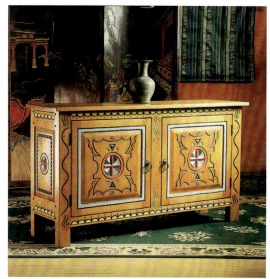

If you are looking for quality wood furniture with classic appeal, you must visit Ernest Thompson Furniture in Albuquerque. President Mike Godwin, along with 50 craftsmen, offers high end, handcrafted furniture, assembled at the Albuquerque workshop. Custom orders are always welcome. The Ernest Thompson style is a fusion of many cultures and design inspirations. Styles include American Southwest, Ranch, Lodge and Mission, along with European Country. From French-inspired armoires for the bedroom to regional pieces like the Tesuque dining table with Durango armchairs, Ernest Thompson has been delivering quality furniture, plus cabinets, doors and shutters for 35 years. The furnishings honor design traditions long established in New Mexico, a place where European culture and native colors and forms have blended to produce distinctive styling. Some furniture boasts carvings based on classic Spanish Colonial, Tuscan and French country designs. Branch-covered screens and shutters, called Sombraje, use willows and salt cedar to produce pieces with a unique character. Ernest Thompson has a second showroom in Scottsdale, Arizona and recently finished cabinetry for 38 upscale homes in that area. You can view a large assortment of work online or order a catalog, but to experience the full impact of these pieces, crafted with Old World techniques, you will want to come to the spectacular showroom, where heirloom quality pieces promise to become lasting and meaningful parts of your home.

4531 Osuna Road NE, Albuquerque NM
(505) 344-1994 or (800) 568-2344
www.ernestthompson.com

Honey Do Home Repair and Closets Too

People of Santa Fe have been referred to Honey Do Home Repair since Douglas Maahs founded the local company in 1996. Honey Do has set the standard for quality in home repair and remodeling. Douglas says, "Show up on time, return phone calls and do what you say you're going to do. That's what creates success." In 2006, Honey Do was a top five finalist for the Santa Fe Small Business of the Year award and won three awards from the Santa Fe Area Home Builders Association, including two Best Kitchen awards. From small home repairs and new doors and windows, to full kitchen and bath remodels, a highly skilled team of professional repair technicians, designers and craftspeople will handle your job personally. The company promises free estimates and a job that is done right the first time, at a fair price. Closets Too provides high quality custom kitchen cabinets or custom closets and storage solutions. The Closets Too showroom is filled with great product displays and a design team to help you create or recreate your cabinet and storage solutions. With the custom kitchen cabinets, Honey Do offers a complete, one-stop solution to the design and implementation of your new kitchen or bath. The custom closets are manufactured at the local facility for fast service and impeccable follow up after the sale. They are proud members of the Santa Fe Alliance, Better Business Bureau and the Remodelors Council. Honey Do boasts a 95-percent customer satisfaction rate, and clients who are always happy to serve as references. Call Honey Do Home Repair and find yourself effortlessly checking tasks off your to-do list of home improvements.

2356 Fox Road, Suite 700, Santa Fe NM (505) 992-8382 (Honey Do)
333 W Cordova Road (505) 992-0200 (Closets Too Showroom)
www.honeydo-homerepair.com

Southwest Spanish Craftsmen and Nussbaumer Fine Art Gallery

The tradition of handcrafted furniture and doors has borne the signature of excellence for more than 75 years at the Southwest Spanish Craftsmen workshop. Past Southwest Spanish Craftsmen employees include Eliseo Rodriguez, an artist who was honored by the Smithsonian as a National Treasure in 1992, and Abad Lucero, an elder statesman in the craft of Spanish Colonial furniture. Victor Vera, who once served as Pancho Villa's gunsmith, joined the Southwest Spanish Craftsmen team in his later years. The list of famous customers includes the Von Trapp family, Lucille Ball, Gene Autrey and Randy Travis. The company has gone through several changes in ownership since the passing of founder R.H. Welton, and is now owned by the Nussbaumer family. Today, Southwest Spanish Craftsmen still designs and builds custom furniture and doors and employs some of the most talented artisans in the state. Southwest Spanish Craftsmen specializes in faithful reproductions of museum pieces, as well as innovative new designs of enduring beauty and quality. Examples of the work can be viewed in the Nussbaumer Fine Art Gallery housed in a historic building next to the Guadalupe Chapel. Visit the showroom or plan a consultation to discover the art and craft you need to complete the aesthetic atmosphere in your home.

314 S Guadalupe Street, Santa Fe NM
(505) 982-1767 or (800) 777-1767
www.southwestspanishcraftsmen.com
www.nussbaumerfineart.com

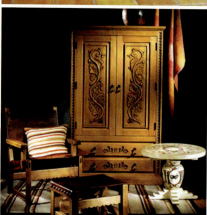

Photos courtesy of southwestspanishcraftsmen.com

Sage Builders

It must be great being Lloyd Martinez. He gets to stroll the Santa Fe plaza knowing he has remodeled some of the most photographed buildings in the country. Through his company, Sage Builders, Lloyd works on landmark buildings and designs new homes, always remembering the deep connection between architecture and place in his native New Mexico. The distinctive adobe architecture, so in tune with the landscape, defines New Mexico as perhaps no other style defines a place in the United States. The style achieves its pinnacle in Santa Fe, where Lloyd's family has lived for so long that he grew up on a street named for them. He sees each project with a native's eyes and feels it with a native's heart. He must also be something of a magician, because his work often requires him to deal with the city's strict building code for historic homes. For the recent transformation of an old carriage house into a new home, he increased the ceiling height without raising the roof. How? He dug down about two feet and lowered the floors. His success on this project won him a Las Casitas award from New Mexico's home magazine, *Su Casa*, and the New Mexico Home Builders Association. The result of Lloyd's ingenious craftsmanship was, according to *Su Casa*, "a nowhere-but-New Mexico home that captures the spirit of old Santa Fe." For native solutions for your building projects, contact Lloyd Martinez at Sage Builders.

7505 Mallard Way, Suite A, Santa Fe NM
(505) 424-7601

ABYDOS

Some furniture is simply furniture, but ABYDOS furniture qualifies as fine art. Owners Clay Cousins and Anne Delling bring expertise and knowledge of graphic and industrial design and applied creativity to the business. Texturally rich wood is adorned with punched or painted tin accents, carvings or metal stands. Furniture is hand-painted to specifications and wood finishes are crackled or hand-rubbed depending on the customer's wishes. ABYDOS utilizes environmentally responsible materials. Their products display the regional Southwest flavor with a distinctive style all their own. The combination of nature and human effort that goes into the creation of the wood and metal accents result in varying finishes that can never be replicated exactly. King-size headboards with stylized outlines and painted tin make a stunning accent in the bedroom. Nightstands, armoires and chests on delicately scalloped iron stands add visual interest to traditional items, fashioning an entirely new category of home furnishings in the process. The furniture handcrafted by ABYDOS today will be tomorrow's heirlooms. This kind of beauty and quality provides a lifetime of use and delight in solid home furnishings that you will pass down to future generations. Your purchases from ABYDOS will last more than a lifetime, so pay their store or website a visit.

7036 Highway 518, Talpa NM
(505) 758-0483 or (888) 900-0863
www.abydosfurniture.com

Re/MAX One

New Mexico is a magical place that draws people to its active lifestyle, gorgeous open landscape and dramatic indigo skies. The independently owned and operated Re/MAX One of Santa Fe helps individuals from all ends of the earth relocate to this enchanted land. With more than 60 years combined experience in Northern New Mexico real estate, owners Bill Schwent and Larry McCarty apply a family-oriented focus to the sale of homes, land and ranches. Their satisfied customers use such Re/MAX One tools as a property search, a current interest rate calculator and buyer how-to tips to find their new homes in Los Alamos and Santa Fe Counties, as well as the rest of Northern New Mexico. Larry, a native of Santa Fe, specializes in historic adobe homes. The company plays an active role in the community as sponsors of the annual 4th of July pancake breakfast on the Plaza, which brings out thousands of citizens, and the annual Rodeo de Galisteo, a traditional rodeo experience that emphasizes small-town values and history. The office also provides a moving van for local nonprofit organizations to use as needed. Bill and Larry encourage you to call today for a relocation packet. They know what awaits you at the end of the Old Santa Fe Trail and invite you to visit Re/MAX One to find a property you will love to call home.

123 W Booth Street, Santa Fe NM
(505) 988-4688 or (800) 257-4688
www.remax-santafe.com

At the end of the Old Santa Fe Trail there are opportunities with REMAX/One

Asian Adobe

Since its 2003 opening in the South Guadalupe district of Santa Fe, Asian Adobe has quickly become the area's prize resource for stunning Asian influenced furnishings, gifts and home décor. The owners of this exclusive home store, Stuart and Fidelia Kirk, travel regularly to China where they hand select the lovely and inspiring products that make up the store's inventory. Asian Adobe specializes in 100 to 200-year-old Chinese furniture, particularly Ming-style pieces, which are characterized by functionality and clean, simple lines. The shop also carries a wide variety of unusual items that would add interest to any room, like red-lacquer armoires, altar tables and screens. Workers crafted all of the furniture in the store during the 1800s utilizing precious woods like walnut, cypress and beech. Throughout the showroom, visitors will also find paintings by Ming Fu, a Beijing artist known for his classic Chinese scenes painted in a colorful and modern style. Asian Adobe has a distinctive collection of fine gifts, as well, including baby hats, shoes and wedding slippers, along with art accessories, rugs, spectacular jewelry and books. They also carry a choice array of Chinese textiles such as handbags, scarves and cashmere clothing. Bring the Far East a lot closer to home with a visit to Asian Adobe.

**530 S Guadalupe Street,
Santa Fe NM
(505) 992-6846**
www.asian-adobe.com

Recreation

Santuario de Chimayo, already a beautiful and legendary church in northern New Mexico, gets some extra beauty as autumn descends upon the mountain landscape.
Photo Courtesy of the New Mexico Tourism Department
Photo by Mark Nohl

Great Southwest Adventures

An afternoon melding searing beauty and personal amusement awaits those with a taste for adventure and history at Great Southwest Adventures. Owners Monique Schoustra and Tom Ribe are dedicated to the place they love and have made a personal commitment to introduce you to the wonders of northern New Mexico, while educating visitors on the subjects of the back country, plant life, culture and natural history of the area. Small groups and quality guides enhance your experience as you tour fascinating communities and beautiful landscapes such as cliff dwellings, Pueblos and Red Rock Country's Ghost Ranch, one of the vistas which inspired Georgia O'Keeffe to capture its brilliance with her paintbrush. Whether you choose to sightsee by vehicle or on foot, Great Southwest Adventures will help you get the most out of New Mexico's splendor. Guided walks through the ruins of prehistoric villages, Taos, the Santa Fe Trail or the surreal, ghostly spires of Tent Rocks will keep you on your toes. The tours are guaranteed to be interesting, and you are encouraged to follow your own personal interests along the way. Great Southwest Adventures believes in the magic of their surroundings and strives to keep them alive for future generations. By donating 10 percent of their profits to environmental and non-profit organizations, they acknowledge that the natural rugged beauty and depth of culture can never be reproduced and must be preserved. Let Great Southwest Adventures turn your trip to New Mexico into a memorable one.

P.O. Box 31151, Santa Fe NM
(505) 455-2700
www.swadventures.com

Tent Rocks National Monument, NM
Photo by Monique Schoustra

Follow the Sun, Inc.

Make the most of your trip to Albuquerque and the surrounding area with the guide services of Follow the Sun, Inc. Whether you are looking for a personal concierge or a group tour by van or motor coach, this company believes that half the fun of any tour should be in getting to your ultimate destination. Tours into the Land of Enchantment can be customized to meet the needs of an individual or group. Follow the Sun professionals work closely with tour groups and convention goers to provide memorable experiences that target your interests. Coaches, vans and cars are clean and luxurious. Individuals can also receive first-class excursions to a spa, a golf course or shopping. Collectors enjoy trips that specialize in American Indian pottery, jewelry, rugs and crafts. Popular day tours include a driving tour of the city of Albuquerque, a tram tour on the world's longest tramway and a tour of nearby mining towns. Customers can also visit the Acoma Pueblo, where several families still reside in the old structures on the mesa. An all-day tour of Santa Fe gives a close-up experience of the adobe architecture, art and fine food of this unusual city. With so much to see and limited time to see it, why not let the friendly and knowledgeable travel experts at Follow the Sun help make your visit to magical New Mexico the experience of a lifetime.

10131 Coors Road NW, Suite 825, Bldg. I-2,
Albuquerque NM
(505) 897-2886 or (866) 428-4SUN (4786)
www.ftstours.com

Cho's Tae Kwan Do New Mexico

Owners Sean and Denise Farrell want to offer you a gift of confidence at Cho's Tae Kwon Do New Mexico. The Farrells have been studying martial arts for 16 years, and each has black belts in both Wusho and Tae Kwon Do. The husband-and-wife team trained with Grandmaster Hee II Cho from 1997 to 2003, when Grandmaster Cho had his world headquarters in Albuquerque. Today, they teach their classes in the manner taught to them by the grandmaster. Sean and Denise have competed widely nationally and internationally and hold many winning titles. The Farrells want to teach others that Tae Kwon Do is not about kicking and punching, it's about self-control, perseverance and being the champion of life. Cho's Tae Kwon Do New Mexico offers classes for all age groups. Children ages four to six focus on building such skills as focus, listening and safety awareness, while those ages seven to 12 practice discipline, respect, self-confidence and academic achievement. Adults can gain self-confidence while enjoying a complete workout designed to release negative emotions. Accept the gift of confidence, and visit Cho's Tae Kwon Do New Mexico.

8214 Montgomery Boulevard NE, Albuquerque NM
(505) 292-4277
www.chostkdabq.homestead.com

Fishback Studio of the Dance

Fishback Studio of the Dance has been teaching Albuquerque residents to dance for more than 50 years, thanks to a family with a strong dance orientation. Four generations of the Fishback family have taken dancers from their first childhood steps to stage performances. Fishback Studio recognizes that dancing is more than a form of art; it's also an athletic activity that promotes health, poise and grace. The studio offers classes to students from three years old through adulthood. Children from three to five enter pre-ballet. Beginning at age six, students can choose classes in ballet, tap, jazz or Scottish dancing. The studio organizes highly regarded competitive dance teams in these four styles. Students must audition for these troupes, which have produced many national dance champions. The studio also offers modern dancing and acrobatics classes. Dr. Charles Fishback and his wife, Katherine, founded Fishback Studio in 1945. Today, their daughter, Kathie Fishback Anthony, and her husband, professional guitarist Michael Anthony, operate the studio. Kathie began training at Fishback Studio when she was three. She enjoyed 12 years of professional dancing in Hollywood and danced at the Academy Awards and on the Carol Burnett and Dean Martin shows, among others. Fishback Studio's 40 instructors include senior faculty members who maintain their excellence through constant study and personal appearances. The senior faculty personally trains assistants. For excellence in dance in a positive learning environment, enroll at Fishback Studio of the Dance.

4529 Eubank Boulevard NE, Albuquerque NM
(505) 298-8828
www.fishbackstudio.com

Skyspan Adventures

How would you like to drift high above the land in a balloon piloted by the first man to fly from the U.S. to Africa in a hot air balloon? Now is your opportunity if you book a flight with Skyspan Adventures. In an ultimate hot air ballooning experience, Skyspan will give you an unforgettable aerial view of the Rio Grande valley. Your adventure will begin in the shadow of the majestic Sandia Mountains in the light of a sunrise launch. Once you are airborne, the experience is much like floating on a cloud. No two flights are the same as you go from literally skimming the treetops to soaring at an altitude high enough to let you see mountain peaks from 70 miles away. The pilot will make you feel right at home with his ability to direct the balloon on waves of air. Once you have landed, your flight will be celebrated with a traditional champagne ceremony and commemorated with a flight certificate suitable for framing. The staff of Skyspan is very experienced with 48 World Aviation Records in altitude, distance and duration. The pilot is also a US National Team Champion, has performed flights worldwide and has more than 4,000 hours of flight time under his belt. Skyspan also provides free hotel pick up. Skyspan has made a lifetime of flying balloons, so have no fear and schedule your adventure today.

5600 McLeod NE, Suite H,
Albuquerque NM
(505) 250-2300
www.skyspanadventures.com

Rainbow Ryders
Hot Air Balloon Company, Inc.

When was the last time you did something for the first time in your life? The largest balloon company in the United States, Rainbow Ryders, considers it their job to help you fulfill your dreams. They will take you on the balloon ride of your life miles above a majestic view of the Rio Grande River. For 24 years, president and vice president Scott and Liz Appelman have been taking passengers on a flight to remember. Scott is the inventor of the famous Balloon Glow and Special Shapes Rodeo. He flies corporate clients and has flown over Super Bowls, Final Fours and numerous PGA Golf Tournaments. Since its establishment, Rainbow Ryders has flown more than 150,000 passengers. Rainbow Ryders has also set the record in hot air ballooning at an altitude of 24,680 feet. Of course, Scott and Liz could not have accomplished all of this with out the help of chief pilots Brooke Owen and Mike Collins, as well as director of operations Kiersten Goddard. Rainbow Ryders is the Official Ride Concession for the Albuquerque International Balloon Fiesta®. They have an impeccable safety record, the newest, top-of-the-line ballooning equipment, and their pilots have thousands of hours of flight experience. Rainbow Ryders specializes in balloon rides for large groups such as conventions or reunions and even offers special group rates. They also have a special occasion package. Try something new and exciting. Give Rainbow Ryders Hot Air Balloon Company a call.

5601 Eagle Rock Avenue NE, Albuquerque NM 87113
(505) 823-1111 or (800) 725-2477(AIRR)
www.rainbowryders.com

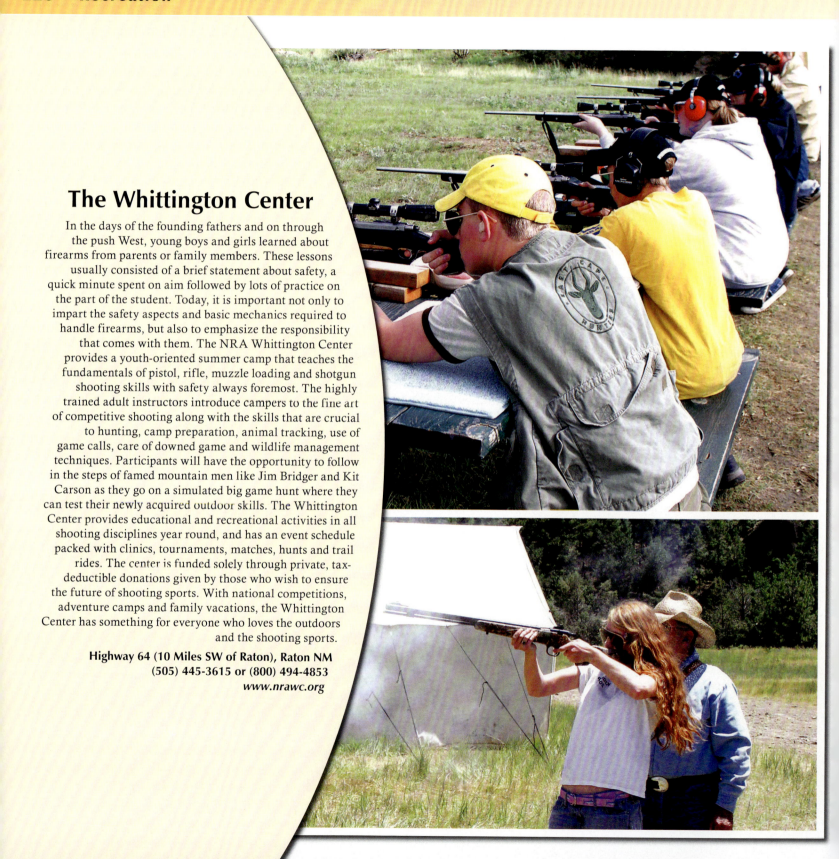

The Whittington Center

In the days of the founding fathers and on through the push West, young boys and girls learned about firearms from parents or family members. These lessons usually consisted of a brief statement about safety, a quick minute spent on aim followed by lots of practice on the part of the student. Today, it is important not only to impart the safety aspects and basic mechanics required to handle firearms, but also to emphasize the responsibility that comes with them. The NRA Whittington Center provides a youth-oriented summer camp that teaches the fundamentals of pistol, rifle, muzzle loading and shotgun shooting skills with safety always foremost. The highly trained adult instructors introduce campers to the fine art of competitive shooting along with the skills that are crucial to hunting, camp preparation, animal tracking, use of game calls, care of downed game and wildlife management techniques. Participants will have the opportunity to follow in the steps of famed mountain men like Jim Bridger and Kit Carson as they go on a simulated big game hunt where they can test their newly acquired outdoor skills. The Whittington Center provides educational and recreational activities in all shooting disciplines year round, and has an event schedule packed with clinics, tournaments, matches, hunts and trail rides. The center is funded solely through private, tax-deductible donations given by those who wish to ensure the future of shooting sports. With national competitions, adventure camps and family vacations, the Whittington Center has something for everyone who loves the outdoors and the shooting sports.

**Highway 64 (10 Miles SW of Raton), Raton NM
(505) 445-3615 or (800) 494-4853**
www.nrawc.org

Far Flung Adventures

Experience the magnificent rivers of the Southwest with Far Flung Adventures. Since 1979, this river excursion guide company has been showing guests what the rivers of the Southwest are all about. Far Flung offers everything from an exciting half-day trip to an incredible three-day river run filled with starlit desert nights and gourmet food. Far Flung Adventures is vigilant about making sure your whitewater experience is not only fun, but, most importantly, safe. One of the excursion options includes the Taos Box Canyon one-day trip. The Taos Box is famous for some of the most thrilling whitewater runs in the West and is punctuated by a long row of big rapids, such as the Pinball that makes up the final five miles of this Class IV run. A second excursion includes the Rio Chama two or three-day excursion. This takes you through Class III whitewater, delightful wooded camps and offers a great view of local wildlife. This is the perfect family trip and a great introduction to the sport of rafting. Every staff member is trained in emergency medical and river rescue, more than half the boatmen are EMTs and all of them are certified Swiftwater Rescue Technicians. While on Class IV sections of the river they use self-bailing rafts exclusively to keep the boats maneuverable. Reservations are required in advance and all trips are dependent upon water levels. If you want to experience some of the most beautiful rivers and exciting rapids in the country, make a reservation for your own Far Flung Adventure.

P.O. Box 707, El Prado NM
(800) 359-2627
www.farflung.com

Fiesta City Tours

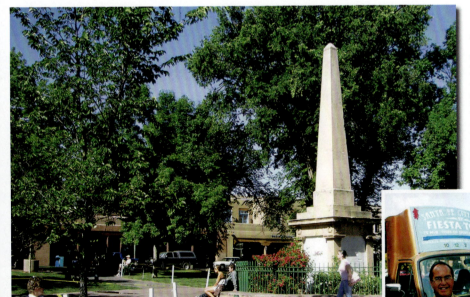

There is an essence of Santa Fe that can only be properly expressed by someone who has experienced years of New Mexico living. Fiesta City Tours' owner Frank Montaño has watched the city of Santa Fe grow since he was a child. With Roberta Flores, a native Santa Fe resident, he offers in-depth tours of the city's historical district that bring the past back to life. The Fiesta City Tours began in 1987 as a walking tour for parties interested in reviving the ghosts of yesteryear. In 1992 it graduated into motorized tours that allow you to enjoy the open-air bus, the Santa Fe Express. Their exciting overview is available year round with multiple tours daily to slip easily into your schedule. It's also an excellent way of orienting newcomers to the area. Regardless of whether you're on a day trip or just arriving to settle in, Frank's experience as City Councilor provides an interesting angle to the event, keeping things exciting and his guests fascinated. Blending current events and historical anecdotes, Fiesta City Tours offers an insightful glimpse into this hub of New Mexico culture. Book your tour today.

1655 Calle Sotero, Santa Fe NM
(505) 983-1570

Taos Sporting Clays

Sporting clays and other target-shooting sports like skeet and trap are among America's fastest growing outdoor sports. With the 2005 opening of Taos Sporting Clays, northern New Mexico is becoming a shooting hotspot. Taos Sporting Clays is a shotgun-only facility located just west of Taos near Tres Piedras. The scenic course sits at 8,200 feet on 648 acres of pinon pine, cedar, sage, rolling hills and arroyos with views of the snowcapped Sangre de Cristo Mountains in one direction and an open mesa dominated by San Antonio Mountain in the other. Presently, 10 stations are positioned around a self-guided walking loop trail. The 100-target course is equipped entirely with automatic trap machines and biodegradable clay targets. The design changes regularly to ensure that both regular shooters and newcomers find the game creative and challenging. Course manager John Rainey is quickly gaining a reputation as a quality course designer. "Taos Sporting Clays is a great place with great terrain and really good equipment. The targets [John] sets are excellent," says Albuquerque's Rick Camuglia, who trained at the facility the week before he won the 2005 Browning All-Around National Championship. The facility includes an office, a pavilion for hosting tournaments and monthly shoot dates registered through the National Sporting Clays Association. Ammo and rental guns are available. Taos Sporting Clays is open year round and some say it's even more fun with snow on the ground. Taos Sporting Clays is open to the public, welcoming beginners as well as national champions.

**126 W Plaza Drive, Taos NM
(Main Office)
N Highway 285, Tres Piedras NM
(Shooting Range)
(505) 770-7648**
www.taossportingclays.com

Los Rios Anglers

To make the most out of your next fly-fishing trip, head to Los Rios Anglers. This full-service guide, outfitter and fly shop has been New Mexico's fly-fishing headquarters since 1985. Los Rios Anglers knows what it takes to make your trip perfect. In the pro shop, you will find the best in waders, books, clothing and accessories. The store even has a collection of fish-related artwork, ideal for the home or office. Additionally, Los Rios is an authorized dealer for top name rods and reels such as Sage, Simms and Ross. Los Rios Anglers features a wide variety of guided trips that range from half a day to overnighters. They have access to some of the finest private-access fishing waters in New Mexico, including streams and easy-access ponds. With more than 50 years of guide experience among them, the guides at Los Rios Anglers are a diverse and interesting group of people who know where the fish are and how to get them on the line. During your excursion, your guide will provide all of your flies, leaders and tippets, as well as lunch for daylong trips. Los Rios Anglers offers instruction as well as excursions for fishermen of all levels, from the beginner who's itching to get that first catch to the experienced pro looking to pick up tips from John Rainey, certified International Game Fish Association guide and fly-fishing world record holder. Take home stories of all the ones that didn't get away with an excursion from Los Rios Anglers.

126 W Plaza Drive, Taos NM
(505) 758-2798 or (800) 748-1707
www.losrios.com

Taos Ski Valley

If you prefer the simple life, leave the crowds and hype behind and head to Taos Ski Valley. This family-owned and operated ski resort has been focused on one thing since 1955–skiing. This world-class resort is consistently ranked as one of the top ski destinations in the nation. Skiers will experience warm and friendly customer service, exceptional ski school instruction and unforgettable terrain. The mountain averages 300 inches of snow and more than 300 days of sunshine annually, perfect conditions for a ski vacation. After a day on the slopes, enjoy the shops, restaurants and evening entertainment offered in the village's locally owned establishments. Snowmobiling, snowshoeing and night snow tubing are available. During the summer, the village of Taos Ski Valley becomes a cool mountain getaway for those wishing to beat the heat. Whether you enjoy a challenging hike up New Mexico's highest peak or a good book under the shade of an aspen tree, Taos Ski Valley has an activity for you. The village hosts many special events throughout the summer, including the Taos School of Music's eight-week Chamber Music concert series, the Jillana School of Ballet and an authentic Oktoberfest. Located high in the peaks of the Sangre de Cristo Mountains, Taos Ski Valley is ideal for family adventures, romantic getaways or weekend trips. Contact the Taos Ski Valley Chamber of Commerce for additional information regarding lodging specials, coming events and dining information, as well as weather and ski conditions. Escape to Taos Ski Valley for cool places and friendly faces.

116 Sutton Place, Taos Ski Valley NM   (800) 517-9816
www.taosskivalley.com

Recreation • 233

HeliNM

For an unforgettable sightseeing tour of New Mexico, HeliNM offers some high adventure with their helicopter tours and combination flight and motorcycle trips. The concept of Manfred Leuthard, this vacation escapade appeals to the romantic as well as the daring. HeliNM offers a variety of services from custom tours, charters and VIP transportation to aerial photography. You can take in New Mexico vistas from the air and have dinner on top of the Pecos mountains, or take a golf tour of the Southwest. The 10-participant tour package combines a Harley-Davidson motorcycle tour with a helicopter flight which takes five people to Santa Fe while the other five ride the bikes to Moab, Utah. Upon their arrival, the Harley group enjoys a flight back to Santa Fe. The Santa Fe group rides in the helicopter to Moab and rides the Harleys back to Santa Fe. The logistics of this trip have proved to provide maximum soul-stirring adventure, all neatly packed into one week of vacation time. HeliNM offers planned vacations combined with the kind of travel not normally accessible to travelers. The aerial view provides an experience of the region not available on the ground, while the combination package allows for a good mix of ground time, fun road trip and air time. The helicopter tours allow some incredible sweeping photography and video opportunities, free from the usual visual obstructions. Be sure to bring your camera to document your HeliNM adventure.

P.O. Box 240, Tesuque NM
(866) 995-1058
www.heliNM.com

High Desert Angler

In the high desert of New Mexico, an entire world of sport fishing and adventure awaits the intrepid vacationer. To ensure that your visit is the best it can be, start your journey at High Desert Angler. Whether you want to fish the local waters or book a fishing trip overseas, High Desert Angler can assist you with all your needs. Owner Jarrett Sasser and his staff focus on education, service and making sure your excursion is a great one. Every trip is customized to suit the individual needs of the participant. Since their guides are on the water 365 days a year, they know right where the fish are biting. Each full-day outing begins with meeting your guide, then you'll travel to the water of your choice and commence fishing. Later in the day, your guide will provide lunch and beverages, while you reflect on the earlier action, relax and enjoy the view. After refreshments, it's time to fish some more. Your guide can provide additional instruction to enhance your skills or just take you to the prime spots. Half-day trips are available. High Desert Angler guides also escort clients on a variety of international fly-fishing trips to exotic locales such as Patagonia and Belize. The company is a serious advocate of the conservation of wild fish, and encourages fishermen to practice catching and releasing. Private classes are offered year round in fly fishing, fly tying and fly casting. Each class is tailored to your specific needs. High Desert Angler strongly encourages women and kids of all ages to participate. The on-site fly shop offers the finest in quality rods, flies and gear. Come and participate in the High Desert Angler experience.

451 Cerrillos Road, Santa Fe NM
(505) 98-TROUT (988-7688)
www.highdesertangler.com

Pueblo Balloon Company

The neatest thing to do in New Mexico is located in Taos, where you can ride in a hot air balloon through the Rio Grande Gorge with Pueblo Balloon Company. The Rio Grande Gorge cuts through the high desert around Taos like a miniature Grand Canyon. You will gently glide on soft desert winds into the 650-foot deep gorge in the basket of a colorful hot air balloon. Pueblo Balloon Company conducts flights through the gorge every morning, year round, weather permitting. You can view the snow-covered Sangre de Cristo mountains in the winter, baby coyotes and deer in the spring, blossoming flowers, shrubs and cacti in the summer and changing foliage in the fall. Your adventure starts bright and early when Pueblo Balloon Company picks you up at your Taos area hotel or bed and breakfast the morning of the flight. The crew and FAA-certified pilots are personable and entertaining and make even the drive out to the gorge an adventure, particularly when the John Dunn Bridge launch site is used, which involves a journey down to the bottom of the Gorge and back up the switchbacks on the other side. At the launch site, the crew re-checks the winds and weather, then begins the set up and inflation of the balloon. The flight lasts anywhere from 60 to 90 minutes, depending on the winds and the location of a landing site. A fearless chase crew will be following. Because balloons can't be steered like planes, the crew is called a chase crew instead of a catch crew. Once you are safely back on terra firma, the chase crew packs up the balloon. After the balloon is again on its trailer, the crew chooses a scenic location for the 223-year-old traditional champagne toast. Pueblo Balloon Company provides a neat little brunch and flight certificates as proof to the world that you are now a lighter-than-air head. Join Pueblo Balloon Company to experience the world's most romantic form of aviation and memories that will last a lifetime.

PO Box 361, Taos NM
(505) 751-9877
www.puebloballoon.com

The Links at Sierra Blanca

The public 18-hole course that is the Links at Sierra Blanca can tempt the gambling nature in anyone. With rolling fairways flanked by thick mounds, this classic Scottish-style course, designed by PGA Senior Tour player Jim Colbert and architect Jeff Bauer, has been consistently ranked by *Golf Digest* as one of the top courses in New Mexico. The Links was built in 1990 on the site of the old Sierra Blanca Regional Airport. The 120-acre project now contains The Links, Hawthorne Suites Resort Hotel, the Ruidoso Convention Center and a public, 2.9-mile walking path. The diverse layout of the course and risk-reward features, together with the well manicured greens, make this course both beautiful and challenging. Because of the beauty of the course, Sierra Blanca is a spike-free golf facility that requires soft spikes or spike-less shoes. The outstanding staff at Sierra Blanca is noted for their friendliness. They specialize in handling group outings, provide lessons from PGA golf pros, and offer a professionalism you would not expect. The season can get busy when the horses are running at Ruidoso Downs Racetrack and Casino, so make sure you call ahead to reserve your tee time. The Links is open year round, weather permitting.

105 Sierra Blanca Drive, Ruidoso NM
(505) 258-5330 or (800) 854-6571
www.trekwest.com/linksgolf

NMSU Golf Course

The New Mexico State University Golf Course is regarded as one of the most outstanding public golf facilities in the Southwest. The course is home to NMSU Men's and Women's Golf Teams, and has played host to some of the biggest collegiate golf tournaments in the nation. This includes three NCAA National Golf Championships (one men's and two women's). Highlighted by beautiful scenery, the 18-hole NMSU Golf Course is framed by the majestic Organ Mountains to the east and the picturesque Mesilla Valley to the west. The golf course provides a challenge to all golfers, with a very nice array of holes ranging in difficulty from very challenging to good birdie opportunities. The golf course features both desert and traditional characteristics and plays to a course rating of 73.0 from the championship tees. In October 2004, a new state-of-the-art clubhouse was opened. The 15,000-square-foot clubhouse is complete with a full service pro shop, a restaurant and a banquet facility. The views from the patio are second to none, with almost every hole being visible from the balcony. Dan Koester, who is in his eighth year as Director of Golf at the University Golf Course, sees the Las Cruces area as a hidden gem when it comes to weather. Temperatures in the mid-60s during the winter months and mid-90s in the summer make for outstanding playing conditions throughout the year.

3000 Champions Drive, Las Cruces NM
(505) 646-3219
www.nmsu.edu/~golf

238 • Restaurants & Cafés

Hiking at the Gila Cliff Dwellings; homes of people of the Mogollon culture who lived in the Gila Wilderness from the 1280s to the early 1300s. Some believe the word "Gila" was derived from a Spanish contraction of "Hah-quah-sa-eel," a Yuma Indian word meaning "running water which is salty." The Gila National Forest is a designated wilderness area.
Photo courtesy of the New Mexico Tourism Department

Restaurants & Cafés

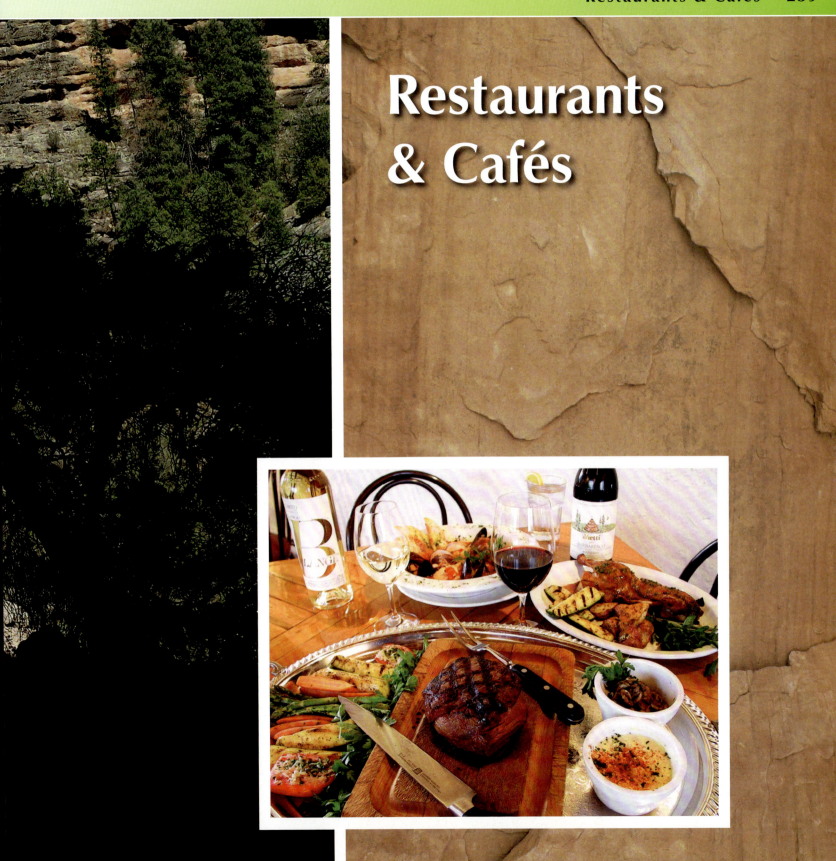

photo by Shelley Mathis

Kelly's Brew Pub

The handcrafted microbrews, the food and the welcome are some of the top reasons for a decade of success enjoyed by Kelly's Brew Pub in Nob Hill. Kelly's Brew Pub has 20 of its handcrafted beers on tap. The pub is friendly to families, businesses and even dogs. Yes, that's right; the outdoor patio welcomes all dogs, a rare find for dog lovers. Canine cuisine is offered on the regular menu, so both you and your dog can feast together. Owners Dennis and Janice Bonfantine run their business in this relaxed, forward-thinking manner, which greatly pleases their patrons. Try their fish tacos with rice and beans or the Reuben sandwich with fries or salad. For dinner, indulge in a fresh fillet of salmon. A choice of house wines and Kelly's pints make fitting accompaniments to your meal. The University of New Mexico's *Daily Lobo* newspaper honored Kelly's with an award for Best Beer Selection, and the weekly *Alibi* newspaper named it Best Brew Pub for three consecutive years. The pub also earned an award from Albuquerque Conservation Association for the restoration and renovation of the former Jones Motor Company building, a tribute to Albuquerque's past and the beginning of a new era for this respected pub. Kelly's can seat more than 100 at one time. You can even call ahead to brew your own beer as part of a party or business gathering at Kelly's. Visit Kelly's Brew Pub for handcrafted beers, great food and friendly surroundings.

3222 Central Avenue SE, Albuquerque NM
(505) 262-BREW (2739)
www.kellysbrewpub.com

Barry's Oasis

Barry's Oasis provides an ample choice of tastes for any palate with an exciting selection of dishes from Spain, Italy and Greece. The choice widens still further with French, American and vegetarian selections. Barry is famous for his lamb dishes, and if you are a lover of this luscious meat, you will find lamb prepared in the styles of many countries. Greek classics at Barry's include moussaka, pastitso and shish-kabob. Italian food lovers might single out the lamb and feta lasagna or shrimp scampi. Spanish temptations include paella or sautéed fish in an almond sauce. Seafood crepes or a juicy Chateaubriand steak can make you think of Paris. The owner and chef at Barry's Oasis, who calls himself simply Barry, has been serving up his global cuisine for 27 years. His loyal following includes third-generation Albuquerque patrons who now frequent a place that has been satisfying their grandparents for many years. Barry's offers an international beer and wine list to complement your dinner choice and desserts made by Barry himself. Barry wants you to relax and enjoy his first-rate food in comfortable clothing. Skip the plane fare and the new wardrobe: Let Barry's Oasis takes your taste buds on a trip around the world.

4451 Osuna NE, Albuquerque NM
(505) 884-2324
www.barrysoasis.com

The St. James Tearoom

In the midst of Albuquerque, a British tearoom offers four-star food, ambience, grace, civility, beauty and excellence. Mary Alice Higbie is the gifted proprietress of this classy endeavor. It was Mary Alice who instituted the Tea Exuberance Society. This club brings a new tea into your home each month, along with a tried-and-true St. James Tearoom recipe. The Exuberance starter kit provides all of the items needed to create a traditional pot of tea. When taking tea at the St. James Tearoom, guests repose in cozy corners fashioned in the English style and named for various English locations. Bannockburn, one of the larger seating choices, accommodates eight and was named for the land where the Scots routed the English army in 1314. Various seating arrangements provide room for three to 12 guests. Full afternoon tea is served on a three-tiered serving tray. This indulgent meal is meant to be savored in slow, serene comfort. All of the tea sandwiches, scones, sweets, desserts and breads are handmade on-site by the expert chef. Specialty loose teas can be purchased to bring a functional memento of the experience home with you. Reserve The St. James Tearoom for an intimate visit with friends or family, for a refreshing change of pace.

901 Rio Grande NE, Suite E-130, Albuquerque NM
(505) 242-3752
www.stjamestearoom.com

Casa de Benavidez

Casa de Benavidez, with its award-winning New Mexican cuisine, beautiful gardens and strolling musicians, has been pleasing Albuquerque patrons for more than 26 years. Yet there was a time when this family-owned and operated restaurant was little more than a dream for founders Paul and Rita Benavidez. Paul and Rita began their dream with a tiny carryout business featuring only three tables. Their daughter Paula worked full time with the couple, and their sons Paul Jr., Mark and Glenn helped out in their free time. Their business, called El Mexicana, became increasingly popular, in part due to the renown of their trademarked Sopaipilla Burger. Twenty-six years ago, they outgrow their tiny beginnings and moved into a 100-year-old house about a mile from their original location. There was a half-finished fountain to the south of the two-story structure and a back section perfect for the take-out business. With carryout flourishing once again, the Benavidez family launched the full-service Casa de Benavidez restaurant, managed today by Paul Jr., Mark and Paula. Casa de Benavidez epitomizes flavorful New Mexican fare, with red and green chile made from freshly roasted peppers. They've won three KOB-TV People's Choice awards for Best Burrito and Best New Mexican Food in Albuquerque, and Best Salsa in New Mexico. Their restaurant features casual dining in delightful surroundings and one of the most beautiful patios in all of New Mexico. Visit Casa de Benavidez and taste for yourself the flavors that put New Mexico cooking in a class by itself.

8032 4th Street NW, Albuquerque NM
(505) 898-3311

El Pinto Foods

Enjoy 42 years of tradition with El Pinto Foods. Located in Albuquerque, this family-run company serves up a true taste of the Southwest. John and Jim Thomas have brought new techniques and technologies to the original recipes of old El Pinto. El Pinto Foods has been the recipient of many awards, including 13 national and nine statewide awards and the coveted Scovie award. Specializing in homemade salsas and packed chiles, the family continues to use only the specially grown and cultivated chiles of the Hatch Valley. Freshly flame roasted and hand peeled, one bite of these spicy favorites will give you a taste of the true flavor of New Mexico. El Pinto Foods produces more than 5,000 jars of product per day using state-of-the-art machinery and bottling processes. It's so good that President George W. Bush, Jr. named El Pinto salsa the official salsa of the White House. El Pinto distributes its products to 2,800 grocers throughout the western United States in conjunction with a website that offers recipes and online purchasing options. For instant gratification, stop in to El Pinto Restaurant, where delicious in-house or take-out meals feature El Pinto products. For traditional Southwestern fare, start with El Pinto Foods.

10500 4th Street NW, Albuquerque NM
(505) 898-1771
www.elpinto.com

El Pinto Restaurant

For more than 40 years, the Thomas family has been serving up traditional New Mexico dishes for the residents of Albuquerque. Featuring recipes from their grandmother Josephina Chavez-Griggs, Jim and John Thomas provide tasty Southwestern favorites that will keep you coming back for more. The stunning restaurant complex holds several dining rooms, along with charming patios that offer scenic views of the North Valley. The focus of this family-run business is to provide good food and a cheerful atmosphere. The very patron-oriented El Pinto can also help you celebrate a special event. The incredible grounds serve as the perfect backdrop for weddings, family reunions, corporate events or other special occasions. The staff will assist you with menu selections and special event coordination. Whether you are planning a big celebration or just stopping in for a quiet dinner, El Pinto can meet your needs. Enjoy flavorful entrées like the house specialty chile con carne enchiladas served with succulent pork and marinated in El Pinto's fresh red chiles. Tostadas, tacos, burritos and rellenos are just a few more of the spicy delicacies that await you. If you're in a hurry or want to pick up something to go, El Pinto has an extensive take-out menu that includes packs of rellenos and burritos sold by the dozen and jars of El Pinto's popular salsas and chiles. For a true taste of New Mexico dine at El Pinto Restaurant.

10500 4th Street NW, Albuquerque NM
(505) 898-1771   www.elpinto.com

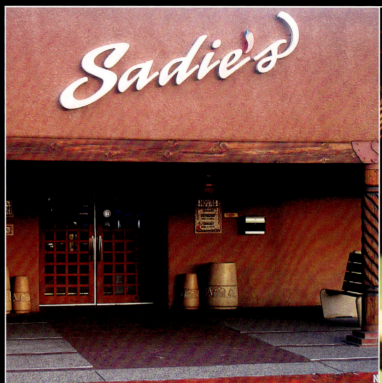

Sadie's Restaurant of New Mexico

Sadie Koury opened the doors of her first restaurant in 1954. The diner seated only nine customers then. The burgers were good and eventually led to bigger and better facilities. Sadie's restaurant now seats 375 and has served diners from Howard Hughes and Bill Clinton to members of the Red Hot Chili Peppers and Van Halen, as well as local townspeople and travelers who are happy to have found this treasure. Sadie passed away in 1986, but she would be proud of the way her family carries on the tradition. Sadie's younger sister, Betty Jo, and her husband Bob Stafford, their children William and Brian and grandsons Isaac and Nicolas are all important members of the operation. Together they provide the excellent New Mexican cuisine and incredible salsa that has made Sadie's Restaurant famous. Sadie's website has expanded the tradition of quality to a wider area, with a variety of award-winning fresh salsas, all made with New Mexico chiles and jalapeños, as well as chips and frozen tamales available for shipping. Bring them to your next event by utilizing their party and catering services with a menu custom-tailored for your occasion. Sadie's serves items as varied as prime rib, chile-crusted rack of pork, prime rib and their renowned burgers and enchiladas. Try anything and you're sure to be back for more.

6230 4th Street NW, Albuquerque NM
(505) 345-5339
www.sadiessalsa.com

Restaurants & Cafés • 247

Sandia Peak Tramway

The 10,378-foot Sandia Peak behind Albuquerque exists due to intense seismic activity in the area millions of years ago that caused the earth's crust to rise well above the surrounding flats. Today you can explore the beauty of this geologic wonder from the Sandia Peak Tramway, the world's longest aerial tramway. The tram was put in motion by Ben Abruzzo and Robert J. Nordhaus and made its first run in May 1966. Sandia Peak Tram Company, with Louis Abruzzo as president, continues to operate and maintain the tram, called a double reversible jigback aerial tramway, meaning that while one car is ascending, the other is descending. The tram takes about 15 minutes to ascend 4,000 feet to the peak and runs at an operating speed of 12 miles per hour. Each of the two cars is equipped to transport 50 passengers, and the cars' expansive windows treat riders to spectacular views as they lift above the desert to canyons and forests on the 2.7-mile sky ride. Skiers and hikers can start a day of adventure from the tramway. Sandia Peak Tramway offers two distinctive dining venues, owned and operated by Russ Zeigler and Doug Smith. Located in the lower tram terminal is Sandiago's Mexican Grill, featuring traditional New Mexican cuisine and oversized, handcrafted margaritas. High Finance Restaurant and Tavern perches atop the peak and specializes in steaks and seafood. Experience everything from a warm welcome and exceptional dining to incredible views and outdoor recreation at Sandia Peak Tramway.

10 Tramway Loop NE, Albuquerque NM
(505) 856-7325
www.sandiapeak.com

Casa Vieja

Bored rigid with the ever-increasing number of interchangeable, characterless restaurant chains? Casa Vieja restaurant and bar provides the antidote. Just off the beaten path, sandwiched between Albuquerque, Rio Rancho and the Rio Grande, scenic Corrales is where you'll find Casa Vieja. Location isn't the only thing that sets this eclectic, Southwestern bistro-style eatery apart. It's been owned and operated by husband-and-wife team Rebecca and Nick Carter since July 2005, and by blending their international culinary heritage, English expertise and love of simple, natural foods, they have created a masterly merger of tastes and textures. The menus combine rustic character with European influences enriched with quality ingredients and flavors. Casa Vieja is an adobe hacienda that is one of the oldest buildings in scenic Corrales. Casa Vieja has 14 rooms and six working fireplaces. Over the years, Casa Vieja has served as a stagecoach stop, a military headquarters, a courthouse, headquarters for a US cavalry unit, a tuberculosis clinic and a nudist colony. It has been a restaurant and bar since 1970. Casa Vieja is open for lunch and dinner every day and serves brunch on Sundays. For lunch a mix of sandwiches, soups, salads and New Mexican dishes are offered. Dinner brings an extensive menu, including more formal Southwestern dishes and a range of meat and fish grill dishes with a European influence. Both menus are available all day and into the evening. Casa Vieja has four rooms available for dining, in addition to the bar and large patio, which is open in the summer months. Private functions can take place for up to 50 guests and exclusive menus can be arranged. Service at Casa Vieja is as friendly and welcoming as it is professional. In the tradition of the Southwest, the dining experience is informal and friendly. For the perfect balance of exceptional food and service presented in intimate, elegant surroundings, visit Casa Vieja.

4541 Corrales Road, Corrales NM
(505) 898-7489

Annapurna Ayurvedic Cuisine & Chai House

In India, Annapurna is the goddess of food and nourishment. In Sanskrit it literally means *complete food*. Annapurna Ayurvedic Cuisine & Chai House is a vegetarian restaurant dedicated to combining delicious food with the philosophy of preventative health and the healing energy found in food. All their food is organic and locally grown, and the menu changes daily according to the day's planetary ruler. Not only is the menu completely vegetarian, many dishes are vegan, and dishes can cater to any kind of food allergy and bring balance to your entire being. Annapurna creates a peaceful environment in which to enjoy this wholesome food. Vegetables are used in many tasty combinations with basmati rice or rice noodles with tofu or flatbread. There is also a daily selection of fresh-baked pastries, tarts, crumbles and ladus. Many desserts are vegan and wheat or egg free. The beverage menu has an immense selection of imported teas, including chai made just as they do in India, as well as fresh smoothies and yogurt and mango lassi. Annapurna also imports traditional Indian clothing, art and antiques for their store. They provide individualized dietary consultations and can cater a variety of functions. The wild success of Annapurna in Albuquerque has led to the opening of a second location in Santa Fe. Discover the healing art of eating well at Annapurna Ayurvedic Cuisine & Chai House.

2201 Silver Street SE, Albuquerque NM
(505) 262-2424
905 W Alameda, Santa Fe NM
(505) 988-9688
www.999dine.com/nm/annapurna/Index.html

Church Street Café

After nearly 300 years as a private residence belonging to the same family, Casa de Ruiz became the Church Street Café. Marie Coleman purchased the ancient dwelling, located in Albuquerque's historic Old Town, and opened a restaurant here in 1990. Church Street Café, serving authentic northern New Mexico fare, may well be the oldest standing former residence in New Mexico. The walls of this early 16th century home are in some places two feet thick for warmth in winter and coolness in summer. With features like this, it's no wonder that Church Street Café has been featured on the Travel Channel's *Ghosts of New Mexico*, in the *Albuquerque Journal, Hispanic Magazine* and *Sunset*. No matter what time of day you choose to visit this café, you'll find something to intrigue your taste buds. Breakfast includes classics like *carne adovada y huevos*, which is oven-cooked pork marinated in red chile with eggs. Luncheon soups and sandwiches also have a distinct northern New Mexico signature. Look for thinly sliced roast beef served with a red chili dip and bowls of posole and menudo. Begin dinner with appetizers like *chicharrones* (fried cubed pork) or deluxe nachos, then go on to enjoy a handmade tamale plate, old-fashioned chile rellenos or one of the vegetarian entrées. Take home a jar of salsa, also available on the website. Let a centuries-old dwelling and the special flavors of northern New Mexico work wonders on your appetite and spirit at Church Street Café.

2111 Church Street NW, Albuquerque NM
(505) 247-8522
www.churchstreetcafe.com

Village Pizza

If you love pizza, saddle up and ride over to Village Pizza in Corrales. This family-owned business is a must-stop for any serious pizza lover. Greg Davidson and his father, Paul, will make your visit to this one-of-a-kind pizza parlor one you'll want to share with all of your friends, especially if they wear chaps, because the Davidson's offer a 10-percent discount to anyone who rides in on horseback. Even if you decide to drive a boring old car, you'll be happy you went. The extensive menu at Village Pizza offers both thick and thin-crust pizza, gourmet soups, good old fashioned pasta, and many other tastes

of Italy. Add the word gourmet to the mix and you get an idea of why this family-owned pizza place is a Corrales favorite. Many of the fresh ingredients come from local farms, and each pizza is generously portioned. Indulge yourself with a pie covered in zesty artichoke hearts, fresh mushrooms and pine nuts. Regardless of what you order, Greg and Paul will give you a pizza worth remembering. Head to Village Pizza, a place where old favorites take on a whole new meaning.

**4266 Corrales Road, Corrales NM
(505) 898-0045**

Pinon Café

Protectively spreading its extensive branches, like the majestic conifer it is named for, Pinon Café takes exceptional pride in its community. John Franklin and Mark Bustamate have spent years carving themselves and their café a tidy niche in local lore. Their most important idcals are met by satisfying guests with home cooking and a strong family atmosphere, cultivating a loyal clientele and taking an active part in many local charity programs and the community. Their breakfasts are well known and well loved.

Whether you're there to enjoy a scrumptious breakfast, a light lunch or an extensive dinner, they will strive to satisfy your hunger and cater to your preferences. They even have a complete vegetarian menu available for those with special dietary needs. The hearty food is so delicious, you may want to grab a bite for take-out as you continue on your way. You may even express the desire to have them assist you with your private party or catering needs. Any day of the week is a good time to stop by Pinon Café. Come see why they've been featured in multiple articles for their success.

**221 Highway 165, Suite D, Placitas NM
(505) 771-1700
www.pinoncafe.com**

Teofilo's Restaurante

Teofilo's Restaurante is a blend of historical importance, family tradition and delicious food. When Pete and Hortencia Torres purchased the house that would become their family restaurant, they were unaware of its history. The house was the home of the first doctor and doctor's office in Los Lunas. Dr. Wittwer was on his way to El Paso in 1899 when he first stopped in Los Lunas, and the house was built for the doctor and his family 15 years after his arrival. He practiced medicine and lived in the house until his death in 1964. Several different families lived in the house until the Torres family found it and decided to restore it and open a restaurant. The Torres were able to keep some of the original fixtures in the building, including the light fixtures. They found several pieces of furniture the doctor had left behind, including a tall wooden chest where he kept his medical instruments, which now sits in the restaurant's lobby. The biggest treasures of all are the two original murals that were painted by Dr. Wittwer's daughter Fanny Bell. These beautiful paintings have been preserved and protected. Teofilo's Restaurante is not only known for its historical building, but also for its authentic New Mexican cuisine. Joelle Torres and Johannah Torres are the daughters of Pete and Hortencia and have kept their traditional family values and cooking alive in their enchiladas, sopaipillas and tacos with red sauce. For a delicious taste of history and New Mexican cuisine, visit Teofilo's Restaurante.

144 Main Street, Los Lunas NM
(505) 865-5511

Rancho de Chimayó Restaurante

Rancho de Chimayó Restaurante in Chimayó, housed in the family home of Arturo Jaramillo, has been serving superior New Mexican cuisine since 1965. The restaurant idea came to Arturo and his wife, Florence, after they became disturbed by the economic changes they saw happening in Arturo's hometown of Chimayó. Taking a cue from Colonial preservation efforts in the South, they hit upon the idea of creating a historic community of their own. In 1959, the Jaramillos inherited a portion of Arturo's grandfather's ranch and were able to purchase the rest from the other inheriting family members. After two years of extensive renovations, the stunning adobe home was ready for business. Opening in the fall of 1965, the restaurant struggled for many years, primarily due to its rural location and exotic menu. The Jaramillos served the same foods that Arturo had grown up on: fiery, flavorful dishes that non-New Mexico natives weren't always comfortable with. Florence ended up taking jobs outside of the restaurant to support her family and did the shopping herself for all of the restaurant's supplies, since no one delivered to Chimayó. Perseverance won out, and by 1971 Rancho de Chimayó was well on its way to fame. Today this inviting restaurant draws customers from several states and has been given accolades by some of the most popular and famous food critics. Forty years later, the restaurant still lives up to its original mission of preserving the early New Mexican way of life. So come, eat and meet the family at Rancho de Chimayó Restaurante.

Santa Fe County Road 98, Drive 300, Chimayó NM
(505) 351-4444 or (505) 984-2100 www.ranchodechimayo.com

Orlando's New Mexican Café

Intrepid entrepreneurs Orlando and Yvette Ortega opened Orlando's New Mexican Café in 1995. Orlando's has become one of the most popular area eateries and for 10 years, its red and green chile sauces have been voted best in Taos. Orlando came to Taos from the Pacific Northwest when his parents went to work there as members of the Park Service. After high school, he began his restaurant career with a vendor's cart selling hot dogs and burritos. Later, he met Yvette. They married and began to plan for a restaurant of their own. Plans quickly became reality, and a fabulous café was born. Orlando's grandmother, Delfina, at his request, created a meatless red chile sauce that is now an award-winning recipe. Orlando's sister Roberta helps manage the restaurant, and Orlando's mother Flora still pitches in to help over vacations. Orlando's New Mexican Café focuses on northern New Mexican cuisine with many savory and flavorful dishes, such as smothered chicken or beef burritos, blue corn cheese enchiladas and Baja-style fish tacos. Orlando's also features that Southwestern favorite, Frito pie, which consists of a large helping of Fritos® corn chips covered in beans, lettuce, tomatoes, beef or chicken and topped with green, red or chile caribe. For dessert, the café offers a wonderful selection of traditional treats, including flan, biscochitos, frozen avocadolie and apple pie. It also has a choice selection of teas, beers and wines. Enjoy all the tantalizing flavors of New Mexico at Orlando's New Mexican Café.

1114 Don Juan Valdez Lane, El Prado NM
(505) 751-1450

Back Road Pizza

Back Road Pizza exemplifies why they call Santa Fe the City Different. Where else can you enjoy great pizza while watching a cabaret show? Cabaret comes to Back Road Pizza once a month, while Back Road features live music every weekend. You will find pool tables upstairs, so drop by and make yourself at home. Owners Piper Kapin and Robin Hardie are proud that their restaurant earned Best of Santa Fe recognition in 2004 and 2005. They make all of their pizzas from scratch, including the popular New Mexican, topped with green chile, and the Gerald, featuring fresh spinach, Roma tomatoes, feta cheese and pesto. Piper describes their thin crust as, "New York-style pizzas with a Santa Fe twist." You won't find another bruschetta like the one at Back Road Pizza, because it's made from a family recipe. Back Road is known for its delicious subs, too, all of which are stone baked to perfection and served with a salad. The veggie sub typifies the Back Road policy of using locally grown ingredients when available. The chicken on the pizzas and in the subs is free of chemicals. It's as if Piper and Robin studied the model for a successful pizza place and then challenged themselves to do theirs differently—and better. If you're looking for a fun and lively place to eat which embodies the spirit of Santa Fe, try Back Road Pizza.

1807 Second Street #1, Santa Fe NM
(505) 955-9055
www.backroadpizza.com

Photos by S.M. Stachler

Stakeout Grill & Bar

"More than a restaurant, it's an adventure!" is the motto at the Stakeout Grill & Bar. The Stakeout is located on top of historic Outlaw Hill on the original Santa Fe Trail. This location is the site of an ancient Taos Native American burial ground, even older than Taos Pueblo, the oldest known continually inhabited dwelling place in North America. Desperados and those on the run could perch here and see any approaching adversaries for miles around with good avenues of escape and a loop for ambushes. The entire Taos Valley, up to 80 miles away, can be seen from the restaurant. It is close to the gorge, a popular retreat for summer activities like fishing, swimming and rafting. Beautiful pinyon, juniper and aspen trees grow on the hill. Chef and owner Mauro Bettini began his study of culinary arts as an apprentice at the age of 14. His mastery and skill with risotto and oysters Rockefeller is a hilltop legend. The Stakeout coldwater lobster and tender filet, fish or steak brandy flambé are all items that must not be missed. The fascinating history, captivating views, overwhelming atmosphere and outstanding dining provide plenty of reasons to stake a claim at Stakeout Grill & Bar for your next meal.

101 Stakeout Drive, Ranchos de Taos NM
(505) 758-2042
www.stakeoutrestaurant.com

Café Des Artistes

Owner, chef, cashier and chief bottle washer Jean-Jacques DeSalle has a gem of a restaurant tucked away on the popular Canyon Road in Santa Fe. Café Des Artistes is a quaint, year round restaurant that features fabulous, fresh fare full of French flair. Jean-Jacques, with his native French accent and dashing personality, purchased the eatery from a friend in 2001. Café Des Artistes has quickly become established as a community favorite. Café Des Artistes caters to an eclectic crowd of locals and international clientele. In true French style, the café offers outdoor seating, French music in the background and, just for fun, flamenco and Middle Eastern dancing. Jean-Jacques offers a great selection of gourmet salads, sandwiches and desserts. All of the restaurant's cookies and cakes are made on-site and include wonderful treats such as oatmeal-cranberry cookies and feather light chocolate-amaretto bundt cake. It also has a fine selection of specialty coffee drinks, imported beers and French wines. This exquisite French café has an adjacent gallery called Elysee Fine Art and Jewelry that displays artistic metal furniture with an emphasis on natural elements and sophisticated elegance. The gallery houses contemporary paintings, sculptures, and designer jewelry in 18 and 22-karat gold set with ancient gems. Enjoy beautiful art, an inviting ambience and a taste of the Old World at Café Des Artistes.

223 B Canyon Road, Santa Fe NM
(505) 820-2535

Cowgirl BBQ & Western Grill

For casual dining with a Western theme, it's hard to beat the Cowgirl BBQ & Western Grill. A Santa Fe hot spot with a lively atmosphere and first-rate service, the restaurant pays homage to the American Cowgirl in its food and style. Located near the historic Plaza, the Cowgirl serves lunch, dinner and weekend brunch, while providing live entertainment every night from local artists and traveling groups. The Cowgirl is a meeting place for Santa Fe residents with a full bar featuring legendary Frozen Margaritas, as well as pool tables on the premises. The Cowgirl's signature barbecue specialties include tender, mesquite-smoked ribs, brisket, and chicken, plus game burgers made from a mixture of elk, buffalo and venison. Chef Patrick Lambert adds seasonal specials ranging from a Cajun-Creole menu and Oktoberfest bratwurst, to savory seafood dishes like seared scallops or mahi tacos. Outdoor dining is available on the patio, and the Mustang room can be reserved for private parties. Diners with children get kid-friendly perks like a seasonal outdoor play area and an engaging children's menu with buckets of crayons. Full service catering completes the picture. Try a different take on the taste of the new West at the Cowgirl BBQ & Western Grill.

319 S Guadalupe Street, Santa Fe NM
(505) 982-2565
www.cowgirlsantafe.com

Maria's New Mexican Kitchen

Everybody in Santa Fe comes to Maria's. Some come for the Margaritas, some for the food and many for both. Whatever the draw, Maria's New Mexican Kitchen is a Santa Fe tradition. Maria's has more than 100 *real* Margaritas. These must contain Tequila certified by the Mexican government, triple-sec liqueur with all-natural ingredients, and fresh-squeezed juice. A bartender shakes them by hand. (Maria's does offer excellent frozen-style fruit concoctions made in a blender, but refuses to call them Margaritas.) Local readers have voted Maria's Margaritas the best in town again and again. Owner Al Lucero has written a book to share the recipes, *The Great Margarita Book*. The Mexican dinners at Maria's taste marvelous, yet the restaurant is unpretentious. Dinners have an average price of only $8.50. Specialties include traditional fajitas, rellenos, steak served with green chile, and dozens of other choices. A Santa Fe classic is the blue corn enchiladas with lean ground beef, cheese and red or green chile. Vegetarians take note: the refried beans are lard-free. The fame of the Margaritas causes many people to overlook Maria's great wine list. Maria's began in 1952 when Maria and Gilbert Lopez started a small take-out in the area that now houses the bar and kitchen. Laurie and Al Lucero bought the restaurant in 1985 and have striven to maintain its Old Santa Fe charm and hospitality. Strolling mariachis perform regularly. For a truly satisfying evening, dine at Maria's New Mexican Kitchen.

555 W Cordova Road, Santa Fe NM
(505) 983-7929
www.marias-santafe.com

Photo by Tara Hunt

San Francisco Street Bar & Grill and Santa Fe Bar & Grill

In 1985, Robert Day looked around the downtown district of Santa Fe and saw the need for a casual, workingman's eatery that served great food and stayed open late. He creatively filled that need with the San Francisco Street Bar & Grill. Success was immediate and continued to boom through the late 1980s. In 2002, the restaurant closed for 18 months before reopening in grand style just half a block away in a new 5,000-square-foot location. The revival was for the best, and today the San Francisco Street Bar & Grill still offers the same terrific cuisine that made it popular more than 20 years ago when it first opened its doors. The restaurant offers a fabulous selection of American-influenced dishes like fresh grilled ruby trout and hamburgers so delicious that both *Esquire* magazine and the *Santa Fe Register* have named them the Best Burgers in Town. In June 2002, Robert opened a second location in the DeVargas Mall and dubbed it the Santa Fe Bar & Grill. In this location he wanted to provide patrons with cuisine that was native to the area, so the new grill features contemporary interpretations of Southwestern favorites like Santa Fe rotisserie chicken and blue corn enchiladas. Both locations offer freshly made soups and salads that burst with flavor at every bite, including Cobb salad and tortilla soup. Experience a dining adventure that goes beyond the pale at the San Francisco Street Bar & Grill or Santa Fe Bar & Grill.

50 E San Francisco Street, Santa Fe NM
(San Francisco Street Bar & Grill)
(505) 982-2044
www.sanfranbargrill.com
187 Paseo de Peralta, Santa Fe NM
(Santa Fe Bar & Grill)
(505) 982-3033
www.santafebargrill.com

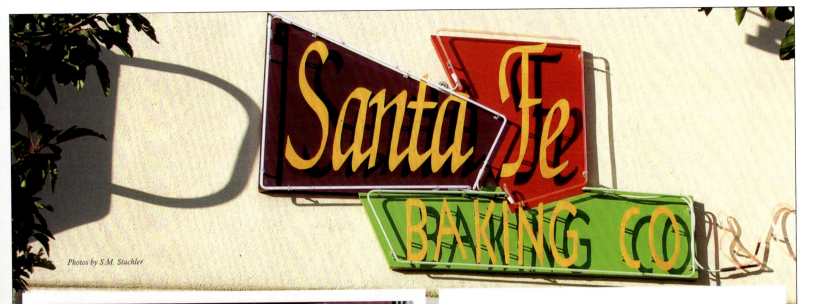

Photos by S.M. Stachler

Santa Fe Baking Company and Café

Brothers Eric, Steve and Kevin Struck offer a winning combination of great food and good prices in an atmosphere that keeps locals coming back and visitors feeling like old friends at the Santa Fe Baking Company and Café. The brothers purchased an existing coffee bar in 1998 and added the restaurant, where diners order heaps of great food without spending much. Enjoy breakfast all day, including the award-winning breakfast burrito, a flour tortilla stuffed full of scrambled eggs, cheese and fried potatoes with a few chile peppers thrown in. The lunch menu offers a choice of burgers, wraps and salads with several vegetarian options. Four house-blend coffees go well with any meal, or ask for your favorite espresso drink. Fruit smoothies and freshly squeezed juice provide a healthful and satisfying snack. The Struck brothers encourage a sense of community at the little café, and have created a place where people feel comfortable to gather. Each weekday morning, Santa Fe public radio station KSFR broadcasts live, giving people a chance to speak their minds about local happenings. Check your email via the free wireless Internet or take a look at the latest pieces on display from local artists. Musician Gerry Carthy plays traditional Irish tunes each Saturday morning. Head over to the Santa Fe Baking Company and Café for flavorful food and great company.

504 W Cordova Road, Santa Fe NM
(505) 988-4292
www.santafebakingcompanycafe.com

Santa Fe Brewing Company

The oldest microbrewery in New Mexico will certainly make a beer lover happy. Santa Fe Brewing Company is ready to make entire families happy, as well, with a new pub and grill next door, a kid's playroom and indoor and outdoor bars featuring at least eight beers, including the company's flagship pale ale. Santa Fe Brewing Company came to the attention of the New Mexico State Fair and the Great American Beer Festival shortly after opening in 1988. Today, the company can boast of many award-winning brews, including the Santa Fe Wheat and Nut Brown, along with the State Pen Porter and the Sangre de Frambusa. All beers are made from the finest hops shipped directly from Washington growers, and specialty malts imported from the United Kingdom. The beers, made without preservatives or pasteurization, are conditioned in the bottle, creating natural carbonization and a rich, complex taste. Call ahead for a Saturday tour or stop by the tasting room Tuesday through Saturday. The new Pub & Grill can treat you to the company's microbrews, as well as breakfast, lunch or dinner seven days a week. Live music, pool tables and a patio add to the fun. Kids can choose from a menu of their favorites, including the largest assortment of Taos Cow ice cream in Santa Fe. The restaurant can be rented for a party or conference. Catering services range from appetizers to elaborate main dishes. For memorable beers served in a casual, non-smoking environment, visit Santa Fe Brewing Company.

27 and 35 Fire Place, Santa Fe NM
(505) 424-3333
www.santafebrewing.com

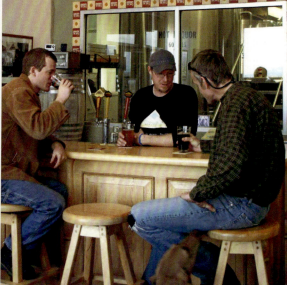

Steaksmith at El Gancho

Since 1973, the Steaksmith at El Gancho has been creating a reputation for excellence. They accomplish this by offering the finest quality aged beef and perfectly prepared seafood, while maintaining praiseworthy service levels in a cozy and comfortable atmosphere. Herb Cohen and several associates established this popular restaurant, which became an immediate hit at its original location in the former De Vargas Hotel. In 1988, when the building was purchased by new owners and renamed the St. Francis, Cohen moved to semi-rural El Gancho and dubbed his restaurant Steaksmith at El Gancho. Today the Steaksmith is thriving under the youthful energy of Tom Vimont, Herb's new partner and former manager of the restaurant. Vimont and 10-year general manager Thomas "Tupper" Schoen are consummate restaurateurs who are attentive to detail and love what they do. Open for dinner only, the menu features an adventurous range of delicious items that will suit nearly everyone's tastes. The appetizer selection features a wide range of American and internationally influenced tidbits, such as Asian-style yellowfin tuna, ceviche and New York-style chicken wings. Follow your appetizers with succulent entrées, including Alaskan king crab, perfectly prepared prime rib with all the trimmings, savory pork ribs and chicken dishes. Steaksmith at El Gancho is a family-friendly restaurant that still manages to maintain that special occasion feeling. Come see why Steaksmith at El Gancho has been a favorite for more than 30 years.

104 B Old Las Vegas Highway, Santa Fe NM
(505) 988-3333
www.santafesteaksmith.com

Tomasita's Restaurant

Tomasita's is a Santa Fe institution and the local favorite for New Mexican cuisine, over and over again receiving rave reviews from local newspapers and national magazines. Both the red and green chile have a well deserved following, and a wait for a table is an opportunity to enjoy a noteworthy margarita. The blue corn chicken and green chile enchiladas have been a standard here for more than 30 years, and the tortilla soup, with its traditional blend of posole, beans and chicken, has just the right level of spiciness. The Friday carne adovada is a standout. Tomasita's is named after the restaurant's first chef, Tomasita Leyba. Tomasita was a perfectionist who dressed as impeccably as she cooked and demanded absolute cleanliness in the kitchen. Long-time owner Georgia Maryol bought a little café in the early 1970s on the strength of Tomasita's cooking. Georgia then organized and promoted the business until people were standing in line to get in. She later moved to the larger quarters at the old railway station. Today, Georgia's cousin Ignatios Patsalis owns the restaurant and continues to honor Georgia and Tomasita with his menu. The restaurant welcomes children—and families appreciate the easy ambience here. Visit Tomasita's, and take your place in the legend.

**500 S Guadalupe Street,
Santa Fe NM
(505) 983-5721**

Photos by S.M. Stachler

Apple Tree Restaurant

When Richard Oakeley planted an apple tree in the backyard of his 1903 Taos home, he had no idea what a symbol the tree would become nearly a century later. In 1979, the Oakeley house began its transformation from residence to restaurant. Years later, the Apple Tree Restaurant's name stemmed from the humble planting and steady growth of that special tree. It still grows where it was planted so long ago, but it is now in the patio and the centerpiece of the restaurant. The apple tree adds a special element of delight to the dining experience, especially when it blooms each spring. Owners Angela and Tony March carefully select quality local vegetables and chemical-free meats as part of their dedication to offering only the best quality and taste to their patrons. They are environmentally conscious and recycle everything that can be recycled. Seasonal favorites such as mango chicken enchiladas are made from scratch and delicious steaks are prepared and offered at extremely reasonable prices. Not only is Apple Tree Restaurant known for its great steak value, it's considered by many to be the finest casual dining experience in Taos. Located one block north of the plaza in the picturesque Bent Street district, Apple Tree Restaurant invites you to delight in carefully prepared cuisine within sight of a beautiful and inspirational apple tree.

123 Bent Street, Taos NM
(505) 758-1900
www.appletreerestaurant.com

The Bean

A great cup of coffee doesn't just happen, it's created. At The Bean, greatness begins with the best beans from around the world that are locally roasted, creating the freshest bean-to-cup experience. This popular community hot spot is owned by Berni Patera, who purchased the eight-year-old business in 2004. Berni masterfully produces excellent made-from-scratch soups, breads, chili, salsas and more. Even the hamburger buns are skillfully handmade on-site by Berni. With two locations in Taos, her coffee houses have quickly become the destination for a perfect cup of coffee and great food. The Bean has been named in *The Best of Taos County* for the past eight years. The Bean serves up a diverse menu of traditional favorites and tasty contemporary dishes. In the morning you can treat yourself to welcoming breakfast entrées such as freshly baked croissants with scrambled eggs, omelets, oatmeal pancakes, breakfast burritos or an assortment of pastries baked daily at their in-house bakery. The lunch menu includes burgers, wraps, sandwiches, homemade soups and varied Mexican dishes, which all feature freshly made-from-scratch salsas and chili. The menu also features fresh salads, bagels with assorted spreads, and a spectacular selection of coffees from around the world. The Bean is home to the New Grounds Gallery, featuring the works of local artists. At the north side location wireless Internet is available. The Bean offers a unique experience with every visit. Come for the brew, stay for the food.

900 Paseo del Pueblo Norte, Taos NM
1033 Paseo del Pueblo Sur #J, Taos NM
(505) 758-5123
www.thebeantaos.com

WilLee's Blues Club

After more than 25 years of life in Santa Fe, it can be said that Wil and Lee, owners of WilLee's Blues Club, have their fingers on the pulse of the town. Wil and Lee draw on their combined experiences and love of music to create a sublime blend of sounds and sights while fulfilling the club's promise of intimacy with ambience. Their knowledge of the bar business, the town and the desires of local customers and visitors makes this club one of Old Santa Fe's hottest venues for live music. WilLee's Blues Club presents local and national acts throughout the year. You'll discover an entrancing mix of musical styles, including the sultry smoothness of the blues with soul influences, Latin sounds, light rock and the varied styles of Austin, New Orleans and Chicago. Flanked by two full bars and offering both indoor and outdoor seating, it's no wonder that WilLee's Blues Club draws a crowd each evening. WilLee's Blues Club is just the right place to put yourself in tune with Santa Fe's distinctive beat.

401 S Guadalupe, Santa Fe NM
(505) 982-0117
www.willees.com

¡Bravo! Fine Wine, Foods & Spirits

Bravo is an Italian word that means brave, wild and excellent. ¡Bravo! Fine Wine, Foods & Spirits in Taos embodies a bit of all three definitions. In 1995, Owner Jo Ann Carolla braved opening a new style of business that combined both a restaurant and a retail package store under one roof. Her wild new concept got attention and garnered a reputation for excellence in service and product quality. ¡Bravo! houses the largest selection of microbrews and fine wines in northern New Mexico, and further carries an extensive variety of tequilas, single malt scotches and other popular spirits. Patrons of this spectacular eatery can choose any bottle of wine they fancy from the retail shelves and enjoy it on-site with their meal and never pay a corkage charge for opening the bottle. Another option is Flights of Wine or Flights of Beer, which offers guests four two-ounce servings of selected draughts or wines. Chef Lionel Garnier utilizes fresh, local products to create flavorful and exciting dining options. To start your meal or for a lighter snack, choose from the appetizer menu, which offers delicious nibbles like petite pizza au fromage and baby crab cakes. ¡Bravo! features daily homemade soups, flavorful salads and spectacular lunch and dinner entrées like Cajun catfish sandwiches, mesquite chicken quesadilla and the ¡Bravo! pizza du jour. ¡Bravo! is a non-smoking establishment, but smoking is allowed on the outdoor dining patio. Raise your glass in an appreciative toast to the excellence that awaits you at ¡Bravo! Fine Wine, Foods & Spirits.

1353-A Paseo del Pueblo Sur, Taos NM
(505) 758-8100
www.bravotaos.com

Rellenos Café by Antonio

Antonio and Sarah Matus shared the dream of someday owning their own restaurant, and realized that dream with the acclaimed Antonio's. They celebrated their success as restaurateurs by opening a second establishment, Rellenos Cafe by Antonio, located near the Plaza in Taos. Rellenos Cafe is the sister restaurant to Antonio's. It is walking distance from the Plaza, and provides an excellent location as well as fantastic food for the lunch-hour crowd. The café is the Matus' delicious way of giving something back to a community that has been good to them. Local workers can get a wonderful meal at a price they can afford. Also, businesses on or near the Plaza can take advantage of free delivery service. Menu favorites include the ever-popular enchiladas and chili rellenos en Nogada. Dishes are smothered in red or green chile, southwestern favorites. Such fare as their tempting tacos, satisfying ceviche and bountiful burgers await you. For a tasty bite on the go, or to savor every bite in comfort within the restaurant, stop by Rellenos Café. Rellenos Café serves lunch Monday through Saturday, 11 am to 3 pm and dinner from 5 to 9 pm.

135 Paseo del Pueblo Sur, Taos NM
(505) 758-7001
www.antoniosoftaos.com

Photo by S.M. Stachler

Roasted Clove

There is someone stirring an interesting flavor in Angel Fire. That someone is chef Thomas Bowles, owner of Roasted Clove. Thomas studied communication at DePauw University, spent three years in medical and telecommunications sales, and then realized that what he really needed to do was follow his passion. Luckily for his patrons, that passion is everything and anything culinary. He enrolled and graduated from Johnson and Wales University in Denver. Before joining the Roasted Clove crew and pursuing restaurant ownership, Thomas made his mark at Strings in Denver, McMurdo Station in Antarctica and worked at a private fly-fishing retreat near Steamboat Springs, where he spent his days cooking and fishing. Thomas' second passion is undoubtedly his love for the outdoors and his free time is generally spent fishing, skiing, snowboarding, hiking and rafting. Thomas also teaches cooking classes. The menu at the Roasted Clove is filled with savory, creative dishes that are pure inspiration and full of flavor. Favorites include pork tenderloin, crab portabella Napoleon and filet mignon. In addition to fabulous contemporary American cuisine, Thomas has selected more than 100 wines with which to pair your delicious food. While away a quiet evening while satisfying your inner epicurean with reservations at Roasted Clove. Enjoy dinner, catering or special events.

48 N Angel Fire Road, Angel Fire NM
(505) 377-0636
www.roastedclove.com

La Trattoria Italian Restaurant & Steakhouse

Edouard Waffelaert is the owner of La Trattoria Italian Restaurant & Steakhouse, which features northern Italian and French cuisine. At the age of 11, Edouard's calling to become a chef began in the foothills of the Pyrenees Mountains of southern France near the Mediterranean Sea. By the age of 16, he had served a rigorous apprenticeship in Perpignan, a place abundant with fresh fish, vegetables and fruit. After military duty, he moved to Paris to work with several master chefs. Edouard's American adventure began in New York, then continued in Santa Fe where he owned two restaurants. Since opening La Trattoria in Las Vegas, many faithful Santa Fe customers happily make the hour-plus drive for a masterfully prepared meal. Edouard works in conjunction with chef and advisor Luca Tossani to create an oft-changing menu featuring seasonally fresh ingredients. Specialties include a flavorful meat lasagna, and penne with a blend of four creamy traditional Italian cheeses in a decadent white sauce. Taste the delightful veal scaloppini in an apple brandy sauce, the classic rib eye steak flambé with cognac in a pepper and cream demi-glace, or savor the citron-stuffed rainbow trout with shrimp and lemon butter sauce. The warm atmosphere is not surprising considering Edouard loves talking with his patrons as well as serving fantastic food. Enjoy your next taste of Italy with a visit to La Trattoria Italian Restaurant & Steakhouse.

**500 Douglas Avenue, Las Vegas NM
(505) 425-3805**

Blackjack's Grill

Since 1997, Blackjack's Grill in Las Vegas has developed a reputation throughout the Southwest for serving fine food and wines in a charming Old World atmosphere. Blackjack's is definitely off the beaten track, but widespread word of mouth has put this little gem on the map. Executive chef and owner Lavinia Fenzi merges her international travels and cooking experience to bring together flavor, texture and color combinations that create savory yet straightforward fare. The basic menu at Blackjack's hasn't changed in years, a testimony to the influence that regulars have in keeping their favorites on the front burner. Timeless Italian classics, plus contemporary Southwestern and Western cowboy cuisine for the local ranchers are solid anchors on the menu. Daily specials take advantage of fresh seasonal ingredients and reflect an element of global fusion. This casual yet elegant dining oasis has been featured in *Gourmet* and *Food & Wine* magazines. Blackjack's invites you to try the seafood enchilada, which has received rave reviews, or any of its celebrated main courses, including margarita salmon, veal scallopini or filet mignon medallions with sherry butter sauce. A dinner at Blackjack's will be a memorable occasion.

1133 Grand Avenue, Las Vegas NM
(505) 425-6791
www.innonthesantafetrail.com

A side street in Santa Fe

Shopping

Lavande Bleu

Do you remember your first whiff of lavender? Do you recall how its soothing scent made you feel? The power of this herb is legendary and is the reason Amy Henne created Lavande Bleu, a shop devoted to all things lavender, along with other luxurious scents, to add a bit of elegance to your everyday life. The delightful scents of Lavande Bleu lure you from the sidewalk into this beautiful European-style gift boutique. You will discover the soothing scent of lavender in lotions and oils, soaps, candles, room fragrances and fabric fragrances for your fine washables. You'll find everything from biodegradable home-keeping products to beautiful night and loungewear in cotton and silk. Gorgeous baby gifts that will be the talk of the shower await you. Lavande Bleu makes it simple. Lavande Bleu's lavender confections have been featured on the Food Network's popular program, *Food Finds*. They include the legendary lavender lemon white chocolate bark, lavender orange shortbreads and lavender chocolate biscotti. All are crafted entirely by hand with organic culinary lavender. The delicate tastes are memorable. You'll enjoy slowly perusing the shelves and antiques of this warm and inviting neighborhood shop. Amy and her marvelous staff will enjoy spoiling you with attention and suggestions for thoughtful gift-giving. Just ask. You'll quickly understand why Lavande Bleu has been featured in a variety of luxury and women's magazines, including *Lucky*. Everything leaves the shop thoughtfully wrapped and bowed with their signature style. Come and indulge your senses. You'll discover a world of luxury and comfort for everyday living.

109 Carlisle Boulevard SE, Historic Nob Hill, Albuquerque NM
(505) 255-5006
www.LavandeBleu.com

The Enchanted Southwest

Located on Albuquerque's west side, The Enchanted Southwest is an emporium specializing in regional home décor and personal adornments. The tremendous variety amassed by owners Robert and Jeanette Whitehead gives residents and out-of-town guests opportunities for one-stop shopping. From handmade furniture to cotton clothing, the Enchanted Southwest evokes the Land of Enchantment at every turn. Look for wall hangings, pottery, religious items and tinwork. Native Southwestern music and books fill shelves and make browsing an enticing prospect. The selection of jewelry includes pieces in gold, silver and platinum, some set with diamonds or semiprecious stones. This family-owned and operated store boasts lower prices than many shops and an unbeatable selection of gift items. The Enchanted Southwest regularly ships items for visitors from outside the area. Many items can be custom ordered, offering still greater opportunity for you to find pieces that will enhance your home and lifestyle. The store provides framing and repair services, and layaways are always welcome. Come experience authentic Native American and Southwestern artwork at The Enchanted Southwest.

9311 Coors Boulevard NW, Suite 015, Albuquerque NM
(505) 898-4808
www.theenchantedsouthwest.com

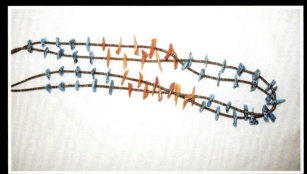

Morningside Antiques

Morningside Antiques, located in Albuquerque's prestigious Nob Hill area, offers collectors such a sensational array of quality antiques, Persian rugs and vintage artwork that it can easily be called a world-class antiquing venue. Jerry McQueen Turner, who was considered by all to be a warm, generous and engaging man until his death in October of 2001, founded this popular antiquing paradise and invested his heart and soul into the business. His exceptional sales staff, many of whom have been with the business for more than 18 years, continues his tradition of excellence by providing the same gracious service to the shop's faithful patrons. Morningside Antiques features an extended selection of period furnishings, as well as oil canvasses and other paintings, sterling and bronze accent pieces and statuary, and a choice array of stained glass work. The buyers at Morningside Antiques are continually buying new pieces and accepting new consignments, so the inventory is always changing, and new treasures are always awaiting the avid collector. Find remembrances of yesterday that will hold their value into tomorrow at Morningside Antiques.

4001 Central Avenue NE, Albuquerque NM
(505) 268-0188

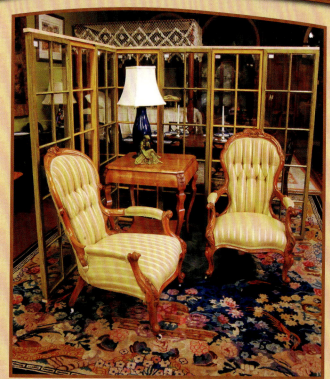

Shopping • 275

Photo courtesy of the New Mexico Tourism Department

Cowboys and Indians Antiques

Museum quality beadwork, textiles, pottery and jewelry are just some of the quality objects found at Cowboys and Indians Antiques on Route 66 in the historic Nob Hill section of Albuquerque. Here, 25 of the country's best known antiques dealers display Native American and Western art along with cowboy gear and Western movie memorabilia. All of the dealers guarantee the authenticity of every item they sell. Owner Terry Schurmeier's favorite childhood pastime was dressing up in Indian costumes while her brothers played cowboys. She created Cowboys and Indians to honor her memories of the fun they had. Together with managers Michael Eros and Skip Scroggins, who have been in the business for more than two decades, Cowboys and Indians procures pre-1950s Native American, Western and New Mexican art and antiques. The nostalgic roadside attraction carries arrowheads, Concho belts and coonskin caps. The equestrian will enjoy the shop's saddle and spur selection. For the jewelry collector, Cowboys and Indians carries vintage Fred Harvey Company bracelets. You might find a fully beaded Sioux vest or a 1920s-era Zia Pueblo pot here. Cowboys and Indians Antiques participates in the Great Southwestern Antiques, Indian & Old West Show every August, a show that attracts more than 200 top dealers from across the country. Let Cowboys and Indians Antiques bring the warmth and historic charm of New Mexico to your home.

4000 Central Avenue SE, Albuquerque NM
(505) 255-4054
www.cowboysandindiansnm.com

The Candy Lady

The Candy Lady is a reflection of the dynamic and compassionate woman who owns it, Deborrah Ball. The business sprang from Deborrah's mother, Diane Davis. When Debby's six-year-old son, Michael, sold some of his grandmother's candy at the sheriff's office, word about her delicious candy spread. Business became so brisk, they outgrew the kitchen and started The Candy Lady. The shop enjoyed some controversy when Deborrah honored the requests of customers to make X-rated candy. The candy was kept in the refrigerator and proved to be an extremely popular item. Picketers protesting the candy drew national press attention and suddenly the business was famous. However, the real heart of the business is the sincere customer service, friendly concern and, of course, the incredible candy. A large portion of the menu is devoted to diabetic candy. Glazed fruits are imported from Australia. The chocolates and fudges are rich and creamy, and New Mexico piñon nuts are used in some of the specialty candies, including a chile piñon brittle. The Candy Lady will create special orders, custom made to satisfy a customer's particular craving. The Candy Lady serves it all, from licorice and caramels to jelly beans, pretzels and mints. If you don't see it, ask for it. The Candy Lady can find what you need and will even ship it to your door. Step into Albuquerque's most talked about candy shop. You'll find it hard to leave empty-handed.

524 Romero NW, Albuquerque NM
(505) 243-6239 or (800) 214-7731
www.thecandylady.com

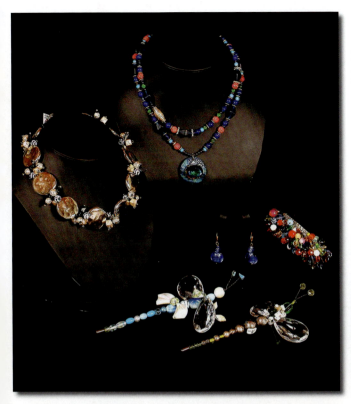

Innovations Gift Gallery

Located just two blocks north of Old Town, Innovations Gift Gallery specializes in affordable local art. Here you'll find mouth-blown, one-of-a-kind glass. These are beautiful pieces that are crafted in New Mexico, as well as imported. Innovations is the only store of its kind in Albuquerque. With more than 25 local artists featured, you will find an array of unique gifts. There are lotions and potions from Datil, antler pen sets and even organic journals. You will also find Native American jewelry and jewelry by Marguerite, as well as works by featured artists Dennis Michael Garcia, Angela Caputi, Greg Analla and Marcelo. You will also discover signed clocks by artist Andy Kirsch. Owner Ron Snodgrass says one of the most important people who contributes to the success of the store is Denise

Blackman, who is very knowledgeable about the products they sell. Come to Innovations Gift Gallery and find a unique and artistic gift that can be cherished for a lifetime.

901 Rio Grande Boulevard NW, Suite A192, Albuquerque NM (502) 242-7230

Pennysmiths Paper

For more than 25 years, people who throw the best parties have come to Pennysmiths Paper. "My mom's loves in life are paper and parties," says Emily Rembe Benak, owner of Pennysmiths Paper. Her mother, Penny Rembe, started the shop. The little girls who were in her sticker club are now grown up and Pennysmiths is helping them with their wedding invitations and kids' birthdays. Nestled in Albuquerque's rural North Valley, Pennysmiths Paper is the favorite neighborhood store in which to pick up handmade greeting cards created by local artists, handsome cocktail napkins and unique gifts. Boxed stationery and stickers, fine writing instruments and sealing wax, leather journals and archival photo albums, handmade papers and beautiful gift wrap are all available here. Pennysmiths Paper is a destination for brides, graduates and many others from all over New Mexico who want the best in invitations. Pennysmiths specializes in custom invitations for all occasions. They feature a knowledgeable, creative staff, including in-house graphic artists who ready to help create the perfect invitation to set the tone for your next party. They've even created their own line of Southwestern invitations. Emily invites you to drop by anytime to see what Pennysmiths Paper can do for you.

4022 Rio Grande Boulevard NW, Albuquerque NM (505) 345-2353
www.pennysmiths.com

Gertrude Zachary Inc.

For almost 30 years, Gertrude Zachary's sense of style and grace has put her on the cutting edge of the Native American Jewelry industry. Gertrude Zachary Inc. produces jewelry handmade by Native American silversmiths using contemporary designs. As Albuquerque's only female jewelry manufacturer in the 1970s, Gertrude drew upon her artistic abilities to develop a new style for Native American jewelry using contemporary designs and gemstones, as well as traditional stones. Gertrude and the Native American silversmiths collaborate on each piece of jewelry. She begins with a drawing of her idea and shows it to one of the silversmiths. The skillful hands of the master artisan then give the piece its shape. Gertrude's team uses only high-quality materials, such as high-grade North American turquoise and rare Mediterranean coral. As a result, many pieces can be made only in limited quantities. In 1991, Gertrude opened a manufacturer's outlet store, Gertrude Zachary Jewelry, Etc., near the Old Town District. Customers flock to the store because they know they will get the best stones and highest quality craftsmanship at a fair price. Five years ago, Gertrude branched out with an Antiques and Fine Gifts Gallery that offers beautiful European and domestic pieces that she handpicks on her travels. Many come from France and Italy. The shop has a first-class selection of chandeliers and European furniture. Many pieces date from the 18th and 19th centuries. Garden and landscaping items include bronze statuary created using the lost wax method and a dazzling assortment of fountains. The collection of antique religious items includes many hard-to-find pieces. The gallery also carries architectural pieces such as windows and doors. Recently, Gertrude opened a third retail outlet that carries both jewelry and antiques. For that special, beautiful item, shop at one of the Gertrude Zachary stores.

Jewelry
  1501 Lomas Boulevard NW, Albuquerque NM
  (505) 247-4442 or (800) 682-5768

Antiques and garden accessories
  416 Second Street SW, Albuquerque NM
  (505) 244-1320 or (800) 682-5768

Jewelry and antiques
  3300 Central Avenue SE, Albuquerque NM
  (800) 682-5768

www.gertrudezachary.com

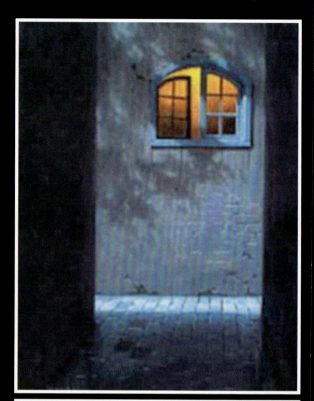

Sumner & Dene

Add touches of whimsy and fun to your everyday life with the diverse collection of fine art, furnishings and jewelry found at Sumner & Dene in Albuquerque. This delightful shop is owned and operated by Roy Sumner Johnson, a noteworthy art dealer for more than 25 years. Johnson holds a Bachelor of Fine Arts degree from the University of San Francisco, along with a degree in advertising and illustration from the San Francisco Academy of Art. He is well recognized throughout New Mexico for his work in developing the first national advertising campaign for the arts, as well as various efforts to promote New Mexico's artistic community. He has mounted traveling art exhibitions throughout the five-state area of New Mexico, Arizona, Colorado, Texas and Oklahoma. Johnson established Sumner & Dene in 1996 as an adjunct to his premier art gallery, the Variant Gallery in Taos. Sumner & Dene exhibits the work of more than 120 different artists from around the world, ranging from contemporary to true Southwestern. The work is original and unlike pieces you will find elsewhere. The shop carries an extensive array of furniture from Normand Couture along with dazzling jewelry from Dawn Estrin. Additional artists include husband-and-wife team Walker and Moore, who each work on the same canvas, and Heather Ramsey, who specializes in figurative mixed media. Find gifts and home décor that reflect your fun side at Sumner & Dene.

517 Central Avenue NW, Albuquerque NM
(505) 842-1400
www.sumnerdene.com

Clear Light • the Cedar Company

The initial inspiration for Clear Light • the Cedar Company came to Joshua Peine while hiking in the high altitude forests of New Mexico in 1971. With a fierce commitment to the basic essence of cedar, he designed a unique facility to dry the needles he gathered and started growing his business by selling the Green Cedar Needle Sachets he made. Since then, Joshua has developed a diverse line of products based on this aromatic and useful ingredient, including a broad range of skin, hair-care and bath products, incense, soap, candles and potpourri. Joshua's cedar and cedar-lavender candles will add an atmospheric glow and ancient mystique to every room in your home, along with a soothing forest-fresh scent. Utilizing the healing properties of cedar long recognized by Southwestern Native American tribes, these products promote well being. Fragrance is becoming more widely recognized in modern day America for its therapeutic benefits to the body and mind, and is the backbone of this refreshing, cleansing and soothing product line. Joshua welcomes visitors to his showroom and workshop, as well as to his gardens and lavender field. Visit Clear Light • the Cedar Company and let the scents inspire you.

686 State Road 165, Placitas NM
(505) 867-2381 or (800) 557-3463
www.clcedar.com

Ghost Town Trading Co.

Sometimes a single piece of furniture can make a room. One piece can have so much character, so much personality, it becomes an inspiration for everything around it. That's exactly what you'll find at Ghost Town Trading Co. Handmade and crafted from recycled wood, each piece of furniture they create is unique and different with that rustic, time-worn look. In addition to recycling old wood, the furniture artisans use other recyclable materials, such as old window screens, antique ceiling tin, rusty metal roofing, old moldings, and whatever else they can creatively incorporate into their designs. Ghost Town Trading Co. carries a full line of rustic furniture and accessories for the entire home, including bookcases, hutches, pantries, entertainment centers, tables, chairs and bedroom furniture. Their rugged line of patio furniture and solid wood kitchen and bathroom cabinetry can imbue your home with lasting beauty. Custom work is available, and the masters at Ghost Town Trading Co. welcome the opportunity to create a special piece just for you. For nearly a decade, they have been a regular source for builders and designers looking for unique and different solutions for their clients' needs. In addition to their own furniture and accessories, Ghost Town Trading Co. carries an eclectic mix of antiques, collectibles, rustic hardware and other eye-catching accessories, as well as works from local artists. Located in historic Nob Hill, the friendly staff at Ghost Town Trading Co. prides itself on customer service. The website has information on the recycling end of their business, as well as notices of upcoming special sales and events.

111 Carlisle Boulevard NE, Albuquerque NM
(505) 255-5656 or (888) 224-8280
www.ghosttowntradingco.com

Terra Firma

Patrick Cox, owner and operator of Terra Firma, Albuquerque's hottest footwear and accessory store, believes life is too short for dull, boring shoes. He and his buyer, Lisa Smith, go out of their way to find the very best for your busy feet, including sexy, fashionable styles that can be worn comfortably all day and into the night. Terra Firma's young, professional staff members, affectionately known throughout the neighborhood as "Terra Firmites," are well versed in the ins and outs of this shop's exquisite collection of contemporary shoes, from such far-flung locales as Denmark, Spain, Holland and Brazil. They will expertly fit these beauties to your foot and your lifestyle. Look for stellar designs from top names like Dansko, Pikolino and Wolky, along with fabulous handbags, clutches and wallets. Additional finds include terrific totes with a pocket for every need and great accessories from Hobo, Baggallinni and Ellington. Terra Firma carries fashionable and functional laptop cases and gadget protectors. Find shoes, clogs and sandals to protect and pamper your feet, along with accessories that organize and protect your things, at either of Terra Firma's convenient Albuquerque locations—in the historic Nob Hill district and in the fashionable Northtown Shopping Center.

113 Carlisle SE, Albuquerque NM
(505) 260-0507
5901 Wyoming Boulevard NE, Albuquerque NM
(505) 856-7200

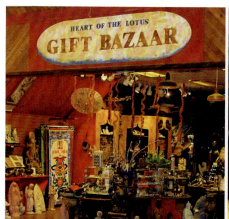

Heart of the Lotus Gift Bazaar

In many Eastern philosophies, the lotus is a good fortune symbol of enlightenment and transformation. To see the heart of the lotus is a gift. The Heart of the Lotus Gift Bazaar in Santa Fe carries meaningful, sacred treasures of every kind. It is unlike any other shopping experience. The presence and open-heartedness of the owners and staff saturate every part of the business. It is grounded in the values of benevolence, acceptance, generosity, love, and honor of the diversity within all life. The store offers the rich cultural and spiritual work of artisans from multiple countries, such as Tibet, India, Nepal, Thailand and many others. Heart of the Lotus Gift Bazaar, located between Mervyn's and Sears, is serenely populated with indoor and outdoor statuary, metaphysical gifts and jewelry. Feng Shui items, crystals, natural stones and Buddhist as well as Hindu items are available. Gifts are created in a variety of media, including wood, stone, ceramics and bronze. There's also a selection of singing bowls, didgeridoos and drums so you can make your own sacred music. Come find something good for your soul and your décor at Heart of the Lotus Gift Bazaar inside the Santa Fe Place Mall.

4250 Cerrillos Road, Santa Fe Place Mall, Santa Fe NM
(505) 438-1896

Dancing Wolf & Narrow Gauge Gifts & Boutique

A visit to the northern New Mexico village of Chama is an opportunity to sink into a culture and landscape that seems in many ways untouched by time. No business better captures the many aspects of life in Chama than Dancing Wolf & Narrow Gauge Gifts & Boutique. The shop is located just steps from the Cumbres and Toltec Narrow Gauge Railroad, one of the prime tourist attractions in this mountain village, located at the base of scenic 10,000-foot Cumbres Pass. The steam locomotive that once hauled precious metals over the pass now labors over the same steep grades to carry tourists into this incomparable landscape. Dancing Wolf celebrates the train and the look and lifestyle of the region with train-oriented gifts and toys in its Narrow Gauge Gift Shop and home accessories and clothing for men and women in the Dancing Wolf Boutique. The store, owned by Ed Kurtz and Jim Martens, opened two years ago and adds greatly to the charm and architectural appeal of historic downtown Chama. Bring home a reminder of the enchanting elements that set Chama and northern New Mexico apart with a visit to Dancing Wolf & Narrow Gauge Gifts & Boutique, where the merchandise captures the rare qualities that make a visit to Chama a magical and memorable experience.

**534 Terrace Avenue, Chama NM
(505) 756-2963**

Tailwater Gallery & Fly Shop

A perfect marriage of interests shared by husband-and-wife team Stephanie and Jack Woolley resulted in the Tailwater Gallery & Fly Shop in Taos. At Tailwater, displays include Stephanie's captivating paintings of fish, wildlife, landscapes and people of the region, as well as a complete line of fly-fishing equipment. Stephanie's command of realism is eloquently expressed through her acrylic and watercolor paintings. The balanced use of color she unfailingly achieves in each new work is her signature. Influences from her childhood near the Brandywine River Valley in Pennsylvania and her life in Taos shine through her vividly painted canvases. Her work is a celebration of the same triumphs and pleasures that prevail in the world of fly fishing. Fly-fishing aficionados love new opportunities for fishing adventures and Tailwater caters to this desire by providing a booking service for fly-fishing expeditions. At Tailwater, you can book fly-fishing adventures for northern New Mexico or southern Colorado. These localized trips are booked with Van Beacham's Solitary Angler Service. International trips are available with Mark Cowan's Pescador Solitario. If art is taking what is consequential in this world and expressing that meaning to others in a beautiful fashion, Tailwater has admirably fulfilled the definition. This is a fine chance to experience what happens when life's passions are channeled into art. Jack and Stephanie invite you to rejoice in the outcome at Tailwater Gallery & Fly Shop.

204 B Paseo del Pueblo Norte, Taos NM
(505) 758-5653 or (866) 502.1700
www.tailwatergallery.com

Artwork by Stephanie Woolley

Las Cosas Kitchen Shoppe and Cooking School

For more than 30 years, the staff of Las Cosas Kitchen Shoppe and Cooking School has been equipping home kitchens with gadgets, fine cookware and beautiful tableware. With an inventory of more than 20,000 items, home cooks will find a wish list of supplies, from small utensils to deluxe coffee machines. Las Cosas also offers an extensive range of specialty foods, including specialty teas, like those from Eden Grove Ceylon Estate. Other treats such as organic oils, vinegars and special chile spices are also available. Las Cosas offers hands-on cooking classes, where the slogan is We Cook for Fun. The Cooking School director, John Vollertsen, joined the Las Cosas team in 1998 and immediately developed a following of loyal customers eager to improve their cooking skills and learn how to use their new equipment. The guest chef series from Las Cosas brings in important chefs from Santa Fe, as well as from neighboring Taos and Albuquerque. John continues to research the wonderful world of food and shares his adventures with his students. He marvels daily at how much good food he has yet to explore. Las Cosas offers a bridal registry and is located in Santa Fe just north of the historic plaza. Come join one of John's eclectic classes, or simply enjoy the shopping experience at Las Cosas Kitchen Shoppe and Cooking School.

181 Paseo de Peralta, Santa Fe NM
(505) 988-3394 or (877) 229-7184
www.lascosascooking.com

Photos by Junior Vaquera

Salman Raspberry Ranch and La Cueva Historic District

The Salman Raspberry Ranch and the La Cueva Historic District are nestled on the Eastern slopes of the Sangre de Cristo Mountains. Six acres of expertly cultivated river bottom land yield enough fresh berries to fill the baskets of tourists and locals alike. Visitors can pick straight from the field or buy flats at the Salman Ranch Store, which is open year round. Across the road from the store is the Salman Ranch Café, open during the you-pick season, offering such delicious homemade New Mexican treats as tacos and tamales, tasty sandwiches with locally baked bread and soft serve ice cream drenched in Salman Ranch raspberry topping and fresh raspberries from the field. Other attractions in the area are the beautifully restored Mission Church of San Rafael, the three-story adobe mill with its water wheel, and the nearby two-story Romero-Salman adobe hacienda dating to the 1800s. The hacienda is still the home of descendants of Colonel William Salman, who purchased the ranch in the 1940s. The buildings, gardens and acequia invite the painter and photographer in all of us. A day with your family at the Salman Raspberry Ranch will be well spent. Once you've picked plenty of berries, feel free to have your lunch under the beautiful willow trees that line the ancient acequia. Just across from the picnic area is one of New Mexico's most colorful gardens. The Ranch Store carries a large variety of drought resistant and sun loving seeds.

The store features the famous Salman Ranch Raspberry jam, topping and vinegar, along with other gourmet food products, ranch-grown dried floral bouquets, farm-grown vegetables and fine art photography and ranch mementos. The raspberry season usually starts in early August and ends with the first killing frost in mid to late October. Be sure to call their toll-free number before visiting to check on field conditions.

Junction of NM 518 and 442
(505) 387-2900 or (866) 281-1515
www.salmanraspberryranch.com

Photo © High Country Gardens

The Critters & Me

For those who adore the various animals in their lives, from pets to barnyard critters to local wildlife, the Critters & Me store in Santa Fe carries a comprehensive assortment of the finest animal products available, along with the information you need to keep those animals healthy. In the animal care business since 1998, owner Laura Moore is committed to animal welfare and communication about animal needs. Critters & Me acts as an information clearinghouse for animal lovers, as well as a supply store with top-of-the-line items for your pets and farm animals. Critters & Me specializes in pet health and provides natural pet foods, homeopathic remedies and supplements designed to prolong and enrich the lives of your pets. You'll find just about anything a pet could need, including great toys, feeding dishes, leashes, collars and grooming equipment. Laura says that love, better food and better care makes for the best pet possible. Anyone who has ever shared a bond with an animal knows there is nothing better than a healthy critter that levels an adoring gaze at you when you come through the door. Whether you care for a bird, horse, dog or cat, the Critters & Me shop has the information and supplies you need.

1403 Agua Fria, Santa Fe NM
(505) 982-5040
www.crittersandme.com

La Paz Imports

The warmth of copper goes straight to the heart, and at La Paz Imports, owners Tamra McLeod and Shelly Martin know this. La Paz Imports boasts the largest and finest collection of Mexican folk art and crafts in Mesilla, a town rich in artistic tradition. La Paz is noted especially for its copper artifacts, many of which were hand-forged in Michocan, Mexico, renowned worldwide for its ancient mastery of metalwork. The pieces at La Paz are high quality, sensuous and difficult to find anywhere else. They carry the work of noted coppersmith Bricio Pureco Falfan, who stamps and certifies all of his works sold at La Paz. In addition, the store features pottery made by the Tarahumara Indians of Copper Canyon, Mexico. You can also find candles, religious icons, baskets and dolls at this treasure trove of authentic Southwestern treasures. To make your shopping experience even better, La Paz offers featuring espresso, cold and smoothies, while a seating area allows you browse through a variety as you enjoy your cup. If copper and the history Southwest call to you, Imports, where the will help you find the will answer the call.

2470 Calle de Guadalupe, (505) 647-9397

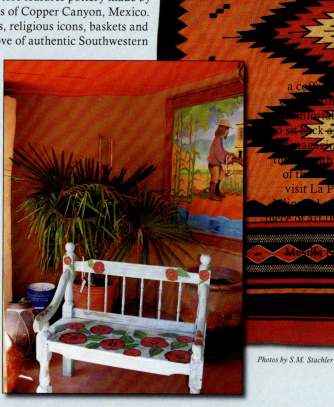

Photos by S.M. Stachler

New Mexico State University Bookstore

School spirit runs high at New Mexico State University's Bookstore, located in the Corbett Center Student Union. University owned and operated, the bookstore is the best source for course material from textbooks to art supplies. Active on campus and in the community, the general reading department places special orders daily and hosts faculty and local author book signings throughout the year. Students can purchase books tax-free and can also reserve books online. The bookstore will hold your reservations until the first day of class. Budget conscious buyers can often find used textbooks and save an extra 30 percent. When you're done with the book, return it during finals week and the bookstore will buy it back. Not sure how much they will pay? Their website will answer that question for you, too. If you miss the deadline or want to sell directly to another student, the bookstore has a classified bulletin board. Those with any change left jingling in their pockets will find the store stocked with a popular selection of gifts and apparel. Bookstore director Ron Benson and his staff look forward to greeting you and assisting with your educational experience.

Corbett Center Student Union, Las Cruces NM
(505) 646-4431
www.nmsubookstore.com

Kokoman Fine Wines & Liquors

How does an old service station in the sleepy New Mexican town of Pojoaque become a gourmet wine shop that attracts the most sophisticated clientele in the Southwest? Since 1984, the shop has become an out-of-the-way hot spot, thanks to one trait—quality products. Kokoman owners Keith Obermaier and Jerome Valdez stay busy keeping up with the constant flow of customers who have heard of this little shop of spirits from word of mouth alone. Coming from all walks of life, Kokoman customers are a diverse group that defies labeling. Local hunters may stop to pick up cold beer, while travelers and jetsetters en route to a casino or the Santa Fe Opera come in search of specialty liquors and cases of champagne. Even a local priest or two come for cases of sacramental wine. With 1,500 square feet devoted exclusively to spirits, a climate-controlled wine cellar and more than 2,000 wines on hand, Kokoman is never idle. On Saturdays winemakers showcase new products and provide tastings from the up-and-coming New Mexican wine country. On your next visit, ask for a sparkling wine from the Albuquerque-based Gruet vineyard, or pick up a good local Pinot Noir or Chardonnay for under $20. With the simple philosophy of quality, Kokoman draws the masses from far and wide. Visit Kokoman, and tell Keith and Jerome you heard about them on the street.

34 Cities of Gold Road, Pojoaque NM
(505) 455-2219

Brown Cow Saddle Blanket Company

When looking for the best in saddle blankets, the equestrian community of Santa Fe heads for the Brown Cow Saddle Blanket Company. Owner Christina Bergh and a team of discriminating saddle blanket aficionados work together to create spectacular, custom-designed blankets that are hand-dyed and woven into truly exquisite patterns. The bi-level weaving studio has nine multi-harness looms, three of which are computer driven. It also employs an extraordinary jacquard loom. The only other loom of its kind and size resides in Egypt. When a customer orders a saddle blanket from the Brown Cow, they are ordering a quality piece of practical art. Each customer's order starts with dyeing virgin wool and mohair in large vats over industrial stoves. The extra attention and hand dyeing produces vibrant hues that would otherwise be unattainable. These custom saddle blanket yarns are then taken to the weaving studio to be lovingly turned into one-of-a-kind blankets. The company carries a choice selection of tapestries, beadwork items and the Schaefer Outfitter line. The Brown Cow got its name from a horse that survived a cattle guard accident and went on to become the ultimate children's horse. When Christina's daughter Doriane was three, she named the horse Brown Cow and learned to ride on the gentle animal. The pair quickly began to win 4-H rodeo competitions. Christina, wanting the duo to look its best, wove her first saddle blanket and went on to create The Brown Cow Saddle Blanket Company.

333 Cordova Road, Santa Fe NM
(505) 820-6297
www.thebrowncow.com

Susan's Christmas Shop

Susan Topp Weber, who has always loved handmade things, began making Christmas ornaments to sell in 1969. Soon her work was in museum shows, and is now in the permanent collection of the Smithsonian in Washington, D.C. In 1978, she opened Susan's Christmas Shop in the small adobe room on East Palace Avenue. What her shop lacks in size is made up for in the vast collection of treasures. Customers return frequently to see what's new. Some items are handmade by local artists and others come from around the world, but what they all have in common is superior design. Susan's Christmas Shop has become a fine source for nativities. She hosted a national convention of The Friends of the Crèche, in Santa Fe in November 2005, and has sold nativities in Europe and the United States. While Susan discovers and nurtures fresh new talent, the pen and ink eggs of one local artist have been sold here for 28 years. German specialties in the shop include Wendt und Kuhn figures and treasures of the Erzgebirge region. Susan is also developing a line of mouth-blown, handpainted glass ornaments called Landmarks of New Mexico whose sale benefits historic preservation in New Mexico. Feel free to browse the website, but the most fun is to visit in person. Located right beside The Shed Restaurant, a favorite for more than 50 years, it's easy to combine the two destinations for a memorable day. The turquoise benches under the portal outside her door are the perfect place for the weary to lean back against the adobe wall and gaze at Cathedral Park. Come to Susan's Christmas Shop, located one-half block east of the plaza in historic downtown Santa Fe.

115 E Palace Avenue, Santa Fe NM
(505) 983-2127
www.SusansChristmasShop.com

294 • Textile Arts

Textile Arts

296 • Textile Arts

History of Wool and Weaving

Since the days of the ancient Anasazi, around 800 AD, weaving has played a starring role in the economic development of what is now New Mexico and southwest Arizona. The descendants of the Anasazi, the Pueblo, continued this practice, growing and weaving cotton on upright or vertical looms. With the coming of the Spanish explorers and conquistadors in the mid-1500s, specifically Coronado and his 5,000 Churro sheep in 1540, new elements were introduced to the Pueblo, including the Spanish creation of a long, narrow, striped blanket, which became known as the Rio Grande blanket. In 1680, the Pueblo united and drove out the Spanish in the Pueblo Revolt. A dozen years later, upon their return, the Spaniards had learned the value of a peaceful co-existence and the evolution of more diverse Pueblo styles of weaving emerged. Today, Pueblo weaving consists of elaborately embroidered mantas and sashas, as well as the popular striped blanket preferred by the Spanish. At around this same time, the Navajo were beginning to spin on their own in western New Mexico and eastern Arizona. For the Navajo, a nomadic tribe, the upright looms and movement of sheep proved advantageous to the development of weaving. Navajo weaving has been influenced by many factors, including the Spanish and Pueblo, and they have injected their textiles with culturally aesthetic and interesting features that exemplified their rich native stories, symbols and crafts. Both tribes drew heavily from the influences of others and the first style truly developed in New Mexico is said to have evolved from the Saltillo, becoming the Vallero, which emerged in the mid 19th century. Today, the Rio Grande textile industry is enjoying a renaissance, fueled by greater tourism and the revival of cottage industries. Weaving begun by the ancient ones has returned full circle to become a dominant player in the future prosperity of New Mexico and the Southwest.

(505) 387-2247

History of the Sheep

For more than 12,000 years, wool has been an integral part of the weave we call civilization. Wool fibers have unique, minute, overlapping plates or scales that all point in the same direction and act like tiles on a roof. Air trapped between these fibers gives wool its sustaining properties. The surface of each wool fiber is water resistant and its interior is highly absorbent, which allows wool to feel warm even when wet. When Don Juan de Onate colonized New Mexico in 1598, he brought with him Churro sheep, which quickly became part of the Pueblo Indian way of life. The Indians immediately began utilizing the Churro wool to weave their blankets, rugs and apparel. After the Pueblo Revolt of 1680, the Spanish colonists began a textile industry that went on to sustain them for the next 300 years. Tierra Wools' handspun yarn and weaving products are made from the wool of locally raised Navajo-Churro sheep, descended from the Iberian breed, a hardy stock with beautiful, coarse fleece. This lustrous wool is perfectly suited for spinning and weaving the fine rugs and blankets displayed inside the shop. The area's local Churro flocks were almost wiped out (although remnants of Churro were found in local flocks) until the 1980s, when a breeding program, developed by local sheepherders and Dr. Lyle McNeal from Utah State University, brought them back from the edge of extinction. The natural beauty and durability of the wool from the Churro sheep is a gift that all can appreciate.

91 Main Street Los Ojos NM
(505) 588-7231 or (888) 709-5979
www.handweavers.com

Textile Arts

History of the Alpacas

Alpacas are small, gentle cousins to llamas and natives of the South American Andes. Alpacas produce one of the world's finest and most luxurious natural fibers. Soft as cashmere and warmer, lighter and stronger than wool, the fiber comes in 22 basic colors with many variations and blends. The fleece is water-resistant, does not soil from oil and is not conducive to static electricity. The fleece, once reserved for Incan royalty, is now enjoyed by spinners and weavers around the world. In place of hooves, alpacas have small, padded, two-toed feet that cause little damage to terrain. They are cud-chewing animals that feed on pasture grass and hay. Their sensitive lips can pick up a single grain of wheat without disturbing the surrounding materials. Each alpaca generally eats less than two pounds of feed a day. A full-grown alpaca adult weighs between 125 and 200 pounds and will measure only four-and-a-half feet to the top of its head. At birth a cria, or baby alpaca, weighs about 15 to 20 pounds. In 30 to 60 minutes the cria is standing and nursing. It begins exploring the world within hours. In the mid 19th century, Sir Titus Salt of England discovered the delights of alpaca fiber and introduced it into world trade. Breeders outside of South America first obtained the animals in the early 1980s, which is when ranchers introduced the alpaca into New Mexico. Still, 99 percent of the world's three million alpacas continue to live in Peru, Bolivia or Chile.

Sangre de Cristo Mill

With the textile industry in America poised for resurgence, Tapetes de Lana's new 11,000-square-foot Sangre de Cristo Mill is ideally located to reap the rewards. For many years, most of the raw wool in the states was produced west of the Mississippi, while most of the industrial textile producing sales took place on the East Coast. "Our mill represents a *cultura nueva* or new culture, in that it ties together the production and processing of wool all in the same region," veteran Mill Manager Robert Donnelly says. "It combines sheep and wool producing capabilities with the weaving capability that has been here for more than 400 years." Donnelly cautiously estimates that by spring of 2006 the mill will be operating at full speed and will be able to conservatively produce about 1,000 pounds of yarn per week. Aside from basic statistics, the important aspect of this new venture is that they will now be able to complete the process from shearing the wool to washing and processing it all in one location. According to Donnelly, the Mora Mill will be the largest mill west of the Mississippi that will process domestically grown fiber. After a two decade decline in the United States textile industry, resurgence is now being fueled by a spike in the tourist trade, a new appreciation for the natural beauty and resilience of woven products and an increase in the number and size of sheep and other fiber-producing herds like alpacas. Donnelly feels that the reversal will be slow but is confident of sustainability for this new era in wool processing.

Junction 518 & 434 Main Street, Mora NM

Tapetes de Lana Gallery

When Don Juan de Onate came to New Mexico in 1598, he brought colonists intent on finding gold of the glittery variety. He never realized that the churro sheep brought by his colonists would plant the seeds for a present day textile industry that is promising weavings of gold for people in the upper Rio Grande valley. Since the days of the Anasazi, weaving has played a major role in New Mexico. For 300 years after Onate, textiles flourished and provided a livelihood for up to 70 percent of Northern New Mexico residents. In 1988, future Tapetes founder Carla Gomez was teaching weaving at New Mexico Highlands University while working as a curator at El Rancho de Las Golondrinas, a living history museum south of Santa Fe. Ten years later, a single mother of six took Gomez' course. She needed a job. So Gomez got her enrolled in a work training program with the Department of Labor. For the woman to qualify, she had to be working with a nonprofit organization. Tapetes de Lana was born. Gomez teamed up with GOAL, a welfare-to-work program, and soon she was teaching a dozen women to weave. With the help of business development grants from the Hitachi Foundation and the United States Department of Agriculture, Tapetes expanded its training program to benefit under-employed and unemployed people. The organizational plans include the operation of an 11,000-square-foot spinning mill, renovation of an old theater, a Culinary Arts Center, Pottery Studio and a 10-room Hostel. The Performing Arts Center will offer cinema, theatrical, and educational benefits to the community of Mora. The purpose of Tapetes de Lana is to create an economic environment that will promote a sustainable economy, so that local residents and especially the young will not have to migrate to cities and other urban centers to obtain employment.

1814 Plaza, Las Vegas NM
(505) 426-8638
www.tapetesdelana.com

Tierra Wools

Tierra Wools is a spinning, hand dyeing, hand weaving workshop and retail store in Los Ojos. Many of the weavers at Tierra Wools are descended directly from Spanish immigrants who settled in the Rio Grande Valley as early as the 16th century or from later waves of settlers who immigrated from Spain and Mexico. Raising sheep was the economic mainstay of these settlers. The textiles produced by them were called Rio Grande Blankets.

This weaving style was influenced by a mix of Spanish, Mexican and Native American designs and characterized by the use of stripes and bands, Saltillo diamonds and Vallero stars.

Tierra Wools pays homage to these traditions by purchasing locally grown wool and hiring and training local people. The owners of Tierra Wools and their experienced staff invite you to glimpse a time when Hispanic weaving was a mainstay for village artisans while they were surviving the long, bitter winters. It was during this time that the Rio Grande weavers would quench their thirst for color by creating stunning pieces for their families and communities. Today, this worker-owned company continues to help ensure that the sheep herding and weaving industries will continue to preserve the land and culture. The showroom at Tierra Wools is an ideal place for visitors to see weavers, spinners and dyers at work and browse through the company's large selection of handwoven creations. Run your fingers across a majestic landscape of fiber, purchase your own stunning yarns and learn more about the Spanish weaving heritage at Tierra Wools.

91 Main Street, Los Ojos NM
(505) 588-7231 or (888) 709-0979
www.handweavers.com

Española Valley Fiber Arts Center

With nearly 350 members, Española Valley Fiber Arts Center is many things to many people. This exciting facility serves as a school, gallery and source of information and supplies. It is also a gathering place and a quiet haven from the hectic world. The arts center was founded in 1995 by a dedicated group of weavers concerned for the survival of the area's textile traditions. Today, under the leadership of founding member Trish Spillman, the organization is a multifaceted nonprofit arts organization that serves all of Northern New Mexico with a mission to preserve and promote the rich textile heritage of the region and its people. This inspiring facility provides both learning and teaching opportunities in the fiber arts for people of any age and background as well as reasonably priced materials and equipment in a welcoming atmosphere. Española Valley Fiber Arts Center also promotes local fiber arts traditions by spreading knowledge to the general public. To support the fiber artists, the center offers entrepreneurial training, studio workspace, marketing assistance and sales opportunities like shows in the new Enchanted Fiber Gallery. Here, artists learn how to sustain themselves as artists in an encouraging environment. The Española Valley Fiber Arts Center offers an array of classes throughout the year, including weaving, knitting, dyeing, spinning, bead weaving and embroidery. The gallery is open Monday through Saturday for viewing and purchasing affordable, local handmade items. Celebrate the beauty and craftsmanship that is fiber art at the Española Valley Fiber Arts Center.

325 Paseo de Oñate, Española NM
(505) 747-3577
www.evfac.org

Centinela Traditional Arts

Working with traditional methods and styles, the artisans at Centinela Traditional Arts in Chimayo create a wide variety of products to grace your home and body including jackets, wall tapestries and purses. Just as in the past, the creation of these stunning pieces requires skill in loom design, loom warping, skirting, scouring, carding, spinning, dyeing and designing as well as finishing and weaving. This artistry requires the mastery and perpetuation of skills and the company is continually developing these due to the patronage of its community as well as outside clients. Owner Irvin Trujillo has been weaving since he learned the craft from his father Jake in 1965 when he was 10. Over the years, Irvin has grown in his art, continually changing his focus and studying every style, technique and method. Additionally, he applies his own sense of artistry to each piece he creates. The development of these skills is an ongoing process and his intriguing ideas of color and proportion are subject to change. Prominent museums and individuals worldwide collect Irvin's work. His wife Lisa learned the trade after marrying Irvin and has developed a special interest in the Saltillo and Vallero styles. Lisa's work is often detailed and delicate and examines the endless possibilities in elements and patterns. Centinela has several weavers on staff, who work to provide a variety of unique pieces in a multitude of sizes and styles. Centinela Traditional Arts is the ideal place to learn about and view the rich heritage of New Mexico weavers.

HCR 64, Chimayó NM
(505) 351-2180
www.chimayoweavers.com

Ortega's Weaving Shop

As a young man Gabriel Ortega came to the northern Rio Grande Valley with a group of immigrants to settle what is now Chimayo. At the time, the area was the last frontier for New Spain, and people were called upon to be self-sufficient. Of the many skills needed to survive, weaving was one of the most important, since it supplied the colonies with clothing, blankets and even mattresses. Gabriel and his son filled their days with weaving, farming and making do with what they had. For the next several generations, the Ortegas' lifestyle remained much the same. Then in 1885, a few years after the birth of fifth generation son Nicacio, the railroad came to nearby Espanola, changing the economic landscape of the area. American culture began to mix with the isolated Native American and Spanish cultures of Northern New Mexico, and new products such as canned goods, tools and sewing machines were being fervently traded for chile ristras, Indian pottery, hand woven Chimayo blankets and other indigenous products. In the early 1900s, Nicacio and his wife Virginia, who was also from a weaver's family, opened a general store in Chimayo. Here, Nicacio housed his loom and sold his weavings, alongside the work of his sons, relatives and friends. After World War II, Nicacio's sons Jose Ramon and David and their spouses joined Nicacio's business, which continued to grow so much that the family hired on other weaving families to keep up with the demand. Now, nearly 300 years later, David's sons Robert, Andrew and Chris continue Ortega's Weaving Shop's legacy of creating intricate and masterful weavings for you and your family.

53 Plaza de Cerro, Chimayó NM
(505) 351-4215 or
(877) 351-4215

Toadlena Trading Post

Toadlena Trading Post is a busy place that offers a glimpse into the past. This trading post maintains a lifestyle that the Navajo and traders have played out for over 100 years and nurtures a centuries-old weaving tradition. The Navajos arrived from the North and learned the weaving techniques from the Pueblo Indians. Navajo weaving utilizes the upright loom of the Anasazi, the weaving techniques of the Pueblo people and the wool of the Spanish. Early fur trappers traded the Navajo red cloth for access to their land. The Navajo coveted the red cloth because they could not create this color on their own. Permanent trading posts sprouted around the reservation. The demand for Navajo rugs increased and by 1900 the traders and weavers were working together to develop marketable textiles that appealed to the white man. Thirteen regional designs within seven weaving districts emerged inside the Navajo Nation, each named for its trading post. Each district offered spectacular textiles. The most coveted Navajo textile today is the Two Grey Hills from Toadlena. It is far superior because it possesses more wefts to the linear inch, resulting in a finer weave. Traders Bloomfield and Davies encouraged the weavers of Toadlena to weave more finely, create more intricate designs and use only hand spun native wool in the natural colors of the sheep. The result is intricate geometric designs in variations of black, brown, gray, beige and cream.

Toadlena operates today in the same way trading posts did in the 1870s, directly with the weaver and their family. At Toadlena Trading Post, you are offered the unique opportunity to acquire a textile of timeless beauty and lasting value.

(505) 789-3267 or
(888) 420-0005
www.toadlenatradingpost.com

Photos by John Andrews

Victory Alpaca Ranch

Garments made from luxurious Alpaca fibers are treasures that often become family heirlooms. Victory Ranch in Mora provides a place for you to learn more about these lovely animals. Alpacas are small, gentle cousins to llamas and natives of the South American Andes. Victory Ranch is proud to have one of the largest and finest alpaca herds in the United States and stands behind the bloodlines of its excellent breeding stock. Alpacas come in 22 varied colors, and their wool can be used in various textiles. The fleece is extremely lightweight and coveted for its warmth and softness. Products created from alpaca fiber can easily last a lifetime. The fleece is water-resistant, does not soil from grease or oil and is not conducive to static electricity. Alpacas can be traced to the Incan civilization, where they were considered a measure of a person's wealth. In place of hooves, Alpacas have small, padded, two-toed feet that cause little damage to terrain. They are cud-eating animals that feed on pasture grass and hay. Each alpaca generally eats less than two pounds of feed a day. A full-grown alpaca adult weighs up to 175 pounds and will measure only four and a half feet to the top of its head. Alpacas have a life expectancy of about 20 years, and Victory Ranch is home to one of the oldest living alpacas, a female named Fuzzy who is now 23. Ken and Carol Weisner, owners of Victory Ranch Alpacas, invite you to come and explore 1,100 acres of spectacular scenery in the mountains of northern New Mexico while enjoying the opportunity to hug and feed these charming and friendly creatures.

North of Mora on Route 434 at mile marker 1, Mora NM
(505) 387-2254
www.victoryranch.com

The other-worldly landscape of the 4000 acre Bisti Badlands, with its surreal geologic formations, is within the fossil-rich 22,500 acres of washes and mesas of the De-Na-Zin Wilderness. This hiking and backpacking attraction is about 35 miles south of Farmington, in northwestern New Mexico.
Photo Courtesy of the New Mexico Tourism Department

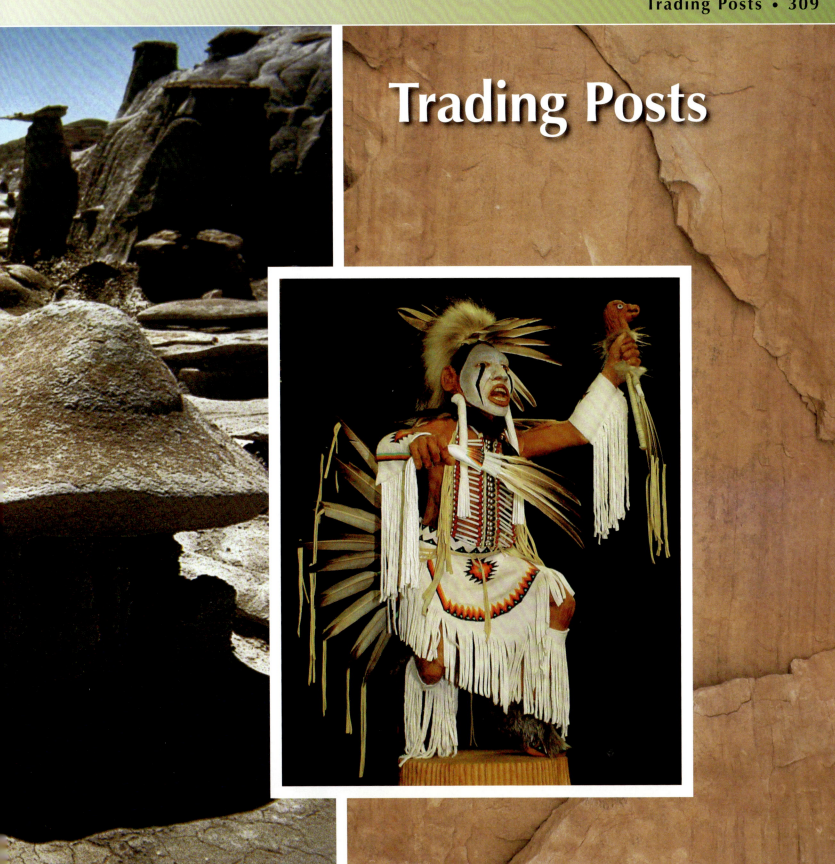

Trading Posts

Hatch Brothers Trading Post

R.S. "Stewart" Hatch built his trading post in 1949 at the intersection of two wagon roads, between two fords on the San Juan River. He grew up on the Navajo and Ute reservations and attended Indian school near Gallup. His father, Joe, who was half Paiute, owned and operated a trading post in the area in 1891. He worked his own turquoise mine and brought beads and stones to Navajo silversmiths. Joe passed away while his sons were serving in the military during WWII. Stewart and his brother, Claude, inherited the trading post and built the business into what it is today. Claude has since retired, but Stewart is still in charge of the post. With the help of his youngest son, Chuck, he continues to serve the needs of the Native Americans who have had a long-standing relationship with the Hatch family. Stewart is a confidante, banker, counselor and postman for his customers. A thumbprint on a government check is all that Hatch requires of his local patrons to cash it. He always treats his customers with respect and still speaks in his native Navajo tongue. Stewart and his wife Elsie raised five sons, but Stewart doesn't think any of them will carry on the business that he spent his life building. The Hatch Trading Post is still the way it was back in the 1950s. It's a rewarding trip back in time to meet Mr. Hatch and spend a few hours hearing and seeing him work with such dedication. Blankets, pottery, jewelry and collectible items are available for purchase, along with soft drinks and cookies. Hatch's Trading Post lies off the beaten track, at the end of a dirt road in the village of Fruitland, between Shiprock and Farmington. Take the Fruitland turnoff from highway 550, and turn right past the post office and Fruitland Trading Company. The road ends, but your history lesson will begin at Hatch Brothers Trading Post.

36 Road 6677, Fruitland NM
(505) 598-6226

Photos by: S.M. Stachler

Ellis Tanner Trading Company

"Near Gallup on a rocky hilltop stands Ellis Tanner Trading Company, with 90 percent Navajo employees...."
—*National Geographic Magazine*

"'Turquoise is still sacred to the Navajo,' says Ellis Tanner, owner of one of the biggest trading posts in Gallup, near the Navajo Nation Reservation."
—*Smithsonian Magazine*

When in Gallup, make time to see Ellis Tanner Trading Company. This modern-day trading post is owned and operated by a fourth-generation trader. You will witness the everyday transactions of the Native American people who shop there, and find yourself surrounded by museum-quality art. And when we say surrounded, we don't just mean all the beautiful jewelry and original artwork for sale. You'll see inspiring murals portraying Navajo people who are role models for success in their lives and chosen fields. Taking six years to complete, the murals were created by award-winning Navajo artist Chester Kahn. The murals completely fill the upper walls of the store. Featuring doctors, lawyers, business people, spiritual leaders, entertainers and the Navajo Code Talkers, the murals were conceived to help Navajo youth set their goals high. For nearly 40 years now, Ellis Tanner has worked hard to build a solid reputation in the Indian trading business. When you shop at Ellis Tanner Trading Company, you'll find a huge selection of handmade turquoise and silver jewelry and artwork in all price ranges. Everywhere you turn inside Ellis Tanner Trading Company, you'll see something to delight your senses. Fetishes and carvings abound. Baskets and pottery line shelves and hang from walls. Native American music CDs delight your ears. Your eyes will feast upon walls covered in awarding-winning paintings and artwork. If you're looking for Pendleton blankets, Ellis Tanner is an authorized Pendleton dealer. You'll find a full line of Pendleton products like backpacks, purses, picnic sets, and even mousepads. Experience the true spirit of the

Indian Touch of Gallup

Located in the old White Café building constructed circa 1928, Indian Touch of Gallup is a fabulous gallery displaying authentic Native American artwork, including rugs, pottery and silver jewelry. Indian Touch of Gallup is owned and overseen by the Ayesh family, with three generations of traders who have worked closely with the Native American population. This is the ideal place to find the work of your favorite Native American artists, such as Calvin Begay, Daniel Etcitty and Lori Smith of the Navajo tribe. Zuni artists represented here include Effie Calavaza and Bobby Shack. Indian Touch of Gallup has an in-house silversmith who will happily show you how Native American Indian jewelry is made. Many of the artists featured at Indian Touch have taken to restructuring traditional motifs into more contemporary pieces, which keeps the market more demanding while allowing local families to retain their heritage. The shop keeps long hours, open daily from 8 am to 8 pm, and someone is always available and happy to give visitors a complimentary tour of shop and the unique pieces that line its shelves. Find exquisite pieces of the past and modern day Native American art destined to become treasures of the future at Indian Touch of Gallup.

106 W Historic Highway 66, Gallup NM   (505) 722-6807 or (877) 507-2923

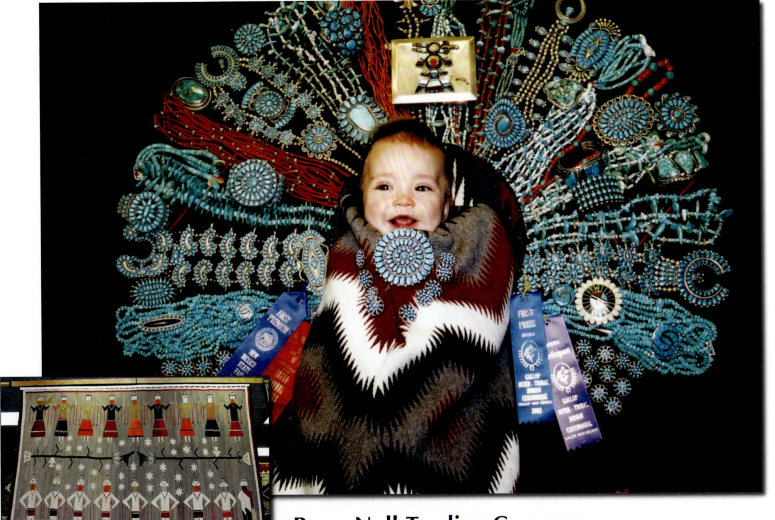

Perry Null Trading Company

Tobe Turpen's Trading Post opened in 1939 and served as a bank, store and community gathering place for area tribes, which included the Hopi, Zuni and Navajo. In 2003, Perry Null, who had 36 years of experience in the trading post business, purchased the historic post and renamed it Perry Null Trading Company. Although the name has changed, this popular hub continues to serve as a bank for Native Americans who come each week to cash paychecks, pawn their art for cash and trade news. Null continues to work with the artists, teaching them how to keep their valuable work safe, which is far easier to do in a pawn vault than in a hogan. The Perry Null Trading Company offers a vast selection of original and often one-of-a-kind collector's pieces, including old silver and turquoise jewelry, Navajo rugs and kachina dolls. You can also find wonderful fetishes, bolos and belt buckles. Perry Null Trading Company is an ideal place to learn the history of pawn, which is far different from what the seedy pawn shops lining urban streets would lead you to believe, and find out how these trading posts influenced both American and Native American history. Explore New Mexico's past while relishing the art of many generations at Perry Null Trading Company.

1710 S Second Street, Gallup NM (505) 863-5249 or (505) 722-3806
www.pntrader.com   www.tobeturpens.com

Richardson's Trading Company

Nestled into the heart of downtown Gallup is New Mexico's oldest and most colorful trading post, Richardson's Trading Company. Established in 1913, this fabulous post has been continually family owned and operated. Fourth generation owner Bill Richardson learned the trade as a small boy on the reservation circa 1916, and he continues today to be an active part of the business along with the fifth generation Richardson, Bill's daughter Frances. The company moved to its current location in 1935, where it has continued to draw a large and faithful clientele. Richardson's Trading Company is an echo of the past, and continues to be run in much the same way as it was almost 100 years ago. The post gleams with nostalgia, from the polished hardwood floors to the pew-like benches and the old pawn jewelry. Here you can find everything from rugs and baskets to pottery and fine art paintings by some of the country's top Native American artists. Indian trading makes up about 90 percent of the Richardson's business even today, with the other 10 percent going to retail and wholesale trade. Richardson's Trading Company boasts numerous third and fourth generation customers, and many deals are still sealed over a handshake. Whether you're searching for antique pieces or scoping out contemporary Native American art, you can find it all at Richardson's Trading Company, where the Richardsons have been garnering a reputation for quality and integrity for nearly a century.

222 W Historic Route 66, Gallup NM
(505) 722-4762
www.richardsontrading.com

Photo by Eddie Rivera

Photos by John Andrews

Toadlena Trading Post

Toadlena Trading Post is a busy place that offers a glimpse into the past. This trading post maintains a lifestyle that the Navajo and traders have played out for over 100 years and nurtures a centuries-old weaving tradition. The Navajos arrived from the North and learned the weaving techniques from the Pueblo Indians. Navajo weaving utilizes the upright loom of the Anasazi, the weaving techniques of the Pueblo people and the wool of the Spanish. Early fur trappers traded the Navajo red cloth for access to their land. The Navajo coveted the red cloth because they could not create this color on their own. Permanent trading posts sprouted around the reservation. The demand for Navajo rugs increased and by 1900 the traders and weavers were working together to develop marketable textiles that appealed to the white man. Thirteen regional designs within seven weaving districts emerged inside the Navajo Nation, each named for its trading post. Each district offered spectacular textiles. The most coveted Navajo textile today is the Two Grey Hills from Toadlena. It is far superior because it possesses more wefts to the linear inch, resulting in a finer weave. Traders Bloomfield and Davies encouraged the weavers of Toadlena to weave more finely, create more intricate designs and use only hand spun native wool in the natural colors of the sheep. The result is intricate geometric designs in variations of black, brown, gray, beige and cream. Toadlena operates today in the same way trading posts did in the 1870s, directly with the weaver and their family. At Toadlena Trading Post, you are offered the unique opportunity to acquire a textile of timeless beauty and lasting value.

(505) 789-3267 or (888) 420-0005
www.toadlenatradingpost.com

Palms Trading Post

Palms Trading Post is the only business that can boast of having the largest selection of both Pueblo pottery and Native American jewelry in the Southwest, and the most affordable prices. You can find this great shop just east of Historic Old Town on the corner of 15th and Lomas Streets. Owner Guy Berger makes it his goal to provide the magic of Southwestern art for the wholesale and retail trade. The Palms Trading Post is the bridge between Native American artisans and Native American art collectors. As a trusted source for more than 30 years, Guy and his staff will give you honest advice and help you purchase the craft that is best suited to your taste and budget. Palms Trading Post purchases art from Acoma, Santa Clara, Jemez and numerous other places. Guy goes to great lengths to get as much information about the artists as possible, so that every piece of pottery tells a story and becomes a symbol of the artist's life. Palms Trading Post carries gorgeous products that you are sure to appreciate, so come to the shop and view the great selection.

1504 Lomas Boulevard NW, Albuquerque NM
(505) 247-8504
www.palmstrading.com

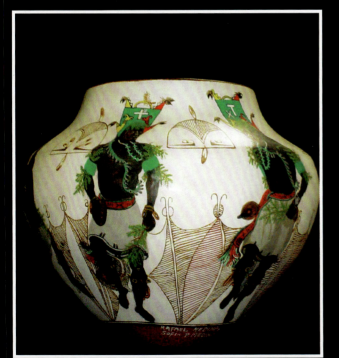

Gus's Trading Company

As you travel along historic Route 66 through Old Town Albuquerque, make time for a visit to Gus's Trading Company, where you will find the best prices in town on traditional native art and artifacts. Owner Gus Archuletta, an area resident for more than 65 years, opened his popular shop in 1981 and offers a wonderful selection of work by Native American Zuni, Navajo and Santo Domingo tribes. Gus's Trading Company carries extraordinary jewelry, as well as other Native American arts and crafts. Look

for kachina dolls, handmade pottery, paintings and numerous artifacts from New Mexico's prominent Pueblo cultures. Gus himself is perhaps best known for the jewelry he wears, which amounts in value to nearly $70,000 dollars and turns Gus into a walking advertisement for the stunning collection of Native American jewelry and collectibles that he exhibits at the store. Gus's Trading Company specializes in providing quality merchandise at a great price, which has led to a faithful following of customers from across the country and around the world. Find the pieces you will adore at prices you can afford with a trip to Gus's Trading Company, a Route 66 tradition for more than 25 years.

2026 Central Avenue SW, Albuquerque NM
(505) 843-6381

Wind River Trading

If you want the real thing, head to Wind River Trading in Santa Fe. Carrying authentic Native American jewelry, pottery, rugs and artifacts, Wind River Trading has all your home décor needs. Sisters Jean, Marie and Barbara have owned this unique shop for more than six years, and their passion for Native American artifacts really shows. They travel directly to reservations throughout the West to purchase the most beautiful and authentic products for their store. Additionally, they travel to Mexico for pottery and folk art and 19 different Pueblos for exquisitely handmade goods. The shop features a large estate jewelry section and a specialty moccasin shop. These hard-working women don't run their family-owned business from afar. Their parents originally owned it, and you'll find each of them working in the shop on a regular basis. Their hands-on involvement and dedication to their work attracts collectors from all over the United States.

112 E Palace Avenue, Santa Fe NM
(505) 989-7062

Shiprock rises from the terrain in northwestern New Mexico. The 1,700-foot volcanic plume is renowned not just for its rugged beauty, but also for the legends and spiritual power it contains. Shiprock is a sacred site to the Navajo people.
Photo by Mark Nohl, courtesy of the New Mexico Tourism Department

320 • Wineries & Breweries

Known as "Sky City," the Pueblo of Acoma's main village is situated on a 367-foot-high sandstone rock. It is considered to be the oldest inhabited village in the United States. In the background is Acoma's legendary Enchanted Mesa.
Photo Courtesy of the New Mexico Tourism Department

Wineries & Breweries

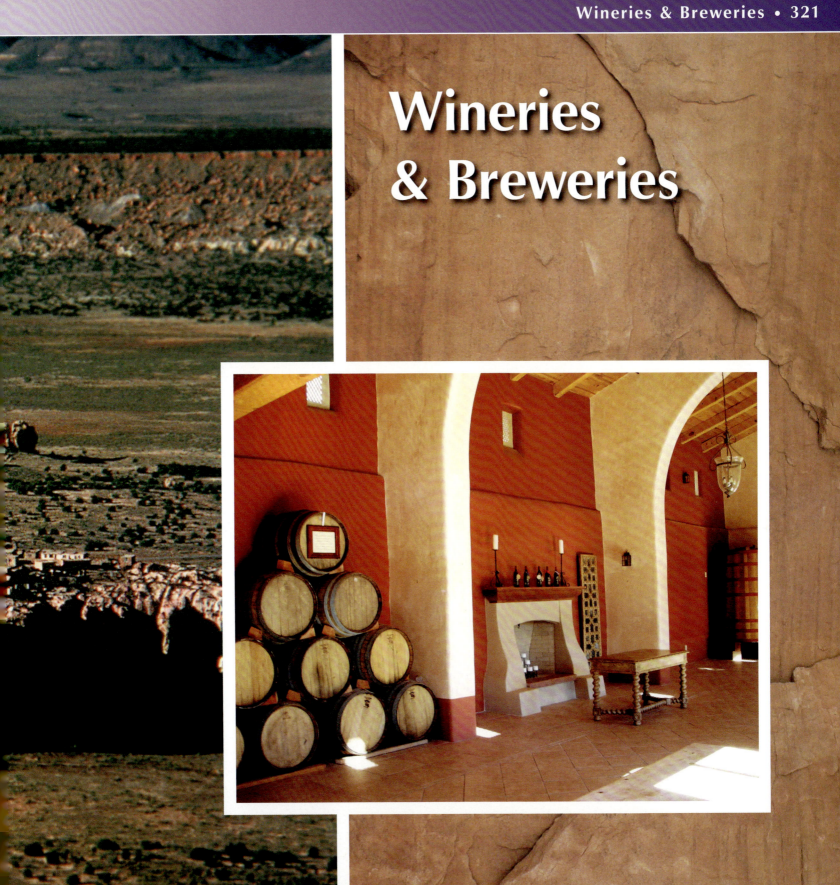

Tierra Encantada Vineyards & Winery

Tierra Encantada means "enchanted land." What better name for a winery located deep within New Mexico, the Land of Enchantment? Tierra Encantada Vineyards & Winery has been winning state fair ribbons ever since it opened its doors in 2004. In 2002 and 2003, it took best of show in the noncommercial category. The winery, located in Albuquerque's South Valley, one of the oldest agricultural regions in New Mexico, is a dream come true for owners Jim Dowling and Pat Coil, who have spent many years studying, sampling and collecting the great wines of the world, as well as experimenting with wine production. At Tierra Encantada, they present New World versions of their favorite grape varietals, including a white Viognier with a hint of gardenia; a smooth, dry Sauvignon Blanc; and a refreshing blend of Vidal, Seyval and Villard, known as VSV. The winery's red wines are equally delightful and include a Chambourcin-Merlot blend that goes well with New Mexico's spicy dishes; a Syrah that tastes of black pepper and spices and has a long, lingering finish; and a classic Cabernet Sauvignon. Tierra Encantada, just a 10-minute drive from Old Town, is open Friday, Saturday and Sunday afternoons. Let your spirit and taste buds experience an enchanted land with a visit to Tierra Encantada Vineyards & Winery.

1872 Five Points Road SW, Albuquerque NM
(505) 764-WINE (9463)

Gruet Winery

Even 100 years ago it was common knowledge that the best cigars came from Havana, the best chocolate came from Belgium and the best sparkling wine from Champagne, France. Fortunately, a lot changes in 100 years, and the Gruet Winery in Albuquerque has been producing a lovely selection of champagne-style sparkling wines since 1989. After scouting out California wine country for a place to begin a new venture, the family traveled to New Mexico, where they met with a group of European winemakers who had successfully planted vineyards in Engle. Patriarch Gilbert Gruet, the creator of the Gruet Champagne house in Béthon, France in 1952, decided to plant an experimental vineyard exclusively with Pinot Noir and Chardonnay, the two main grapes of Champagne. Gilbert's children, winemaker Laurent and daughter Nathalie, along with family friend Farid Himeur, relocated to New Mexico to pursue a U.S.-based winemaking adventure. Their success has been astounding. Since their first release in 1989, Gruet sparkling wines have won hundreds of gold medals at national and international wine competitions. Their elegant barrel-fermented Chardonnays and barrel-aged Pinot Noirs have received considerable attention and praise, garnering gold medals. Located at 4,300-feet elevation, the Gruet vineyards are some of the highest in the United States. This means that regardless of how hot the days are, the nights are cool, which slows down ripening and produces grapes that have a wonderfully piquant acidity, making Gruet sparkling wines crisp, lively and refreshing. Experience these exciting and distinctive New Mexican wines at the Gruet Winery.

**8400 Pan American Freeway NE,
Albuquerque NM
(505) 821-0055 or (888) 857-WINE (9463)**
www.gruetwinery.com

Casa Rondeña Winery

Let the sound of sparkling fountains soothe you in the spring, or the warmth of a crackling fire protect you from winter's chill air, while sipping fine wine in sensuous surroundings at Casa Rondeña Winery in Albuquerque. Stroll through the Great Hall, complete with cathedral ceilings, an antique oak fermentation tank and Indian-carved sandstone-shaded windows. The elegant visions of John Calvin gave rise to this winery. Since 1990, Calvin has dedicated himself to making New Mexico's best red wines and has become a pioneer of premium wine making in the state. He has increased the popularity of New Mexican wine making and has been turning heads and winning medals for his vintages in competitions from California to Florida. Although Calvin is a native of the Rio Grande Valley, his passion for world music led him to study the classical music of India and the Flamenco of southern Spain. It was there that he began to form his own philosophy that wine, music and architecture all allow us to experience beauty and weave the diverse elements of nature and earth into a delicate pattern. With this firmly in mind Calvin created Casa Rondeña, a harmonious blending of all things alluring. Magnificent symmetry and construction are wedded with fine wine and exquisite music. From the tasting room and tours to private celebrations and music festivals, the Casa Rondeña Winery is an enchanting salute to the beauty that is life.

**733 Chavez Road NW,
Los Ranchos de Albuquerque NM
(505) 344-5911 or (800) 706-1699
www.casarondena.com**

 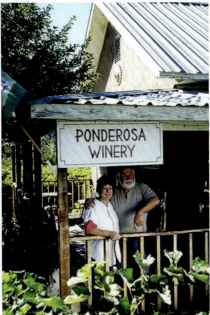 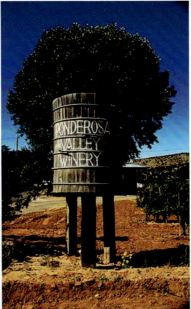 

Ponderosa Valley Vineyards & Winery

Comfortably situated on the southern slopes of the Jemez Mountains is a small, intimate valley where you'll find the beautiful Ponderosa Valley Vineyard & Winery. The area is considered one of the region's premier areas for growing wine grapes. Owners Henry and Mary Street purchased three acres in the valley for a camping retreat in 1975. It wasn't long before they noticed numerous small vineyards in the area. The families who owned these vineyards held on to strong family traditions of winemaking and grape growing. The seed was planted for the Streets to establish their own vineyard. After taking a course in winemaking and researching viticulture varietals, the first plantings were French Hybrids. In 1978, on the advice of a California winemaker, they were encouraged to try Rieslings, and this proved to be incredibly successful. Since then, Henry has added a cold-hardy Pinot Noir varietal and expanded the vineyard to more than eight and a half acres. The area's climate, combined with the richness of volcanic soil, has proven to be a winning combination when it comes to producing wines. By carefully picking the grapes at differing levels of ripeness, they produce four distinct, award-winning signature wines. You can sample their wines in their tasting room along with numerous other releases. Henry and Mary encourage you to bring your entire family, tour their vineyards and winery and discover how handcrafted award-winning wines are produced.

3171 Highway 290, Ponderosa NM
(505) 834-7487 or (800) WINE MKR
www.ponderosawinery.com

Vivác Winery

In the fall of 2003, two brothers who grew up in Dixon started a winemaking venture. Their goal was to make wine they would enjoy drinking, and have a good time doing it. Jesse and Chris Padberg, inspired by rural lifestyles in France and Italy, started Vivác (pronounced Vee-vok) on land owned by their father. Today, the Padbergs' red wines rival those found at high altitudes in Germany, in Italy's Piedmonte and in Walla Walla, Washington. Vivác is a Spanish mountaineering term, which refers to a high altitude refuge or high base camp. The Padbergs' vineyard is probably the northernmost planting in New Mexico. You can find Jesse and Chris working with passion and enthusiasm at their boutique winery, where all steps are meticulously performed by hand. Vivác participates in several wine festivals throughout the state and hosts shows by New Mexico artists. The winery is open for tasting and more information can be found on the website. Stop by Vivác Winery for a unique and fun winery experience.

7075 State Highway 68, Embudo NM
(505) 579-4441
www.vivacwinery.com

Pecos River

Madison Vineyards and Winery

Madison Vineyards and Winery is in an area rich in the history of its trade. New Mexico is the oldest wine-producing area in the United States. In the early 1500s, Spanish settlers brought European grapes to the new territory. By the 1580s, the missionary priests extended the vineyards and began tending to the fruits of their sacramental wines. By the 19th century, wineries and vineyards dotted the entire Rio Grande Valley. Prohibition curtailed regional production, but a recent resurgence has more than 5,000 acres under cultivation for the production of superior wine. Northern New Mexico has a long, proud tradition of wine production. Today, the family-owned and operated Madison Vineyards and Winery quietly produces 4,000 gallons of award-winning dry and semi-sweet wines a year in the village of El Barranco. Bill and Elise Madison work together on the wine, with help from daughters Lisa and Heather. The beautiful Pecos River runs alongside their vineyards. The vines sink their roots into the sandy and red-soiled clays of the region, with spectacular results. Some of the offerings are French hybrids. These New Mexico natives claim to have started the winery to avoid the typical eight-to-five job, but their passion for the craft has turned the enterprise into a labor of love. The Madison Vineyard and Winery is truly an asset to the wine-making world. The Madison family invites you to browse the gallery and visit their well-crafted tasting room for a taste of the nectars.

HCR 72, Box 490, Ribera NM
(505) 421-8028
www.madison-winery.com

Cottonwood Winery

After major surgery and a doctor's recommendation to drink two glasses of wine or grape juice every day to extend his life, Dale Taylor prepared to experiment with some varieties of grapes on the 1,500-acre family farm north of Artesia to see what might grow best in the area. Cottonwood Winery is the creation of Dale and his wife, Penny. With the help of friends and family members, the winery is quickley expanding. The winery provides limited bottling of several notable wines, including Gewurztraminer, a white wine with a spicy bouquet. The Taylors also sell Merlot and a popular black muscat, a sweet dessert wine. The winery mainly serves as a tasting room for regional New Mexico wines and is a gift shop and carrier of New Mexico food products. Dale and Penny encourage the public to stop by and try the wines or take it easy by the nearby pond. The winery's rural setting, surrounded by horses and llamas grazing on serene pastures, makes a great place to stage a special gathering and Cottonwood Winery can cater parties of up to 100 people. Younger visitors are also welcome, with non-alcoholic beverages available for their enjoyment. The gift shop offers gourmet mustards, relishes and other foods that go great with a bottle of fine wine. Take a drive into the farm country near Artesia and stop to drink to your health at Cottonwood Winery.

1 E Cottonwood Road, Artesia, NM
(505) 308-9391

Willmon Vineyards

Willmon Vineyards has been a favorite with the people of Ruidoso for a long time, and now the rest of the world is finding out what locals already knew about these artful wines. Recently, the Willmon Vineyards Quatro won a silver medal in the Bordeaux blend class at the prestigious San Francisco Wine Competition. This speaks volumes for the high quality of the wines Willmon Vineyards is producing, considering that there were more than 3,300 entries in the competition from all over the country. You can stop by and taste these award-winning wines at either of Willmon Vineyards' two unique retail stores, End of the Vine and Viva New Mexico. End of the Vine carries a wide selection of gourmet cheeses, stemware and other gift items to complement the wines. Regular customers often drop in to pick up fresh bread from a local baker and a bottle of wine to go with dinner. If you can stay a little longer, the wine bar is a great place to relax with friends. Viva New Mexico showcases the talents of local artists and carries all New Mexico-made products. Both stores display the talents of owners Jessica and Scott Willmon, who have backgrounds in art and interior design. Stop by either location for some great wine and good food.

2801 Sudderth Drive, Ruidoso NM
(505) 630-WINE (9463)

La Viña Winery

La Viña Winery, which sits alongside the Don Juan de Onate trail in La Union, is the state's oldest winery and specializes in the creation of some of New Mexico's finest vintages. Winemaking in the region began around 400 years ago when Spanish colonists, who were led north by conquistadors, established vineyards along the Rio Grande. Today this area, known as the Mesilla Valley, is able is produce a wide variety of distinctive world-class wines due to high desert elevation, rich soil and controlled irrigation. This family-owned and operated winery was established in 1977 and has been a community favorite since its inception. La Viña produces a full spectrum of estate-bottled wines, including a nice variety of dry reds and whites, along with a pleasing assortment of sweet wines, such as Rojo Loco, and sparkling wines like La Dolce Viña, the winery's bestseller. Proprietors Ken and Denise Stark host numerous annual events, including an old fashioned country picnic for the Fourth of July, and the sylvan grounds are the ideal spot for weddings and other special events. The winery is composed of a 24-acre vineyard, along with two acres of park-like grounds and a patio area where patrons can enjoy picnics and other events. During the spring, summer and fall, the tasting room at La Viña Winery is open every day except Wednesday from noon to five pm, and wine tours are offered at 11:30 am. Call for winter hours. Enjoy a new kind of high desert experience with a visit to La Viña Winery.

4201 S Highway 28, La Union NM (505) 882-7632 *www.lavinawinery.com*

Wineries & Breweries • 331

332 • Wineries & Breweries

Gila Cliff Dwellings National Monument offers a glimpse of the homes and lives of the people of the Mogollon culture who lived in the Gila Wilderness from the 1280s through the early 1300s. The surroundings probably look today very much like they did when the cliff dwellings were inhabited.
Photo and text courtesy of the National Park Service

Tractor Brewing Company

The Tractor Brewing Company™ honors the good things in life, like beer, tractors, family and good friends. Tractors are as prominent as beer at the brewery, affectionately called the Beer Farm. Outside you'll find antique tractors restored by the president of the company. Inside look for hundreds of tractor models mounted on walls and positioned on a carousel and a Ferris wheel. The tasting room continues the farm theme with a roof reminiscent of a barn. The beer is everything you could hope to find, with farm fresh flavor sure to enliven your day or evening. Try Tractor's Hay Maker Honey Wheat™ or Sod Buster Pale Ale™. Taste the naturally rich flavor of earth in the Double Plow Oatmeal Stout or the crisp flavor of the Farmer's Tan Red Ale™. The beers are natural accompaniments to Ribs Hickory Pit Barbecue, located next door to the brewery. Continue your celebration of the good life with collectible hats and shirts emblazoned with the Tractor Brewing Company logo and Getplowed.com, Tractor's catchy web address. The website is a great place to check for upcoming events sponsored by Tractor, such as the large bike rally, which touts bikes, bands, barbecue, brew and babes. For a homegrown microbrewery experience just 25 tasty miles south of Albuquerque, visit Tractor Brewing Company.

120 Nelson Lane, Los Lunas NM
(505) 866-0477
www.getplowed.com

Sierra Blanca Brewing Co.

New Mexico's largest brewery, Sierra Blanca Brewing Co., recently moved to the Albuquerque Metro Area. Richard and Suzanne Weber started the brewery 10 years ago in Carrizozo and it went on to become one of the top 100 breweries in America. Their microbrews include the top seller among New Mexico-made beers, Alien Amber Ale, as well as a Pilsner, Pale Ale, Nut Brown, Stout, IPA, Lager and Wheat. Sierra Blanca Brewing Co. also brews two sodas, root beer and ginger ale, under the label Way 2 Cool. The brewery's number one objective remains the consistency and quality of the product. Their state-of-the-art equipment plays a role in masterfully producing flavored crystal clear beers. Enjoy a gift shop and tasting room, with free tours Monday through Friday 10 am to 4 pm. Cheers!

1016 Industrial Avenue E, Moriarty NM
(505) 257-BEER (2337)
www.sierrablancabrewery.com

Kelly's Brew Pub

The handcrafted microbrews, the food and the welcome are some of the top reasons for a decade of success enjoyed by Kelly's Brew Pub in Nob Hill. Kelly's Brew Pub has 20 of its handcrafted beers on tap. The pub is friendly to families, businesses and even dogs. Yes, that's right; the outdoor patio welcomes all dogs, a rare find for dog lovers. Canine cuisine is offered on the regular menu, so both you and your dog can feast together. Owners Dennis and Janice Bonfantine run their business in this relaxed, forward-thinking manner, which greatly pleases their patrons. Try their fish tacos with rice and beans or the Reuben sandwich with fries or salad. For dinner, indulge in a fresh fillet of salmon. A choice of house wines and Kelly's pints make fitting accompaniments to your meal. The University of New Mexico's *Daily Lobo* newspaper honored Kelly's with an award for Best Beer Selection, and the weekly *Alibi* newspaper named it Best Brew Pub for three consecutive years. The pub also earned an award from Albuquerque Conservation Association for the restoration and renovation of the former Jones Motor Company building, a tribute to Albuquerque's past and the beginning of a new era for this respected pub. Kelly's can seat more than 100 at one time. You can even call ahead to brew your own beer as part of a party or business gathering at Kelly's. Visit Kelly's Brew Pub for handcrafted beers, great food and friendly surroundings.

3222 Central Avenue SE, Albuquerque NM
(505) 262-BREW (2739)
www.kellysbrewpub.com

Santa Fe Brewing Company

The oldest microbrewery in New Mexico will certainly make a beer lover happy. Santa Fe Brewing Company is ready to make entire families happy, as well, with a new pub and grill next door, a kid's playroom and indoor and outdoor bars featuring at least eight beers, including the company's flagship pale ale. Santa Fe Brewing Company came to the attention of the New Mexico State Fair and the Great American Beer Festival shortly after opening in 1988. Today, the company can boast of many award-winning brews, including the Santa Fe Wheat and Nut Brown, along with the State Pen Porter and the Sangre de Frambusa. All beers are made from the finest hops shipped directly from Washington growers, and specialty malts imported from the United Kingdom. The beers, made without preservatives or pasteurization, are conditioned in the bottle, creating natural carbonization and a rich, complex taste. Call ahead for a Saturday tour or stop by the tasting room Tuesday through Saturday. The new Pub & Grill can treat you to the company's microbrews, as well as breakfast, lunch or dinner seven days a week. Live music, pool tables and a patio add to the fun. Kids can choose from a menu of their favorites, including the largest assortment of Taos Cow ice cream in Santa Fe. The restaurant can be rented for a party or conference. Catering services range from appetizers to elaborate main dishes. For memorable beers served in a casual, non-smoking environment, visit Santa Fe Brewing Company.

27 and 35 Fire Place, Santa Fe NM
(505) 424-3333
www.santafebrewing.com

Wineries & Breweries • 337

A reliable waterhole hidden at the base of a massive sandstone bluff made El Morro (*the bluff*) a popular campsite. Ancestral Puebloans settled on the mesa top over 700 years ago. Spanish and American travelers rested, drank from the pool and carved their signatures, dates and messages for hundreds of years. Today, El Morro National Monument protects over 2,000 inscriptions and petroglyphs, as well as Ancestral Puebloan ruins.
Photo and text courtesy of the National Parks Service

Index by Business

A

Aboot About Santa Fe 100
Absolute Nirvana Spa, and the Madeleine Inn 18, 209
ABYDOS 217
Adobe Silver at Naranjo's Arts 169
Albuquerque Biological Park 80
Alma del Monte "Spirit of the Mountain"
    Bed & Breakfast 21
American International Rattlesnake Museum 81
Anderson-Abruzzo Albuquerque
    International Balloon Museum 82
Andrews Pueblo Pottery & Art Gallery 164
Angels' Ascent Retreat & Spa 7, 207
Annapurna Ayurvedic Cuisine & Chai House 249
Apple Tree Restaurant 263
Art Divas Gallery 152
Artifacts Gallery and The Studios 193
Art is OK Gallery & Sculpture Garden 166
Asian Adobe 219
Austing Haus Bed & Breakfast 20

B

Back At The Ranch 139
Back Road Pizza 254
Barry's Oasis 241
Bavarian Lodge and Restaurant, The 17
Bean, The 264
Bear Creek Cabins 38
Beauty and the Beads 49
Best Western Adobe Inn 29
Best Western Kachina Lodge 23
Best Western Mesilla Valley Inn 36
Best Western Sands 28
Big River Raft Trips 99
Billy the Kid Museum 69
Blackjack's Grill 269
Blue Dome Gallery 187
Bodywise Massage & Day Spa 204
Böttger Mansion of Old Town 11
Bradbury Science Museum 102
¡Bravo! Fine Wine, Foods & Spirits 265
Brazos Fine Art 148
Brown Cow Saddle Blanket Company 292
Burnt Well Guest Ranch 31

C

Café Des Artistes 256
Candy Lady, The 276
Carlsbad Caverns National Park 115
Casa Blanca Inn 40
Casa de Benavidez 243
Casa de la Chimeneas Inn & Spa 24
Casa Rondeña Winery 324
Casa Verde Salon and Spa 206
Casa Vieja 248
Celebro Natural Fiber Clothing 132
Centinela Traditional Arts 304
Cho's Tae Kwan Do New Mexico 224
Christopher Thomson Ironworks 180
Church Street Café 249
Clear Light • the Cedar Company 281
Closets Too 215
Coleman Gallery of Contemporary Art 169
Cottonwood Winery 328
Courtyard By Marriott 42
Cowboys and Indians Antiques 275
Cowgirl BBQ & Western Grill 257
Cozy Jewel Gallery 179
Critters & Me, The 289

D

Dancing Wolf & Narrow Gauge
    Gifts & Boutique 285
Day Spa at Serenity Gardens 205
Desert Designs 134
Destination Southwest 72
Dragonfly Journeys 156

E

Elaine's, A Bed and Breakfast 6
Elemental Arts 186
Ellis Store Country Inn, The 30
Ellis Tanner Trading Company 311
Elodie Holmes Liquid Light Glass 154
El Pinto Foods 244
El Pinto Restaurant 245
El Rancho de las Golondrinas 98
El Rancho Hotel & Motel 41
Enchanted Southwest, The 273
Enchanted Trails RV Park & Trading Post 10
Ernest Thompson Furniture 214
Española Valley Fiber Arts Center 303

F

Far Flung Adventures 229
Farnsworth Gallery Taos 149
Fiesta City Tours 229
Fishback Studio of the Dance 224
Follow the Sun, Inc. 223
Fountain Theatre, The 124
Framing Concepts Gallery 168

G

GALERIA 200 184
Gallery Between
    & Head in the Clouds Productions, The 181
Gallup Historical Society 128
Garcia's Colonial Gallery 157
Geronimo Trail Scenic Byway 56
Gertrude Zachary Inc. 279
Ghost Town Trading Co. 282
Glowing Maternity & Baby Boutique 133
Grace Corn Heritage House 113
Grasshopper Silk 63, 183
Great Southwest Adventures 222
Gruet Winery 323
Guilloume's Fine Art 177
Gus's Trading Company 317

H

Hacienda Nicholas 15
Hacienda Vargas 7
Hatch Brothers Trading Post 310
Heart of the Lotus Gift Bazaar 284
HeliNM 233
High Country Gardens 198
High Desert Angler 234
Historic Pelham House Sanctuary and Retreat 35
Honey Do Home Repair and Closets Too 215
Hotel Albuquerque at Old Town 9
Hotel Encanto de Las Cruces–
    A Heritage Hotel and Resort 37
Hotel Plaza Real 26
Hotel St. Francis 19
Hubbard Museum of the American West, The 118

I

Indian Pueblo Cultural Center 83
IndianTouch of Gallup 312
Inger Jirby's Taos Guest Houses 146
Inger Jirby Gallery 147
Inn at Paradise, The 10, 207
Innovations Gift Gallery 277
International UFO Museum and Research Center, The 117

J

J&R Vintage Auto Museum 88
Jd Challenger Studio/Gallery 150
Joseph's Bar & Grill 71

K

Kelly's Brew Pub 240, 335
Kioti 138
Kit Carson Home and Museum 94
Kokoman Fine Wines & Liquors 292

L

La Bella Spa and Salon 202
La Paz Imports 290
La Trattoria Italian Restaurant & Steakhouse 268
La Quinta Inn & Suites of Deming 39
La Quinta Inn & Suites Roswell 33
La Viña Winery 330
Las Cosas Kitchen Shoppe and Cooking School 287
Las Cruces City Museums 122
Lavande Bleu 272
Leyba & Ingalls Arts – Supplies and Gallery 188
Links at Sierra Blanca, The 236
Lodge at Santa Fe, The 22
Lois Duffy Art 189
Los Rios Anglers 231

M

Mabel Dodge Luhan House 21
Madison Vineyards and Winery 327
Maria's New Mexican Kitchen 257
Mesilla, Town of 121
Mesilla Valley Maze 120
Millicent Rogers Museum 95
Montezuma Castle 104
Morningside Antiques 274
Mountain Arts Gallery 182
Museum of Archaeology and Material Culture 87
Museum of Fine Arts 96
Museum of Indian Arts & Culture 93
Museum of International Folk Art 90

N

Nancy Kozikowski at DSG Fine Art 170
National Atomic Museum 84
National Solar Observatory 111
Native Jackets 141
Nativo Lodge 12
New Grounds Print Workshop & Gallery 165
New Mexico Farm & Ranch Heritage Museum 123
New Mexico Museum of Space History 116
New Mexico State University Bookstore 291
New Mexico State University Golf Course 237

O

Ojo Caliente Mineral Springs & Spa 14
Old Pass Gallery 178
Ooh! Aah! Jewelry 133
Orlando's New Mexican Café 253
Ortega's Weaving Shop 305
Oviedo Carvings & Bronze 160

P

Palace of the Governors 97
Palette Contemporary Art & Craft 172
Palms Trading Post 316
PaperGami 46
PATRICIAN DESIGN Caliente, It's Hot! 173
Pendaries Village, Mountain Resort and Golf Community 105
Pennysmiths Paper 277
Perry Null Trading Company 313
Peterson-Cody Gallery, Ltd. 157
Philmont Scout Ranch Museums 109
Pine Cone Inn 8
Pinon Café 250
Ponderosa Valley Vineyards & Winery 325
Potteries, The 185
Prairie Dog Glass 155
Pueblo Balloon Company 235

R

R.C. Gorman/Nizhoni Gallery 167
Rainbow Ryders Hot Air Balloon Company, Inc. 227
Ramada Inn Ruidoso 32
Rancho de Chimayó Restaurante 252
Rare Earth Studio Gallery 158
Re/MAX One 218
Refugio Verde 208
Rellenos Café by Antonio 266
Richardson's Trading Company 314
RioBravoFineArt, Inc. 62, 190
Rio Grande Zoo, The 80
Roasted Clove 267
Route 66 Auto Museum 70
Rural Museums of Sierra County 55

S

Sadie's Restaurant of New Mexico 246
Sage Builders 217
Salman Raspberry Ranch and La Cueva Historic District 199, 288
Sandia Peak Tramway 73, 247
San Francisco Street Bar & Grill and Santa Fe Bar & Grill 258
Sangre de Cristo Mill 300
Santa Fe Baking Company and Café 259
Santa Fe Brewing Company 260, 336
Santa Fe Greenhouses 198
Santa Fe Opera, The 101
Santa Fe Weaving Gallery 162
Santa Rosa, City of Natural Lakes 65
Santa Rosa Blue Hole 67
Santa Rosa Golf Course & Country Club 68
Santa Rosa Park Lake 68
Sarabande Bed & Breakfast 8
Schelu Gallery 171
Seventh Goddess 135
Sierra Blanca Brewing Co. 78, 334
Sierra County Arts Council 58
Sierra County Birding 59
Sierra County Lakes and Rivers 61
Sierra Grande Lodge and Spa 34, 210
Silver City Museum, The 125
Silver Sun 136
Skyspan Adventures 225
Smokey Bear Historical Park 119
Smokey Bear Museum 119
Solano's Boot & Western Wear 140

Southwest Spanish Craftsmen 216
Spencer Theater 110
Sportsman's Lodge 16
St. James Tearoom, The 242
Stakeout Grill & Bar 255
Starving Artists Gallery 152
Steaksmith at El Gancho 261
Stone Mountain Bead Gallery 47
Sumner & Dene 174, 280
Susan's Christmas Shop 293

T

Tad Tribal Art Gallery 159
Tailwater Gallery & Fly Shop 162, 286
Taos Gallery Association 145
Taos Ski Valley 232
Taos Sporting Clays 230
Tapetes de Lana Gallery 301
Teofilo's Restaurante 251
Terra Firma 283
Tierra Encantada Vineyards & Winery 322
Tierra Wools 302
Tinkertown Museum 89
Toadlena Trading Post 306, 315
Tomasita's Restaurant 262
Touchstone Inn and Riverbend Spa 25
Tractor Brewing Company 77, 333
Tropic of Capricorn 196
Truth or Consequences Hot Springs and Spa Association 57
Truth or Consequences Museums 54
Turquoise Museum, The 85

U

University of New Mexico, The 75
University of New Mexico Bookstore, The 76
Unser Racing Museum 86

V

Very Large Array Radio Telescope, The 126
Victory Alpaca Ranch 107, 307
Vietnam Veterans Memorial State Park 106
Village Pizza 250
Vivác Winery 326

W

Weems Galleries and Framing 176
White Sands National Monument 103
Whittington Center, The 228
Wilder Nightingale Fine Art 151
WilLee's Blues Club 265
Willmon Vineyards 329
Wind River Trading 318
Wright's Indian Art 175

Z

Zane Wheeler Gallery 153

Index by Category

Accommodations

Albuquerque
  Böttger Mansion of Old Town 11
  Enchanted Trails RV Park & Trading Post 10
  Hotel Albuquerque at Old Town 9
  Inn at Paradise, The 10
  Nativo Lodge 12
  Sarabande Bed & Breakfast 8
Algodones
  Hacienda Vargas 7
Cedar Crest
  Angels' Ascent Retreat & Spa 7
  Elaine's, A Bed and Breakfast 6
Deming
  La Quinta Inn & Suites of Deming 39
Farmington
  Casa Blanca Inn 40
  Courtyard By Marriott 42
Gallup
  El Rancho Hotel & Motel 41
Hatch
  Historic Pelham House Sanctuary and Retreat 35
Las Cruces
  Best Western Mesilla Valley Inn 36
  Hotel Encanto de Las Cruces 37
Lincoln
  Ellis Store Country Inn, The 30
Ojo Caliente
  Ojo Caliente Mineral Springs & Spa 14
Pinos Altos
  Bear Creek Cabins 38
Raton
  Best Western Sands 28
Red River
  Sportsman's Lodge 16
Roswell
  Burnt Well Guest Ranch 31
  La Quinta Inn & Suites Roswell 33
Ruidoso Downs
  Ramada Inn Ruidoso 32
Sandia Park
  Angels' Ascent Retreat & Spa 7
  Pine Cone Inn 8
Santa Fe
  Absolute Nirvana Spa, and the Madeleine Inn 18, 209
  Hacienda Nicholas 15
  Hotel Plaza Real 26
  Hotel St. Francis 19
  Lodge at Santa Fe, The 22
Santa Rosa
  Best Western Adobe Inn 29

Taos
  Alma del Monte "Spirit of the Mountain"
      Bed & Breakfast 21
  Best Western Kachina Lodge 23
  Casa de la Chimeneas Inn & Spa 24
  Mabel Dodge Luhan House 21
  Touchstone Inn and Riverbend Spa 25
Taos Ski Valley
  Austing Haus Bed & Breakfast 20
  Bavarian Lodge and Restaurant, The 17
Truth or Consequences
  Sierra Grande Lodge and Spa 34

Arts & Crafts

Albuquerque
  PaperGami 46
  Stone Mountain Bead Gallery 47
Santa Fe
  Beauty and the Beads 49
  PaperGami 46

Attractions

Alamogordo
  New Mexico Museum of Space History 116
Albuquerque
  Albuquerque Biological Park (aquarium and botanic
      garden) 80
  Albuquerque Biological Park (Tingley Beach) 80
  American International Rattlesnake Museum 81
  Anderson-Abruzzo Albuquerque International
      Balloon Museum 82
  Destination Southwest 72
  Indian Pueblo Cultural Center 83
  National Atomic Museum 84
  Rio Grande Zoo 80
  Sandia Peak Tramway 73
  Turquoise Museum, The 85
  University of New Mexico, The 75
  University of New Mexico Bookstore, The 76
  Unser Racing Museum 86
Alto
  Spencer Theater 110
Angel Fire
  Vietnam Veterans Memorial State Park 106
Capitan
  Smokey BearHistorical Park 119
  Smokey Bear Museum 119
Carlsbad
  Carlsbad Caverns National Park 115
Cedar Crest
  Museum of Archaeology and Material Culture 87
Cimarron
  Philmont Scout Ranch Museums 109

Elephant Butte
  Grasshopper Silk 63
Embudo
  Big River Raft Trips 99
Fort Sumner
  Billy the Kid Museum 69
Gallup
  Gallup Historical Society 128
Holloman Air Force Base
  White Sands National Monument 103
Las Cruces
  Las Cruces City Museums 122
  Mesilla Valley Maze 120
  New Mexico Farm & Ranch Heritage Museum 123
Las Vegas
  Montezuma Castle 104
Los Alamos
  Bradbury Science Museum 102
Los Lunas
  Tractor Brewing Company 77
Mesilla
  Fountain Theatre, The 124
  Mesilla, Town of 121
Mora
  Victory Alpaca Ranch 107
Moriarty
  Sierra Blanca Brewing Co. 78
Rio Rancho
  J&R Vintage Auto Museum 88
Rociada
  Pendaries Village, Mountain Resort
      and Golf Community 105
Roswell
  Grace Corn Heritage House 113
  International UFO Museum
      and Research Center, The 117
Ruidoso Downs
  Hubbard Museum of the American West, The 118
Sandia Park
  Tinkertown Museum 89
Santa Fe
  Aboot About Santa Fe 100
  El Rancho de las Golondrinas 98
  Museum of Fine Arts 96
  Museum of Indian Arts & Culture 93
  Museum of International Folk Art 90
  Palace of the Governors 97
  Santa Fe Opera, The 101
Santa Rosa
  Joseph's Bar & Grill 71
  Route 66 Auto Museum 70
  Santa Rosa, City of Natural Lakes 65
  Santa Rosa Blue Hole 67
  Santa Rosa Golf Course & Country Club 68
  Santa Rosa Park Lake 68
Silver City
  Silver City Museum, The 125

Socorro
  Very Large Array Radio Telescope, The 126
Sunspot
  National Solar Observatory 111
Taos
  Kit Carson Home and Museum 94
  Millicent Rogers Museum 95
Truth or Consequences
  Geronimo Trail Scenic Byway 56
  RioBravoFineArt, Inc. 62
  Rural Museums of Sierra County 55
  Sierra County Arts Council 58
  Sierra County Birding 59
  Sierra County Lakes and Rivers 61
  Truth or Consequences Hot Springs
      and Spa Association 57
  Truth or Consequences Museums 54

Fashion

Albuquerque
  Celebro Natural Fiber Clothing 132
  Desert Designs 134
  Glowing Maternity & Baby Boutique 133
  Ooh! Aah! Jewelry 133
  Seventh Goddess 135
  Silver Sun 136
Raton
  Solano's Boot & Western Wear 140
Santa Fe
  Back At The Ranch 139
  Kioti 138
  Native Jackets 141
  Silver Sun 136

Galleries

Albuquerque
  Adobe Silver at Naranjo's Arts 169
  Andrews Pueblo Pottery & Art Gallery 164
  Art is OK Gallery & Sculpture Garden 166
  Coleman Gallery of Contemporary Art 169
  Framing Concepts Gallery 168
  Nancy Kozikowski at DSG Fine Art 170
  New Grounds Print Workshop & Gallery 165
  Palette Contemporary Art & Craft 172
  PATRICIAN DESIGN Caliente, It's Hot! 173
  R.C. Gorman/Nizhoni Gallery 167
  Schelu Gallery 171
  Sumner & Dene 174
  Weems Galleries and Framing 176
  Wright's Indian Art 175
Chimayó
  Oviedo Carvings & Bronze 160
Deming
  GALERIA 200 184
Elephant Butte
  Grasshopper Silk 183

Index

Embudo
   Rare Earth Studio Gallery 158
Farmington
   Artifacts Gallery and The Studios 193
Ilfeld
   Christopher Thomson Ironworks 180
   Cozy Jewel Gallery 179
Mesilla
   Potteries, The 185
Peñasco
   Garcia's Colonial Gallery 157
Raton
   Head in the Clouds Productions 181
   Old Pass Gallery 178
   Gallery Between, The 181
Ruidoso
   Mountain Arts Gallery 182
Sandia Park
   Guilloume's Fine Art 177
Santa Fe
   Elodie HolmesLiquid Light Glass 154
   Peterson-Cody Gallery, Ltd. 157
   Prairie Dog Glass 155
   Santa Fe Weaving Gallery 162
   Tad Tribal Art Gallery 159
Silver City
   Blue Dome Gallery 187
   Elemental Arts 186
   Leyba & Ingalls Arts – Supplies and Gallery 188
   Lois Duffy Art 189
Taos 152
   Brazos Fine Art 148
   Dragonfly Journeys 156
   Farnsworth Gallery Taos 149
   Inger Jirby's Taos Guest Houses 146
   Inger Jirby Gallery 147
   Jd Challenger Studio/Gallery 150
   Starving Artists Gallery 152
   Tailwater Gallery & Fly Shop 162
   Taos Gallery Association 145
   Wilder Nightingale Fine Art 151
   Zane Wheeler Gallery 153
Truth or Consequences
   RioBravoFineArt, Inc. 190

Gardens, Plants & Flowers

La Cueva
   Salman Raspberry Ranch
      and La Cueva Historic District 199
Santa Fe
   High Country Gardens 198
   Santa Fe Greenhouses 198
   Tropic of Capricorn 196

Health & Beauty

Albuquerque
   Casa Verde Salon and Spa 206
   Inn at Paradise 207
   La Bella Spa and Salon 202
Corrales
   Bodywise Massage & Day Spa 204
   Day Spa at Serenity Gardens 205
Ribera
   Refugio Verde 208
Sandia Park
   Angels' Ascent Retreat & Spa 207
Santa Fe
   Absolute Nirvana Spa, and the Madeleine Inn 18, 209
Truth or Consequences
   Sierra Grande Lodge and Spa 210

Home

Albuquerque
   Ernest Thompson Furniture 214
Santa Fe
   Asian Adobe 219
   Closets Too 215
   Honey Do Home Repair and Closets Too 215
   Re/MAX One 218
   Sage Builders 217
   Southwest Spanish Craftsmen
      and Nussbaumer Fine Art Gallery 216
Talpa
   ABYDOS 217

Recreation

Albuquerque
   Cho's Tae Kwan Do New Mexico 224
   Fishback Studio of the Dance 224
   Follow the Sun, Inc. 223
   Rainbow Ryders Hot Air Balloon Company, Inc. 227
   Skyspan Adventures 225
El Prado
   Far Flung Adventures 229
Las Cruces
   NMSU Golf Course 237
Raton
   Whittington Center, The 228
Ruidoso
   Links at Sierra Blanca, The 236
Santa Fe
   Fiesta City Tours 229
   Great Southwest Adventures 222
   High Desert Angler 234
Taos
   Los Rios Anglers 231
   Pueblo Balloon Company 235
   Taos Sporting Clays 230
Taos Ski Valley
   Taos Ski Valley 232
Tesuque
   HeliNM 233

Restaurants & Cafés

Albuquerque
   Barry's Oasis 241
   Casa de Benavidez 243
   Church Street Café 249
   El Pinto Foods 244
   El Pinto Restaurant 245
   Kelly's Brew Pub 240
   Sadie's Restaurant of New Mexico 246
   Sandia Peak Tramway 247
   St. James Tearoom, The 242
Angel Fire
   Roasted Clove 267
Chimayó
   Rancho de Chimayó Restaurante 252
Corrales
   Casa Vieja 248
   Village Pizza 250
El Prado
   Orlando's New Mexican Café 253
Las Vegas
   Blackjack's Grill 269
   La TrattoriaItalian Restaurant & Steakhouse 268
Los Lunas
   Teofilo's Restaurante 251
Placitas
   Pinon Café 250
Ranchos de Taos
   Stakeout Grill & Bar 255
Santa Fe
   Annapurna Ayurvedic Cuisine & Chai House 249
   Back Road Pizza 254
   Café Des Artistes 256
   Cowgirl BBQ & Western Grill 257
   Maria's New Mexican Kitchen 257
   San Francisco Street Bar & Grill
      and Santa Fe Bar & Grill 258
   Santa Fe Baking Company and Café 259
   Santa Fe Brewing Company 260
   Steaksmith at El Gancho 261
   Tomasita's Restaurant 262
   WilLee's Blues Club 265
Taos
   Apple Tree Restaurant 263
   Bean, The 264
   ¡Bravo! Fine Wine, Foods & Spirits 265
   Rellenos Café by Antonio 266

Shopping

Albuquerque
  Candy Lady, The 276
  Cowboys and Indians Antiques 275
  Enchanted Southwest, The 273
  Gertrude Zachary Inc. 279
  Ghost Town Trading Co. 282
  Innovations Gift Gallery 277
  Lavande Bleu 272
  Morningside Antiques 274
  Pennysmiths Paper 277
  Sumner & Dene 280
  Terra Firma 283
Chama
  Dancing Wolf & Narrow Gauge
     Gifts & Boutique 285
La Cueva
  Salman Raspberry Ranch
     and La Cueva Historic District 288
Las Cruces
  New Mexico State University Bookstore 291
  New Mexico State University Golf Course 237
Mesilla
  La Paz Imports 290
Placitas
  Clear Light • the Cedar Company 281
Pojoaque
  Kokoman Fine Wines & Liquors 292
Santa Fe
  Brown Cow Saddle Blanket Company 292
  Critters & Me, The 289
  Heart of the Lotus Gift Bazaar 284
  Las Cosas Kitchen Shoppe and Cooking School 287
Taos
  Tailwater Gallery & Fly Shop 286

Textile Arts

Chimayó
  Centinela Traditional Arts 304
  Ortega's Weaving Shop 305
Española
  Española Valley Fiber Arts Center 303
Las Vegas
  Tapetes de Lana Gallery 301
Los Ojos
  Tierra Wools 302
Mora
  Sangre de Cristo Mill 300
  Victory Alpaca Ranch 307
Newcomb
  Toadlena Trading Post 306

Trading Posts

Albuquerque
  Gus's Trading Company 317
  Palms Trading Post 316
Fruitland
  Hatch Brothers Trading Post 310
Gallup
  Ellis Tanner Trading Company 311
  IndianTouch of Gallup 312
  Perry Null Trading Company 313
  Richardson's Trading Company 314
Newcomb
  Toadlena Trading Post 315
Santa Fe
  Wind River Trading 318

Wineries & Breweries

Albuquerque
  Gruet Winery 323
  Kelly's Brew Pub 335
  Tierra Encantada Vineyards & Winery 322
Artesia
  Cottonwood Winery 328
Embudo
  Vivác Winery 326
La Union
  La Viña Winery 330
Los Lunas
  Tractor Brewing Company 333
Los Ranchos de Albuquerque
  Casa Rondeña Winery 324
Moriarty
  Sierra Blanca Brewing Co. 334
Ponederosa
  Ponderosa Valley Vineyards & Winery 325
Ribera
  Madison Vineyards and Winery 327
Ruidoso
  Willmon Vineyards 329
Santa Fe
  Santa Fe Brewing Company 336

Index by City

A

Alamogordo
Attractions
New Mexico Museum of Space History 116

Albuquerque
Accommodations
Böttger Mansion of Old Town 11
Enchanted Trails RV Park & Trading Post 10
Hotel Albuquerque at Old Town 9
Inn at Paradise, The 10
Nativo Lodge 12
Sarabande Bed & Breakfast 8
Arts & Crafts
PaperGami 46
Stone Mountain Bead Gallery 47
Attractions
Albuquerque Biological Park 80
American International Rattlesnake Museum 81
Anderson-Abruzzo Albuquerque International Balloon Museum 82
Destination Southwest 72
Indian Pueblo Cultural Center 83
National Atomic Museum 84
Rio Grande Zoo, The 80
Sandia Peak Tramway 73
Turquoise Museum, The 85
University of New Mexico, The 75
University of New Mexico Bookstore, The 76
Unser Racing Museum 86
Fashion
Celebro Natural Fiber Clothing 132
Desert Designs 134
Glowing Maternity & Baby Boutique 133
Ooh! Aah! Jewelry 133
Seventh Goddess 135
Silver Sun 136
Galleries
Adobe Silver at Naranjo's Arts 169
Andrews Pueblo Pottery & Art Gallery 164
Art is OK Gallery & Sculpture Garden 166
Coleman Gallery of Contemporary Art 169
Framing Concepts Gallery 168
Nancy Kozikowski at DSG Fine Art 170
New Grounds Print Workshop & Gallery 165
Palette Contemporary Art & Craft 172
PATRICIAN DESIGN Caliente, It's Hot! 173
R.C. Gorman/Nizhoni Gallery 167
Schelu Gallery 171
Sumner & Dene 174
Weems Galleries and Framing 176
Wright's Indian Art 175
Health & Beauty
La Bella Spa and Salon 202
Casa Verde Salon and Spa 206
Inn at Paradise, The 207
Home
Ernest Thompson Furniture 214
Recreation
Cho's Tae Kwan Do New Mexico 224
Fishback Studio of the Dance 224
Follow the Sun, Inc. 223
Rainbow Ryders Hot Air Balloon Company, Inc. 227
Skyspan Adventures 225
Restaurants & Cafés
Annapurna Ayurvedic Cuisine & Chai House 249
Barry's Oasis 241
Casa de Benavidez 243
Church Street Café 249
El Pinto Foods 244
El Pinto Restaurant 245
Kelly's Brew Pub 240
Sadie's Restaurant of New Mexico 246
Sandia Peak Tramway 247
St. James Tearoom, The 242
Shopping
Candy Lady, The 276
Cowboys and Indians Antiques 275
Enchanted Southwest, The 273
Gertrude Zachary Inc. 279
Ghost Town Trading Co. 282
Innovations Gift Gallery 277
Lavande Bleu 272
Morningside Antiques 274
Pennysmiths Paper 277
Sumner & Dene 280
Terra Firma 283
Trading Posts
Gus's Trading Company 317
Palms Trading Post 316
Wineries & Breweries
Casa Rondeña Winery 324
Gruet Winery 323
Kelly's Brew Pub 335
Tierra Encantada Vineyards & Winery 322

Algodones
Accommodations
Hacienda Vargas 7

Alto
Attractions
Spencer Theater 110

Angel Fire
Attractions
Vietnam Veterans Memorial State Park 106
Restaurants & Cafés
Roasted Clove 267

Artesia
Wineries & Breweries
Cottonwood Winery 328

C

Capitan
Attractions
Smokey Bear Historical Park 119
Smokey Bear Museum 119

Carlsbad
Attractions
Carlsbad Caverns National Park 115

Cedar Crest
Accommodations
Angels' Ascent Retreat & Spa 7
Elaine's, A Bed and Breakfast 6
Attractions
Museum of Archaeology and Material Culture 87

Chama
Shopping
Dancing Wolf & Narrow Gauge Gifts & Boutique 285

Chimayo
Restaurants & Cafés
Rancho de Chimayó Restaurante 252
Textile Arts
Centinela Traditional Arts 304
Ortega's Weaving Shop 305

Chimayó
Galleries
Oviedo Carvings & Bronze 160

Cimarron
Attractions
Philmont Scout Ranch Museums 109

Corrales
Health & Beauty
Bodywise Massage & Day Spa 204
Day Spa at Serenity Gardens 205
Restaurants & Cafés
Casa Vieja 248
Village Pizza 250

D

Deming
Accommodations
La Quinta Inn & Suites of Deming 39
Galleries
GALERIA 200 184

E

Elephant Butte
Attractions
Grasshopper Silk 63
Galleries
Grasshopper Silk 183

El Prado
Recreation
Far Flung Adventures 229
Restaurants & Cafés
Orlando's New Mexican Café 253

Embudo
Attractions
Big River Raft Trips 99
Galleries
Rare Earth Studio Gallery 158
Wineries & Breweries
Vivác Winery 326

Española
Textile Arts
Española Valley Fiber Arts Center 303

F

Farmington
Accommodations
Casa Blanca Inn 40
Courtyard By Marriott 42
Galleries
Artifacts Gallery and The Studios 193

Fort Sumner
Attractions
Billy the Kid Museum 69

Fruitland
Trading Posts
Hatch Brothers Trading Post 310

G

Gallup
Accommodations
El Rancho Hotel & Motel 41
Attractions
Gallup Historical Society 128
Trading Posts
Ellis Tanner Trading Company 311
IndianTouch of Gallup 312
Perry Null Trading Company 313
Richardson's Trading Company 314

H

Hatch
Accommodations
Historic Pelham House Sanctuary and Retreat 35

Holloman Air Force Base
Attractions
White Sands National Monument 103

I

Ilfeld
Galleries
Christopher Thomson Ironworks 180
Cozy Jewel Gallery 179

L

La Cueva
Gardens, Plants & Flowers
Salman Raspberry Ranch
and La Cueva Historic District 199, 288
Shopping
Salman Raspberry Ranch
and La Cueva Historic District 199, 288

La Union
Wineries & Breweries

Las Cruces
Accommodations
Best Western Mesilla Valley Inn 36
Hotel Encanto de Las Cruces–
A Heritage Hotel and Resort 37
Attractions
Las Cruces City Museums 122
Mesilla Valley Maze 120
New Mexico Farm & Ranch Heritage Museum 123
Recreation
New Mexico State University Golf Course 237
Shopping
New Mexico State University Bookstore 291

Las Vegas
Attractions
Montezuma Castle 104
Restaurants & Cafés
Blackjack's Grill 269
La Trattoria Italian Restaurant & Steakhouse 268
Textile Arts
Tapetes de Lana Gallery 301
La Viña Winery 330

Lincoln
Accommodations
Ellis Store Country Inn, The 30

Los Alamos
Attractions
Bradbury Science Museum 102

Los Lunas
Attractions
Tractor Brewing Company 77, 333
Restaurants & Cafés
Teofilo's Restaurante 251
Wineries & Breweries
Tractor Brewing Company 77, 333

Los Ojos
Textile Arts
Tierra Wools 302

M

Mesilla
Attractions
Fountain Theatre, The 124
Mesilla, Town of 121
Galleries
Potteries, The 185
Shopping
La Paz Imports 290

Mora
Attractions
Victory Alpaca Ranch 107, 307
Textile Arts
Sangre de Cristo Mill 300
Victory Alpaca Ranch 107, 307

Moriarty
Attractions
Sierra Blanca Brewing Co. 78, 334
Wineries & Breweries
Sierra Blanca Brewing Co. 78, 334

N

Newcomb
Textile Arts
Toadlena Trading Post 306, 315
Trading Posts
Toadlena Trading Post 306, 315

O

Ojo Caliente
Accommodations
Ojo Caliente Mineral Springs & Spa 14

P

Peñasco
Galleries
Garcia's Colonial Gallery 157

Pinos Altos
Accommodations
Bear Creek Cabins 38

Placitas
Restaurants & Cafés
Pinon Café 250
Shopping
Clear Light • the Cedar Company 281

Pojoaque
Shopping
Kokoman Fine Wines & Liquors 292

Ponderosa
Wineries & Breweries
Ponderosa Valley Vineyards & Winery 325

R

Ranchos de Taos
Restaurants & Cafés
Stakeout Grill & Bar 255

Raton
Accommodations
Best Western Sands 28
Fashion
Solano's Boot & Western Wear 140
Galleries
Gallery Between
 & Head in the Clouds Productions, The 181
Old Pass Gallery 178
Recreation
Whittington Center, The 228

Red River
Accommodations
Sportsman's Lodge 16

Ribera
Health & Beauty
Refugio Verde 208
Wineries & Breweries
Madison Vineyards and Winery 327

Rio Rancho
Attractions
J&R Vintage Auto Museum 88

Rociada
Attractions
Pendaries Village, Mountain Resort
 and Golf Community 105

Roswell
Accommodations
Burnt Well Guest Ranch 31
La Quinta Inn & Suites Roswell 33
Attractions
Grace Corn Heritage House 113
International UFO Museum
 and Research Center, The 117

Ruidoso
Galleries
Mountain Arts Gallery 182
Recreation
Links at Sierra Blanca, The 236
Wineries & Breweries
Willmon Vineyards 329

Ruidoso Downs
Accommodations
Ramada Inn Ruidoso 32
Attractions
Hubbard Museum of the American West, The 118

S

Sandia Park
Accommodations
Pine Cone Inn 8
Attractions
Tinkertown Museum 89
Galleries
Guilloume's Fine Art 177
Health & Beauty
Angels' Ascent Retreat & Spa 207

Santa Fe
Accommodations
Absolute Nirvana Spa, and the Madeleine Inn 18, 209
Hacienda Nicholas 15
Hotel Plaza Real 26
Hotel St. Francis 19
Lodge at Santa Fe, The 22
Arts & Crafts
Beauty and the Beads 49
Attractions
Aboot About Santa Fe 100
El Rancho de las Golondrinas 98
Museum of Fine Arts 96
Museum of Indian Arts & Culture 93
Museum of International Folk Art 90
Palace of the Governors 97
Santa Fe Opera, The 101
Fashion
Back At The Ranch 139
Kioti 138
Native Jackets 141
Galleries
Elodie Holmes Liquid Light Glass 154
Peterson-Cody Gallery, Ltd. 157
Prairie Dog Glass 155
Santa Fe Weaving Gallery 162
Tad Tribal Art Gallery 159
Gardens, Plants & Flowers
High Country Gardens 198
Santa Fe Greenhouses 198
Tropic of Capricorn 196
Health & Beauty
Absolute Nirvana Spa, and the Madeleine Inn 18, 209
Home
Asian Adobe 219
Closets Too 215
Honey Do Home Repair and Closets Too 215
Re/MAX One 218
Sage Builders 217
Southwest Spanish Craftsmen 216
Recreation
Fiesta City Tours 229
Great Southwest Adventures 222
High Desert Angler 234
Restaurants & Cafés
Back Road Pizza 254
Café Des Artistes 256
Cowgirl BBQ & Western Grill 257
Maria's New Mexican Kitchen 257
San Francisco Street Bar & Grill
 and Santa Fe Bar & Grill 258
Santa Fe Baking Company and Café 259
Santa Fe Brewing Company 260, 336
Steaksmith at El Gancho 261
Tomasita's Restaurant 262
WilLee's Blues Club 265
Shopping
Brown Cow Saddle Blanket Company 292
Critters & Me, The 289
Heart of the Lotus Gift Bazaar 284
Las Cosas Kitchen Shoppe and Cooking School 287
Susan's Christmas Shop 293
Trading Posts
Wind River Trading 318
Wineries & Breweries
Santa Fe Brewing Company 260, 336

Santa Rosa
Accommodations
  Best Western Adobe Inn 29
Attractions
  Joseph's Bar & Grill 71
  Route 66 Auto Museum 70
  Santa Rosa, City of Natural Lakes 65
  Santa Rosa Blue Hole 67
  Santa Rosa Park Lake 68
  Santa Rosa Golf Course & Country Club 68

Silver City
Attractions
  Silver City Museum, The 125
Galleries
  Blue Dome Gallery 187
  Elemental Arts 186
  Leyba & Ingalls Arts – Supplies and Gallery 188
  Lois Duffy Art 189

Socorro
Attractions
  Very Large Array Radio Telescope, The 126

Sunspot
Attractions
  National Solar Observatory 111

T

Talpa
Home
  ABYDOS 217

Taos
Accommodations
  Alma del Monte "Spirit of the Mountain"
    Bed & Breakfast 21
  Best Western Kachina Lodge 23
  Casa de la Chimeneas Inn & Spa 24
  Mabel Dodge Luhan House 21
  Touchstone Inn and Riverbend Spa 25
Attractions
  Kit Carson Home and Museum 94
  Millicent Rogers Museum 95
Galleries
  Art Divas Gallery 152
  Brazos Fine Art 148
  Dragonfly Journeys 156
  Farnsworth Gallery Taos 149
  Inger Jirby's Taos Guest Houses 146
  Inger Jirby Gallery 147
  Jd Challenger Studio/Gallery 150
  Starving Artists Gallery 152
  Tailwater Gallery & Fly Shop 162, 286
  Taos Gallery Association 145
  Wilder Nightingale Fine Art 151
  Zane Wheeler Gallery 153

Recreation
  Los Rios Anglers 231
  Pueblo Balloon Company 235
  Taos Sporting Clays 230
Restaurants & Cafés
  Apple Tree Restaurant 263
  Bean, The 264
  ¡Bravo! Fine Wine, Foods & Spirits 265
  Rellenos Café by Antonio 266
Shopping
  Tailwater Gallery & Fly Shop 162, 286

Taos Ski Valley
Accommodations
  Austing Haus Bed & Breakfast 20
  Bavarian Lodge and Restaurant, The 17
Recreation
  Taos Ski Valley 232

Tesuque
Recreation
  HeliNM 233

Tres Piedras
Recreation
  Taos Sporting Clays 230

Truth or Consequences
Accommodations
  Sierra Grande Lodge and Spa 34
Attractions
  Geronimo Trail Scenic Byway 56
  RioBravoFineArt, Inc. 62, 190
  Rural Museums of Sierra County 55
  Sierra County Arts Council 58
  Sierra County Birding 59
  Sierra County Lakes and Rivers 61
  Truth or Consequences Hot Springs
    and Spa Association 57
  Truth or Consequences Museums 54
Galleries
  RioBravoFineArt, Inc. 62, 190
Health & Beauty
  Sierra Grande Lodge and Spa 210